SHORT CUTS

The Dictionary of *USEFUL* Abbreviations

Steven Kleinedler

Printed on recyclable paper

NTC Publishing Group
Lincolnwood, Illinois USA

Library of Congress Cataloging-in-Publication Data
Kleinedler, Steven Racek.
  Short cuts : the dictionary of useful abbreviations / Steven Kleinedler.
      p. cm. — (Artful Wordsmith series)
  Rev. ed. of: NTC's dictionary of acronyms and abbreviations.
© 1993.
  ISBN 0-8442-0905-8 (pbk.)
  1. Acronyms—Dictionaries. 2. Abbreviations, English.
I. Kleinedler, Steven Racek. NTC's dictionary of acronyms and abbreviations. II. Title. III. Series.
PE1693.K533 1993
423'.1—dc20   96-26178
                                                         CIP

© 1997 by NTC Publishing Group, 4255 West Touhy Avenue,
Lincolnwood (Chicago), Illinois 60646-1975 U.S.A.
All rights reserved. Except for use in a review, the reproduction or
utilization of this work in any form or by any electronic, mechanical,
or other means, now known or hereafter invented, including scanning,
photocopying, and recording, and in any information storage and retrieval
system, is forbidden without the written permission of the publisher.

Manufactured in the United States of America.

6 7 8 9 0 VP 9 8 7 6 5 4 3 2 1

ABOUT THIS DICTIONARY

An acronym is a shortened form of a compound or a phrase where the initial letters are pronounced as if they spelled a single word. An abbreviation is a shortened form of a word, compound, or phrase, usually consisting of the first letter(s) of the word, compound, or phrase. If the abbreviation is pronounced, the letters are sounded one by one. The term "abbreviation" includes initialisms, blends, clippings, and shortened written forms. In these pages, the reader will find the acronyms and abbreviations that appear on food packaging, in the sports and financial pages of the newspaper, in recipes, in the telephone book, in the hardware store, and in hundreds of other places. The following paragraphs give a more detailed description of the different types of shortened forms.

ACRONYMS

An acronym is a word formed from the first letter or letters of a compound or phrase. The resulting string of letters is pronounced as a word, rather than a list of letters. For example, **scuba** is from 'self-contained underwater breathing apparatus.' Sometimes, the initial letters of articles or prepositions are excluded, as with **GATT** 'General Agreement on Tariffs and Trade,' in order to make the acronym more manageable. **GATT** is easier to remember and pronounce than **GAOTAT** would be. Sometimes, as with **VTOL** 'vertical takeoff and landing' or **PSAT** 'Preliminary Scholastic Aptitude Test,' a vowel is inserted to make a sequence of sounds that is easy to pronounce:

VEE-tol and PEE-sat. These special pronunciation problems are noted in the appropriate entries. An acronym also can be formed from the first letters of the *syllables* in long polysyllabic words, e.g., **PABA** 'para-aminobenzoic acid.'

INITIALISMS

An initialism is made up of the first letter or letters of one or more words. The resulting letters are not pronounced as a word, but are sounded out one by one as in **CIA** 'central intelligence agency' and **FBI** 'federal bureau of investigation.' **CIA** is pronounced SEE I A, not SEE-ah. **FBI** is pronounced EF BEE I. An initialism also can be formed from the first letters of the *syllables* of long polysyllabic words as in **DDT**, 'dichlorodiphenyltrichloroethane,' an insecticide.

BLENDS

A blend is a combination of the beginning of one word and the end of another, such as **caplet** from *capsule* and *tablet* or **Oxbridge** from *Oxford* and *Cambridge*.

CLIPPINGS

A clipping is the shortening of a polysyllabic word by deleting part of the word's ending. Consequently, *chemotherapy* becomes **chemo** and *examinations* becomes **exams.** Clippings do not end with a period. Words that are formed from the beginnings of two or more words, such as **pixel** from *picture* and *element*, are acronyms.

SHORTENED WRITTEN FORMS

There are many abbreviations that are not usually

pronounced. For instance, **rm.** 'room' is not usually said aloud. Forms falling into this category usually end with a period.

General Pronunciation Patterns

In the entries, the labels Acronym, Blend, Clipping, or Initialism are used to indicate the way the entry is pronounced. An entry lacking one of these four labels is considered to be a shortened written form that is usually not pronounced even though is has the form of a clipping or initialism. These entries are usually pronounced in their full form, i.e., **min.** is pronounced *minute*, **RR** is pronounced *railroad*, etc. All entries labeled as acronyms, blends, or clippings are pronounced as single words. All words labeled as initialisms are pronounced by sounding out each letter name, one by one. The entries not labeled as acronyms, blends, clippings, or initialisms are not usually pronounced. See number **6** in the "Guide to the Use of the Dictionary" on page vii.

Punctuation and Capitalization

It is difficult to generalize about punctuation and capitalization in shortened forms. Most acronyms are written and printed with capital letters, e.g., **GRAS** 'generally regarded as safe.' Some acronyms have become regular English words and are written and printed in lower case, e.g., **scuba, radar, laser.** Many abbreviations that do not belong to one of the other categories are left in lower case: **in.** 'inch,' **nt. wt.** 'net weight.' Abbreviations that usually or always are written with capital letters are also capitalized in this dictionary. Traditionally, initialisms are written or printed with a period after each letter, but that practice is declining. Acronyms, however, usually do not have periods after each letter. Blends never end in periods. Although there is a trend toward not using periods with initialisms, some of them are always written with periods. For instance, **e.g.** 'for example,' from the Latin *exempli gratia*; **i.e.** 'that is,' from the Latin *id est*; and **etc.** 'and so on,' from the Latin *et cetera*. In this dictionary, abbreviations that usually or always have periods are shown with periods. Please remember that practice differs considerably on this point and is often determined by editorial style.

Acknowledgements

Among the many people who have contributed ideas for entries in this dictionary, I would like to thank especially Jon Vincent, Elizabeth Senger, Dr. Douglas Files, Mom and Dad, J. Dallas Smith, Wayne Dunn, Ted Young, Renae Theodore, Zeke from the Zoo, Frank from the Bank, LeRoy Bach, Sheryl A. Smith, Charles C. Valauskas, Darren Hoffman, and Richard Spears.

Guide to the Use of the Dictionary

1. Entry heads are alphabetized according to an absolute alphabetical order that ignores punctuation, spaces, and hyphens.

2. Entry heads appear in **boldface type**. When words or expressions that are not entries in this dictionary are cited, they appear in *italics*.

3. Examples appear in *italics* and follow an arrowhead "▶."

4. An entry head may have one or more alternate forms. The alternatives are printed in **boldface type** and are preceded by "AND." Alternative forms containing commas are separated by semicolons, otherwise by commas.

5. The word or words for which the entry head stands appear in roman type. Alternative or closely related definitions and paraphrases are separated by semicolons.

6. The word *initialism* indicates that the entry head is pronounced by sounding out its letters one by one. The words *acronym, blend,* or *clipping* indicate that the entry head is pronounced as a normal whole word. The absence of one of the words *initialism, acronym, blend,* or *clipping* indicates that the entry in question is usually pronounced aloud in its full

form. Note, however, that people may attempt to spell out any of the entry heads or pronounce them as normal words.

7. A definition or explanation of the entry head appears in parentheses. The information in parentheses may include additional information about the abbreviation.

8. Many expressions have more than one major sense or meaning. These meanings are numbered with boldface numerals.

9. Sometimes a numbered sense will have an alternative form that does not belong to the other senses. In such cases the "AND" and the alternative form follows the numeral.

10. In some entries, comments direct the reader to other entries for additional information through the use of the terms "compare with," "see," or "see also." Entries appearing as cross-references are in *slanted type*.

11. The symbol "<" means "is derived from" or "comes from" when used in the description of the origins of words. For example, the expression *zero < Ar sifr* means "zero is derived from the Arabic word *sifr*."

A

A **1.** a grade indicating superior work. (Initialism. In the series *A, B, C, D, E* and *A, B, C, D, F*.) ▶ *Susan's parents gave her $25 for every A she received.* **2.** a musical tone. (Initialism. The sixth note of the scale of C major.) ▶ *Orchestras use the A above middle C to tune up before a concert.* **3.** a blood type. (Initialism.) ▶ *The blood bank had several pints of A positive and A negative blood.* ▶ *People with Type A blood can receive Type O or Type A.* ▶ *Type A blood can be used by people with Type AB or Type A.* **4.** ace. (Used on playing cards. In the series *J, Q, K, A*.) ▶ *Tina yelled "Blackjack!" as the dealer turned over an A.* **5.** alto. (In most choral music arrangements, the lowest range of a female voice. In the series *S, A, T, B*.) **6.** ampere. (A unit of the strength of electrical current.) ▶ *W = VA (watts = volts times amperes)* ▶ *60-A fuse* **7.** AND **ans.** answer. (Initialism. Often used in conjunction with *Q* = Question.) ▶ *Q: 2 × 5 A: 10* **8.** AND **Apr.** April. (Often used in graph columns or rows to chart the month-by-month progress of something. See also *Apr*.) ▶ *Easter—A 18* **9.** AND **Aug.** August. (Often used in graph columns or rows to chart the month-by-month progress of something. See also *Aug*.) ▶ *Fall quarter classes begin A 28.*

a acceleration. (A physics abbreviation, used in formulas and equations. Acceleration is equal to the change in velocity divided by the change in time. The example indicates an acceleration of 32.17 feet per second each second.) ▸ *a = 32.17 feet per second per second.*

A-1 superlative; the best. ▸ *They ate an A-1 steak and shrimp dinner.*

Å angstrom. (A unit of linear measurement equal to one ten-billionth [1/10,000,000,000] of a meter. The same as *AU*.)

A.A. Associate in Arts. (Initialism. A two-year college degree.) ▸ *After receiving an A.A. at a city college, Jim transferred into a four-year state university to earn a bachelor's degree.*

AA Alcoholics Anonymous. (Initialism. An organization founded in 1935 whose members help each other achieve and maintain sobriety.) ▸ *When Jerry was caught drinking on the job, his supervisor allowed him to keep working as long as he attended AA meetings.*

AAA American Automobile Association. (Pronounced "Triple A." Founded in 1902, a travel organization whose services include planning trips and vacations, placing hotel and transportation reservations, and providing insurance and road service.) ▸ *After the record snowfall, stranded motorists flooded the AAA office with phone calls.*

AAAS American Association for the Advancement of Science. (Initialism. Founded in 1848, the largest federation of scientific groups, whose goals include furthering the progress of science and promoting human welfare.) ▸ *Through the AAAS, Larry's chemistry group was able to share information with scientists across the country.*

AARP American Association of Retired Persons. (Initialism, also pronounced as an acronym. A nonprofit organization open to anyone fifty years of age or older that addresses the needs of older people and promotes independence and dignity.) ▶ *AARP publishes the periodical Modern Maturity.*

AAU Amateur Athletic Union. (Initialism. A nonprofit volunteer organization established in 1888 to promote amateur sports and physical fitness programs.) ▶ *Each year the AAU presents the James E. Sullivan Award to America's outstanding amateur athlete.*

AB **1.** Alberta, Canada. (The official two-letter post office abbreviation. Used in addresses. See also *Alta.*) ▶ *Grand Prairie, AB T8V 4C4* **2.** a blood type. (Initialism.) ▶ *Since Anna had a rare blood type, AB negative, she donated blood frequently.* ▶ *People with Type AB blood can receive blood from all blood types.*

ABA American Bar Association. (Initialism. Founded in 1878, an organization of lawyers, judges, law students, and teachers pledged to uphold legal education and ethics. The ABA determines accreditation for law schools.) ▶ *Joan joined the ABA to network with other lawyers in the area.*

abbr. abbreviation. (A shortened word or phrase. Found in dictionaries and other texts dealing with word lists.) ▶ *res. (abbr.) = reservation*

ABC **1.** very simple; rudimentary. (Initialism.) ▶ *Baking a cake these days is as easy as ABC.* **2.** already been chewed. (Initialism. Gum that is not fresh but that has been chewed.) ▶ *There's ABC gum on the bottom of your chair.* **3.** American Broadcasting Company. (Initialism. A radio and television network in the U.S. See also *CBS, NBC.*) ▶ *I prefer the news broadcast on ABC.*

ABC Islands Aruba, Bonaire, and Curaçao Islands. (Initialism. Three islands in the Caribbean governed by The

ABC's

Netherlands.) ▸ *During winter break, Tiffany spent two luxurious weeks in the ABC Islands.*

ABC's the alphabet. (Initialism. The basics of literacy. Used primarily with children.) ▸ *Johnny, do you know your ABC's?*

ABD all but dissertation. (Initialism. The status of a student who has completed all the requirements for a graduate degree except for writing the final dissertation.) ▸ *After two years Tony was still ABD, so he postponed his graduation party once again.*

abl. ablative. (A grammatical case found in some Indo-European languages that denotes separation, direction away from, manner, or agency. The meanings associated with the ablative case are conveyed in English by prepositions such as *from* and *out of*. Found in language textbooks and dictionaries.) ▸ *(Latin) igne—"by or with fire" (sing. abl. of ignis)*

ABM antiballistic missile. (Initialism. A military missile designed to destroy ballistic missiles in flight.) ▸ *The ABM veered off course because of an electrical malfunction.*

A-bomb atomic bomb. (Initialism-*bomb*. A highly explosive bomb created from the fission of uranium or plutonium atoms.) ▸ *The terrorist claimed to own an A-bomb that he would detonate in the capital unless his demands were met.*

a.c. *ante cibum*. (Initialism. Latin: before a meal. A pharmaceutical term found on prescriptions, indicating that the medication is to be taken before a meal.) ▸ *1 tablet orally, a.c.*

AC **1.** air conditioner. (Initialism. An appliance that keeps air temperature and humidity at a specific level.) ▸ *When* *the building's AC unit broke down, management bent the dress code to allow the office workers to wear shorts.* **2.** air conditioning. (Initialism. The cooling produced by an air conditioner.) ▶ *Who turned on the AC?* **3.** alternating current. (Initialism. Electric current that reverses its electric flow back and forth. The opposite of *direct current*. See also *DC*.) ▶ *Nikola Tesla is responsible for making AC electricity a reality.*

Ac actinium. (The chemical symbol for Element 89.)

acc. AND **accus.** accusative. (A grammatical case that marks the direct object of a transitive verb, expressing the goal of an action or a motion. Found in explanatory material in language textbooks and dictionaries.) ▶ *He gave the pen to me. "the pen"/acc.*

acct. account. (A ledger entry established by a firm or bank to record transactions made by specific clients and customers.) ▶ *Midtown Bank Acct. #40-20392-129A was closed on May 4th.* ▶ *Video Club Acct. 1902-C*

AC/DC **1.** alternating current/direct current. (Initialism. Referring to a device or appliance that works on either alternating current or direct current. See *AC* and *DC*.) ▶ *Some appliances are AC/DC.* **2.** bisexual. (Initialism. A slang term, derived metaphorically from devices that operate on either alternating or direct current.)

ACLU American Civil Liberties Union. (Initialism. An organization that defends constitutionally protected rights and freedoms.) ▶ *The ACLU reached a settlement with the nightclub that had discriminated against Steven.*

ACT American College Test. (Initialism. A standardized exam required by several colleges for admission. It tests academic aptitude in English, mathematics, social studies, and natural sciences.) ▶ *Jane received a score of 31*

ACTH

on the ACT and subsequently was courted by several colleges.

ACTH adrenocorticotropic hormone. (Initialism. A hormone secreted by the pituitary gland that regulates the adrenal glands and plays a role in digestion and the body's response to stress.) ▸ *Irregular sleeping habits affect the release of ACTH.*

ACT-UP AIDS Coalition to Unleash Power. (Acronym. An activist organization committed to direct action to end the AIDS crisis.) ▸ *ACT-UP is directly responsible for shortening the Food and Drug Administration's approval process of new treatments and drugs.*

A/D analog to digital. (Initialism. A conversion process that changes analog data to digital data. Compare with *D/A*.) ▸ *The mixer has very fine A/D filters.*

AD **1.** active duty. (Initialism. Full-time service, particularly as it relates to the military.) ▸ *When he returns to AD, he will do a good job.* **2.** *anno Domini*. (Initialism. Latin: in the year of our Lord. Denotes years after the approximate birth date of Christ. Commonly seen abbreviated with periods [A.D.] or in small capitals [AD, A.D.]. The *AD* was originally placed before the date in edited writing, but that practice is declining. Compare with *BC*. See also Common Era at *CE*.) ▸ *Honduras obtained independence from Spain on September 15, AD 1821.* **3.** assistant director. (Initialism. A motion picture or theater term, the person whose assistance allows the director to concentrate primarily on directing.) ▸ *The AD coached Barry until his soliloquy was letter perfect.*

ad advertisement. (Clipping. A public announcement or commercial.) ▸ *Fifteen-second ads on TV can be annoying.* ▸ *After being laid off, Jimmy looked through the want ads in the paper every day.*

ADA American Dental Association. (Initialism. A national organization of dentists established in 1859.) ▶ *The ADA helps support dental research, accredits dental schools, and examines legislation regarding dentistry.*

ADC Aid to Dependent Children. (Initialism. A governmental agency providing support for children of poor families.) ▶ *Cassie was able to feed her three children after they became eligible to receive ADC checks.*

adj. adjective. (A word used to modify or restrict the meaning of nouns and nominals. Found in language textbooks and dictionaries.) ▶ *blue,* adj.

adm. 1. administration. (The management, staff, and policies of an agency, institution, or political office.) ▶ *Adm. Building, Room 204* ▶ *The Vietnam Conflict escalated during the Johnson Adm.* 2. administrative. ▶ *adm. asst.*

Adm. Admiral. (The highest rank in the U.S. Navy, a four-star commanding officer.) ▶ *Adm. William J. Crowe*

ADR American depositary receipt. (Initialism. A security issued in the United States representing a security issued in a foreign country. ADRs can be bought and sold in the United States just like the underlying shares.) ▶ *Harriet asked her broker if she should sell her French ADRs.*

adv. adverb. (A word or phrase that modifies a verb, adjective, sentence, or another adverb. Found in language textbooks and dictionaries.) ▶ *sad*—adj; *sadly*—adv.

ad val. AND **A/V** *ad valorem.* (Latin: according to value.) ▶ *The store outlet sold products ad val. The goods had been bought below cost at bankruptcy sales, liquidations, and the like.*

AEC Atomic Energy Commission. (Initialism. From 1946 to 1974, a government agency that oversaw the development and use of atomic energy for nonmilitary uses. In

AF

1974, the duties of the AEC were split between the newly created Energy Research and Development Administration and the Nuclear Regulatory Commission. See *ERDA* and *NRC*.) ▸ *The electric company worked with the AEC to develop energy from atomic sources.*

AF 1. air force. (Initialism. The aviation branch of a nation's military forces.) ▸ *USAF* 2. audio frequency. (The range of sound frequencies audible to humans, ranging from 20 to 20,000 hertz.) ▸ *One blast from Terry's dog whistle, which was pitched above AF, sent all the neighborhood canines into a barking rage.* 3. auto focus. (Referring to a camera that focuses automatically. Used in advertising and as a model designation.) ▸ *Features built-in flash and AF lens!*

AFB air force base. (Initialism. The headquarters of an air force division.) ▸ *Wright-Patterson AFB*

AFC 1. American Football Conference. (Initialism. One of two divisions of the National Football League. See also *NFC* and *NFL*.) ▸ *The AFC consists of three divisions: Eastern, Central, and Western.* 2. automatic frequency control. (Initialism. A circuit that locks in on a specific frequency in electrical devices such as television, radio, and radar.) ▸ *Without AFC, radio stations would drift in and out.* ▸ *An AFC circuit in a television set prevents the horizontal hold from rolling.*

AFDC aid to families with dependent children. (Initialism. A government aid program within the department of Health and Human Services. Individual states determine eligibility and the benefits received.) ▸ *Between 1960 and 1980, the number of AFDC recipients tripled.*

AFL 1. American Federation of Labor. (Initialism. A powerful labor organization that merged with the CIO in 1955. See *AFL-CIO*.) ▸ *The AFL has many members.* 2.

American Football League. (Initialism. A professional football league from its inception in 1960 until its merger with the National Football League in 1970. See *NFL*.) ▸ *The first Super Bowl pitted the Green Bay Packers (NFL) against the Kansas City Chiefs (AFL).*

AFL-CIO American Federation of Labor and Congress of Industrial Organizations. (Initialism. A federation of over 100 trade and industrial unions that assists unions in organizing and promotes the activities of union members. The AFL and the CIO merged in 1955.) ▸ *Each Democratic candidate for president sought the endorsement of the AFL-CIO.*

Afr. **1.** Africa. (One of seven continents of the earth. Found on maps and in texts.) ▸ *Nairobi, Kenya, Afr.* **2.** African. ▸ *Afr. studies* ▸ *History 201: 1960's Afr. Political Change*

AFT **1.** American Federation of Teachers. (Initialism. Founded in 1916, an organization of education workers that promotes professionalism, wages, and job security and addresses classroom issues such as class size and equal opportunity.) ▸ *The striking teachers had the support of the AFT.* **2.** automatic fine tuning. (Initialism. A circuit found in radios that was turned on after an FM station had been tuned in, keeping it from drifting.) ▸ *The sales clerk kept emphasizing the AFT feature in an attempt to persuade Aunt Louise to purchase the radio.*

AFTRA American Federation of Television and Radio Artists. (Acronym. The labor union for people working in live and videotaped television programming, commercials, and radio broadcasting.) ▸ *More auditions were open to Elaine after she received her AFTRA card.*

AG **1.** Adjutant General. (Initialism. In the U.S. Army, the head administrative officer in charge of the personnel

Ag

records department. Also, the administrative officer for the National Guard in each state.) **2.** AND **Atty. Gen.** Attorney General. (A member of the cabinet of the president of the United States and the chief of the U.S. Department of Justice; the head law officer and legal representative of each state government.) ▸ *Robert F. Kennedy (AG: 1961-1964)* ▸ *Max Ryan (Atty. Gen., Nebraska)*

Ag silver. (The chemical symbol for Element 47. The symbol is derived from Latin *argentum*.)

AGI adjusted gross income. (Initialism. Used in reference to tax returns and statistics on the economy. A taxpayer's total income less adjustments to income, such as IRA deductions, alimony payments, Keogh retirement plan deductions, etc.) ▸ *If your AGI is less than $21,250 and a child lives with you, you may be eligible to claim Earned Income Credit.*

agr. agriculture. (The science of farming and raising livestock.) ▸ *Robert Bergland (Dept. of Agr. Secty. under Pres. Carter)* ▸ *College of Agr.*

Ah AND **A-h, AH, ah** ampere-hour. (Initialism. The unit used to measure electricity, equal to the flow of a current on one ampere for one hour.) ▸ *7 Ah.*

AI **1.** Amnesty International. (Initialism. An independent international organization that tracks violations of human rights and campaigns for the release of political prisoners.) ▸ *AI campaigned for the release of Vaclav Havel, a political prisoner under the communist Czech government.* **2.** artificial intelligence. (Initialism. The capacity of machines, computers, and computer programs that produce thought processes as humans do, particularly the areas of reasoning and learning.) ▸ *Brad majored in computer science, and his specialty was AI.* **3.**

AI

artificial insemination. (Initialism. The process of making a female pregnant by means other than copulation.) ▸ *Most hybrid cows are produced by AI.*

AID Agency for International Development. (Acronym. A division of the United States International Development Cooperation Agency, it provides economic assistance and self-help programs in developing nations.) ▸ *One goal of AID is to promote economic stability.*

AIDS acquired immunodeficiency syndrome. (Acronym. A viral illness that suppresses the body's immune system and makes patients very susceptible to fatal infections. See also *ARC.*) ▸ *In 1989, the number of Americans diagnosed with AIDS passed the 100,000 mark.*

AK Alaska. (The official two-letter post office abbreviation. See also *Alas.*) ▸ *Anchorage, AK 99501*

a.k.a. also known as. (Initialism.) ▸ *The police apprehended William T. Hagleton, a.k.a. Billy the Bullet and Bill Hagle.*

AL **1.** Alabama. (The official two-letter post office abbreviation. See also *Ala.*) ▸ *Enterprise, AL 36330* **2.** American League. (Initialism. Usually not abbreviated when spoken. One of two professional baseball leagues in the United States and Canada. Known as the American Association until 1890 and reestablished as the American League in 1901. See also *NL.*) ▸ *The 1951 World Series pitted the New York Yankees (AL) against the New York Giants (NL).* **3.** American Legion. (Initialism. Usually not abbreviated when spoken. Founded after World War I, the largest veteran's organization, promoting the interests of veterans and providing disabled veterans with health care.) ▸ *Fish Fry Friday at the AL Lodge, only $5!*

Al aluminum. (The chemical symbol for Element 13.)

Ala. Alabama. (See also *AL*.) ▸ *Montgomery, Ala.* ▸ *Gov. John Smith (Ala.)*

ALA American Library Association. (Initialism. Founded in 1876 to improve the effectiveness of libraries, to provide all people equal access to libraries, and to combat censorship.) ▸ *Several members of the ALA demanded that the city council appropriate funds to make the city library handicapped accessible.*

Alas. Alaska. (See also *AK*.) ▸ *Willow, Alas.* ▸ *Gov. Max Smith (Alas.)*

ald. alderman. (A member of a city or village council representing a particular ward or district.) ▸ *Ald. Helen Walker.*

alg. algebra. (A branch of mathematics that uses symbols to describe arithmetic relationships.) ▸ *Alg. 201* ▸ *Boolean alg.*

alt. altitude. (Found on maps and charts, usually in relation to airplanes and mountains.) ▸ *alt. 20,000 feet*

Alt alternate. (A computer keyboard key, which when pressed in conjunction with other keys, performs various functions, thereby increasing the number of keyboard functions.) ▸ *Pressing Alt + Ctrl + Del will restart most computers.*

Alta. Alberta, Canada. (The same as *AB*.) ▸ *Edmonton, Alta.*

alum alumna; alumnae; alumnus; alumni. (Informally used as a clipping. Graduate(s) of an institution of learning.) ▸ *After graduation ceremonies, the new alums celebrated at a fancy restaurant.*

A&M agricultural and mechanical. (Initialism. Part of the name of a university that specializes, or originally spe-

Ameslan

cialized, in the fields of agriculture and mechanical sciences.) ▸ *Alabama A&M University* ▸ *Texas A&M University*

Am. AND **Amer.** **1.** America. (The lands of the Western Hemisphere; narrowly defined as the United States of America.) ▸ *North Amer.* ▸ *Cent. Am.* **2.** American. ▸ *Am. Indian* ▸ *Am. cheese* ▸ *Amer. Revolution*

AM **1.** amplitude modulation. (Initialism. The system of radio broadcasting that varies the amplitude of the radio carrier wave; the opposite of *FM*.) ▸ *WJR, 760 AM* ▸ *During the blackout, Glenn listened to the news on a small AM transistor radio.* **2.** *anno mundi.* (Initialism. Latin: year of the world. The Jewish calendar system, dated from the year of creation according to the Torah.) ▸ *Rosh Hashanah—1 Tishri 5756 AM corresponds to the Gregorian calendar date of September 25, 1995.* **3.** *ante meridiem.* (Initialism. Latin: before noon. Used to designate the time from midnight to noon. Commonly seen abbreviated with periods [A.M.], small caps [AM, A.M.] or in lower case letters [am, a.m.]. Compare with *PM*.) ▸ *The bus leaves for school at 7:30 AM.*

Am americium. (The chemical symbol for Element 95.)

AMA American Medical Association. (Initialism. Founded in 1847, an organization of doctors that promotes health and wellness.) ▸ *Officials from the AMA charted the outbreak of measles in the city hospitals.*

Amer. See *Am.*

Ameslan AND **ASL** American Sign Language. (Acronym AND initialism. A language used by deaf and hearing-impaired people in the United States. It uses hand signs and gestures.) ▸ *Debate raged on campus as to whether proficiency in Ameslan demonstrated knowledge of a foreign language.* ▸ *Do you know ASL?*

AmEx American Express. (Acronym. A charge card company. Unlike a credit card company, the amount charged to an American Express card is due at the end of each billing period.) ▸ *In addition to its charge card, AmEx provides several services, including traveler's checks and travel agencies.* ▸ *Do you take Visa or AmEx?*

Amex American Stock Exchange. (Acronym. A stock market for small investors and organizations that do not meet the size requirements of *NYSE*. The same as *ASE*.) ▸ *Amex is headquartered in New York City's financial district.*

Amoco American Oil Company. (Acronym. The stress is on the first syllable. The name of a large oil company.) ▸ *Eric walked two miles to an Amoco station because his car ran out of gas.*

amp ampere. (Clipping. A unit of the strength of electrical current.) ▸ *Please hand me a 60-amp fuse.* ▸ *60-amp circuit*

AMPAS Academy of Motion Picture Arts and Sciences. (Acronym. Founded in 1927, a nonprofit organization whose members are leaders in all aspects of filmmaking.) ▸ *Each year AMPAS awards Oscars to outstanding contributors in the motion picture industry.*

amt. amount. (A value; a numerical quantity.) ▸ *amt. due as of 5/15/85* ▸ *amt. paid*

Amtrak American Track. (Blend. The corporation that operates passenger rail service between cities in the United States. Officially known as the National Railroad Passenger Corporation.) ▸ *Amtrak is a public corporation that is controlled by the United States government.* ▸ *Airplanes made Kathy nervous, so she always traveled by Amtrak.*

anat. anatomy. (The study of the structure of plants and animals.) ▶ *Anat. Dept.*

ANC African National Congress. (Initialism. A political organization of black Africans established in 1912. In South Africa, the ANC fights for equality by dismantling apartheid and the white minority rule.) ▶ *Nelson Mandela, the leader of the ANC, was released from prison in 1990.*

anon. anonymous. (An unknown person.) ▶ *anon. donor*

ans. See *A*.

a/o account of. (Because of. Used in memos and note taking with *on*.) ▶ *Oil prices are high on a/o the war.*

AOR album-oriented rock. (Initialism. A radio station format geared toward the works of rock artists found on albums, as opposed to individual Top 40 singles.) ▶ *Elizabeth listened to AOR stations because she was sick of Top 40 stations playing the same songs over and over.*

A&P Great Atlantic and Pacific Tea Company. (Initialism. A United States grocery store chain.) ▶ *"Johnny, would you run down to the A&P and pick me up some milk?" his mother asked politely.* ▶ *Jane found some good bargains at the A&P.*

AP Associated Press. (Initialism. A news agency founded in 1848. See also *UPI*.) ▶ *AP Laser Photo*

APB all points bulletin. (Initialism. A bulletin transmitted to law-enforcement agencies, usually to describe a wanted person or persons.) ▶ *Following the shoot-out, an APB was sent out, describing the gunman and his getaway car.*

APC armored personnel carrier. (Initialism. A protected and armed vehicle for transporting members of military forces.) ▶ *The APC lumbered through the hostile terrain, safely arriving behind the front lines.*

APO Army Post Office. (Initialism. A post office on an army base.) ▶ *Please take this down to the APO immediately.*

approx. approximately. (An estimation; almost, but not exactly.) ▶ *The church steeple is approx. 65 feet high.*

appt. appointment. (Used in memos and note taking. A predetermined arrangement to meet someone or be somewhere at a specific time.) ▶ *appt. book* ▶ *dentist appt.—4:15 pm*

Apr. April. (See also *A*.) ▶ *Apr. 15—Tax Day.*

APR annual percentage rate. (Initialism. The effective percentage rate calculated each year on a loan or a savings account.) ▶ *Buy now, and get 0%-APR financing!* ▶ *Stella tore up her 18.6% APR credit card.*

apt. apartment. (A residential rental unit. Used in advertisements and addresses.) ▶ *Roommate wanted to share 2-BR. apt. on the lake.* ▶ *444 St. James Place, Apt. 304*

AQ as quoted. (Initialism. Used on menus and other price lists for items whose value fluctuates day to day with the market.) ▶ *The menu listed several cuts of prime rib in the $30 range and an enticing selection of lobster dishes marked AQ.*

AQU Aquarius. (The astrological abbreviation for the zodiacal constellation of Aquarius.) ▶ *AQU (January 20 to February 19)*

A&R artists and repertoire. (Initialism. Relating to the department at a record company responsible for finding and marketing new talent.) ▶ *A&R representatives from*

arch.

every major label flocked to Seattle to look for new talent.

A/R 1. accounts receivable. (Initialism. Money due a company or an organization for goods or services.) ▶ *A/R May '89 $24,500* 2. accounts receivable [department]. (Initialism. The department of a company or an organization that tracks money due to see that it is paid.) ▶ *A/R Dept. meets tomorrow at 2:00 to discuss inventory control.*

Ar 1. Arabic. (The language of Arabs. Used in dictionaries to show the etymology of a word.) ▶ *zero < Ar sifr* 2. argon. (The chemical symbol for Element 18.)

AR Arkansas. (The official two-letter post office abbreviation. See also *Ark.*) ▶ *Fayetteville, AR 72701*

Arab. 1. Arabia. (A peninsula in southwest Asia surrounded by the Red and Arabian seas, the Persian Gulf, and the gulfs of Aden and Oman.) ▶ *Saudi Arab.* 2. Arabian. ▶ *Arab. Desert.* ▶ *Arab. culture* 3. Arabic. ▶ *Arab. numerals*

ARC 1. American Red Cross. (Initialism. The American branch of the Red Cross, an international organization that administers health programs and provides relief to victims of war and natural disasters.) ▶ *Within hours of the earthquake, ARC volunteers mobilized on the scene to help the survivors.* 2. AIDS-related complex. (Acronym. The medical condition of a debilitated HIV-positive person not diagnosed with AIDS. See also *AIDS.*) ▶ *Todd was diagnosed with ARC.* ▶ *People with ARC are not eligible for most government aid programs available to people with AIDS.*

arch. architecture. (The study and business of design and construction of buildings and other edifices.) ▶ *Dept. of Design & Arch.*

ARI Aries. (The astrological abbreviation for the zodiacal constellation of Aries.) ► *ARI (March 21 to April 20)*

arith. arithmetic. (The part of mathematics that deals with calculations using addition, subtraction, division, and multiplication.) ► *arith. skills: poor* ► *basic arith.*

Ariz. Arizona. (See also *AZ*.) ► *Phoenix, Ariz.* ► *Gov. John Ryan (Ariz.)*

Ark. Arkansas. (See also *AR*.) ► *Little Rock, Ark.* ► *Gov. George Berry (Ark.)*

ARM adjustable rate mortgage. (Acronym. A mortgage interest rate that can be changed upward or downward at regular intervals during the course of the loan term. Compare with *VRM*.) ► *The ARM financing of the shopping mall saved the investors a lot of money when interest rates fell.*

arr. arrival. (Used primarily in scheduling of planes, trains, and buses.) ► *Flight 702—arr. 7:45 PM Gate 12*

art. **1.** article. (A word that precedes a noun to indicate a degree of specificity. In English, the articles are *a*, *an*, and *the*. Found in language textbooks and dictionaries.) ► *a (art.)* ► *indef. art.* **2.** article. (A division of a larger document, such as a constitution or a treaty.) ► *Art. II of the U.S. Constitution outlines the structure and duties of the executive branch of the government.* **3.** artillery. (Mounted guns, cannons, missile launchers, and the like, used on the ground, warships, airplanes, and rockets.)

ARVN Army of the Republic of North Vietnam. (Acronym. Pronounced "AR-vin." During the Vietnam conflict, the communist-supported army in North Vietnam against which the U.S. troops and South Vietnamese fought.) ► *The American soldier broke down after he shot three civilians he had mistaken for ARVN.*

A's (Initialism. The nickname for the Oakland Athletics baseball team.) ▸ *The A's 1989 World Series triumph over San Francisco was interrupted by the Loma Prieta earthquake.*

As. 1. Asia. (One of seven continents of the earth. Found on maps and in texts.) ▸ *SE As. (Singapore, Malaysia, Laos, Vietnam, Cambodia, Thailand, and Myanmar)* **2.** Asian. ▸ *As. studies* ▸ *As. culture*

As arsenic. (The chemical symbol for Element 33.)

AS 1. Anglo-Saxon. (Initialism. The language of the ancient germanic tribes, the Angles and Saxons, more commonly known as Old English. See *OE*. Usually seen in dictionary etymologies.) ▸ *word is possibly AS* **2.** Anglo-Saxon. (Initialism. Someone of English descent, named for the Angles and the Saxons, who [along with the Jutes] populated England around AD 500. See also *WASP*.) ▸ *race: AS*

ASAP as soon as possible. (Initialism and acronym. Pronounced "A-sap" as an acronym. Used to indicate desire that something be done immediately.) ▸ *Pat, please pick up the proofs from the printer ASAP.*

ASCAP American Society of Composers, Authors, and Publishers. (Acronym. An organization of musicians, founded in 1914 by Victor Herbert.) ▸ *Shortly after joining ASCAP, Glenn moved to New York in hopes of writing for a Broadway musical.*

ASCII American Standard Code for Information Interchange. (Acronym. Pronounced "AS-kee." A standard format for representing characters in differing computer programs.) ▸ *By saving her material in ASCII, Melba could access her information on different computers.*

ASE American Stock Exchange. (Initialism. The same as *Amex*. A stock market for small investors and organizations that do not meet the size requirements of the *NYSE*.) ▶ *The ASE is headquartered in New York City's financial district.*

ASL See *Amselan*.

ASPCA American Society for the Prevention of Cruelty to Animals. (Initialism. An organization that promotes animal welfare and protection laws, shelters abandoned animals, and provides animal birth control. See also *SPCA*.) ▶ *The producer invited the ASPCA to the movie set to prove that animals were not mistreated during the production.* ▶ *Shari took her puppy to the local ASPCA to have it neutered.*

assn. AND **assoc.** association. (A group united by a common purpose.) ▶ *Assoc. of Barbershop Quartets.* ▶ *home owners assn.*

assoc. **1.** See *assn.* **2.** associate; associates. (A business partner or partners.) ▶ *Dan Zellner & Assoc.*

ASSR Autonomous Soviet Socialist Republic. (Initialism. One of sixteen divisions within the former Russian Soviet Federated Socialist Republic. See *RSFSR*.) ▶ *Chuvash ASSR* ▶ *Yakut ASSR*

asst. assistant. (Someone who helps out someone in a superior position.) ▶ *asst. director* ▶ *asst. principal* ▶ *asst. to the president*

astrol. astrology. (The nonscientific study of the effect of the positions of celestial bodies, used to predict the future.) ▶ *astrol. chart*

astron. astronomy. (The study of the universe and its components.) ▶ *astron. student*

ASU Arizona State University. (Initialism.) ▸ *ASU Sun Devils*

AT **1.** automatic transmission. (Initialism. In a vehicle, a device that shifts from gear to gear automatically.) ▸ *Repair to AT, $450.* ▸ *1988 Chevy Citation, good condition, AT, $4,000.* **2.** advanced technology. (Initialism. A type of IBM™ and compatible computer designed around the 80286 chip. Compare with *XT.*) ▸ *Is your computer an AT or a 386?*

At astatine. (The chemical symbol for Element 85.)

ATC air traffic control. (Initialism. The body that is responsible for the safe and speedy movement of aircraft in the air and on the ground.) ▸ *As airspace becomes more limited and air traffic becomes heavier, the need for ATC becomes greater.* ▸ *If ATC procedures had been followed, the aircraft would not have crashed.*

ATF automatic transmission fluid. (Initialism. A product that enables a vehicle's automatic transmission to work properly.) ▸ *Jon tripped over a wrench and spilled a quart of ATF onto the hood of his car.*

Atl. Atlantic. ▸ *Atl. Ocean* ▸ *Atl. City*

ATM automatic teller machine; automated teller machine. (Initialism. A machine that handles simple banking transactions such as withdrawals and deposits.) ▸ *Since the ATM machine would not accept Ollie's bank card, he could not withdraw any money.*

ATP adenosine triphosphate. (Initialism. A chemical compound in all living cells, essential in the production of protein and a source of cellular energy.) ▸ *In advanced organisms, ATP is found in the mitochondria of cells.*

AT&T American Telephone and Telegraph. (Initialism. An information processing and telecommunications com-

attn.

pany that provides communication products and services worldwide.) ▶ *Smithco chose AT&T as its long-distance provider.*

attn. attention. (Used primarily in addresses and salutations of letters and documents to indicate the intended recipient or department.) ▶ *Attn. Ms. Ellen Waite* ▶ *Attn. Circulation Department*

atty. attorney. (A lawyer. See also *Esq.*) ▶ *Charles Reichart, Atty. at Law*

Atty. Gen. See *AG*.

ATV all terrain vehicle. (Initialism. A rugged motor vehicle designed for off-road use.) ▶ *The environmentalists protested against the ATVs, which were destroying topsoil and plant growth.*

AU 1. astronomical unit. (Initialism. A unit of linear measurement in astronomy, equal to 93,000,000 miles, the average approximate distance between the earth and the sun.) ▶ *Light travels 1 AU in about 8.5 minutes.* 2. angstrom unit. (Initialism. A unit of linear measurement equal to one ten-billionth [1/10,000,000,000] of a meter. The same as Å.)

Au gold. (The chemical symbol for Element 79. The symbol is derived from Latin *aurum*.)

AUC *ab urbe condite.* (Initialism. Latin: from the year of the founding of the city. A calendar system in which Year 1 is the year Rome was founded. Commonly seen abbreviated with periods [A.U.C.] or in small capitals [AUC, A.U.C.].) ▶ *Year 1 AUC corresponds to 753 BC in the Gregorian system.*

Aug. August. (See also *A.*) ▶ *School starts—Aug. 28*

Aus. AND **Aust.** **1.** AND **Austral.** Australia. (An island-continent southeast of Asia.) ▶ *Melbourne, Aus.* **2.** Austria. (A landlocked country of central Europe.) ▶ *Vienna, Aus.*

Aust. See the previous entry.

aux. auxiliary. (Helping or subsidiary.) ▶ *aux. verb* ▶ *I decided not to join the women's auxiliary.*

A/V See *ad val.*

Av. AND **Ave.** Avenue. (Used on maps and signs and in addresses.) ▶ *1300 N. Damen Av.* ▶ *Thompson Ave.*

AV audiovisual. (Initialism. Something involving both sight and sound.) ▶ *An AV presentation is more effective than a regular speech because you have images accompanying your words.* ▶ *"Whoever checked out the slide projector, please return it to the AV department."*

avdp. avoirdupois. (A system of weight in which a pound is equal to 16 ounces, as opposed to troy weight.) ▶ *12 oz. avdp.*

Ave. See *Av.*

avg. average. (Used in charts and tables to describe the average of a series of numbers and figures.) ▶ *avg. age of death* ▶ *batting avg.*

AWACS airborne warning and control system. (Partial acronym, pronounced "AY-WAX." A system using aircraft with special radar that can detect and track other objects in the air such as enemy aircraft and missiles.) ▶ *The AWACS installation was expensive, but it saved the pilot's life.*

AWD all-wheel drive. (Initialism. A vehicle whose four wheels are all directly powered by the engine, used primarily for high performance sports cars to improve han-

AWL

dling.) ▶ *She uses an AWD to get to her cabin near the lake.*

AWL absent with leave. (Initialism. A military term for someone not present, but whose absence has been approved. Compare with *AWOL*.) ▶ *It's all right. He is AWL.*

AWOL absent without leave. (Acronym, "A-wall," and initialism. A military term for someone not present and not accounted for.) ▶ *The AWOL soldier tried to sneak through town without getting caught.*

AYH American Youth Hostel. (Initialism. Inexpensive lodging for young foreign travelers in the United States, modeled after European hostels.) ▶ *Jane's restaurant was next door to an AYH, and she enjoyed talking with the people from far-off lands.*

AZ Arizona. (The official two-letter post office abbreviation. See also *Ariz.*) ▶ *Tucson, AZ 85701*

AZT azidothymidine. (Initialism. A drug approved by the FDA to fight AIDS. It delays the severity or the onset of AIDS following HIV infection.) ▶ *Jerry had to stop taking AZT because it was damaging his pancreas.*

B

B **1.** a grade indicating above-average work. (Initialism. In the series *A, B, C, D, E* and *A, B, C, D, F.*) ▸ *After failing the first test, Vince studied every night and worked his grade up to a B.* **2.** a musical tone. (Initialism. The seventh note of the scale of C major.) ▸ *After properly warming up, Rachel's range reached the second B above middle C.* **3.** a blood type. ▸ *Raoul knew he had Type B blood, but he was unsure if it was B positive or B negative.* ▸ *People with Type B blood can receive Type O or Type B.* **4.** ball. (A baseball term. Used on scoreboards to denote the number of balls awarded the present batter. The example is to be interpreted to mean that there is one out and the current batter has two strikes and one ball.) ▸ *O 1 S 2 B 1* **5.** bass. (In most choral music arrangements, the lowest range of a male voice. In the series *S, A, T, B.*) **6.** bishop. (A game piece in chess. See also *Bish.*) **7.** bomber. (Initialism. An aircraft designed to drop bombs.) ▸ *The congressional committee studied alternatives to the expensive B-52 program.* **8.** boron. (The chemical symbol for Element 5.)

B.A. **1.** Bachelor of Arts; *Baccalaureus Artium.* (Initialism. A four-year college degree.) ▸ *Jane received her B.A. in history from Kansas State University.* **2.** Buenos Aires. (A major city of Argentina and a center of immigration in the early twentieth century.) ▸ *B.A., Argentina*

BA bathroom. (Found in house and apartment advertising.) ▸ *Gorgeous 4-BR 2-BA house on lake.* ▸ *Handyman's dream, 3-BR 1-BA, porch.*

Ba barium. (The chemical symbol for Element 56.)

BAC blood alcohol concentration. (Initialism. The percentage of alcohol present in the bloodstream.) ▸ *After the accident, the police officer took a sample of Ivan's blood so the lab could calculate his BAC.*

bact. bacteria. (A one-celled organism.) ▸ *3 types of bact. (cocci, bacilli, spirilla)*

bal. balcony. (Used primarily for theater and auditorium tickets and in classified advertisements describing apartments or houses.) ▸ *1st Bal., Row D, Seat 5.* ▸ *3-BR apt. w/ bal. and fireplace*

BAM Brooklyn Academy of Music. (Acronym. A performing arts space in Brooklyn, New York, which usually showcases newer, less familiar works.) ▸ *Jane's father brought in fifty relatives from Long Island to see her perform at BAM.*

Bap. See the following entry.

Bapt. AND **Bap.** 1. Baptist. (A member of the Baptist Protestant denomination and the denomination itself.) ▸ *Third Bap. Church of Springfield* ▸ *New Hope Bapt. Church* 2. Baptist. (Someone who baptizes, usually in reference to John the Baptist.) ▸ *St. John the Bapt. High School*

bar. 1. barometer. (A device that measures air pressure, used to forecast change in the weather.) ▸ *bar. reading*

2. barometric. (The adjective form of *barometer.*) ▶ *bar. pressure*

Barb. Barbados. (An island in the Caribbean.) ▶ *Bridgetown, Barb.*

bar-b-q AND **BBQ** **1.** barbecue. (An outdoor grill for barbecuing meat.) ▶ *Try a hamburger cooked on the bar-b-q.* **2.** barbecue. (A party where barbecued meat is served.) ▶ *You're invited to John and Mary's bar-b-q next Saturday!* **3.** barbecue. (The spicy, smoky flavor of barbecue. Often found in advertising and on packaging.) ▶ *bar-b-q sauce* ▶ *bar-b-q flavored potato chips* ▶ *bar-b-q style chicken nuggets*

BART Bay Area Rapid Transit. (Acronym. The transportation system of the San Francisco area.) ▶ *When the earthquake damaged the bridge between San Francisco and Oakland, many commuters relied on BART to get to work.*

BASIC Beginner's All-purpose Symbolic Instruction Code. (Acronym. A simple computer language, often used as an introduction to programming.) ▶ *The first assignment of the sophomore computer class was to execute a simple program in BASIC.*

Basic English British, American, Scientific, International, Commercial English. (Acronym. The English language trimmed down to 850 simple words for the purpose of teaching English as a foreign language.) ▶ *Some simple concepts are expressed in Basic English with long phrases, because there are only 850 words to choose from.*

B&B bed and breakfast. (Initialism. An inn, hotel, or home that provides lodging and breakfast for travelers.) ▶ *B&B—Saugatuck resort house, near lake, $250/ weekend (616) 555-1003.*

BB 1. ball bearing. (Initialism. A small steel pellet used as ammunition for a BB gun.) ▶ *Mike's mother refused to buy him a BB gun for Christmas.* **2.** base(s) on balls. (Initialism. A baseball term, also known as a walk. A batter gets a base on balls by accumulating four balls before getting three strikes. The batter then proceeds to first base.) **3.** B'nai B'rith. (An international social, educational, and cultural Jewish organization.) ▶ *The regular BB meeting will be at Mr. Stern's house, due to the meeting room being repainted this week.* **4.** Brigitte Bardot. (Initialism. A French movie star and sex symbol.) ▶ *I just love BB!*

BBB Better Business Bureau. (Initialism. An organization that monitors business activities and alerts and protects consumers from fraud.) ▶ *Sally contacted the BBB to check up on a company that had mailed her a promotional offer that seemed too good to be true.*

BBC British Broadcasting Corporation. (Initialism. A British radio and television network.) ▶ *While living in Oslo, Erik practiced English by listening to the BBC on his shortwave radio.*

bbl. barrel. (A unit of liquid measure equal to 42 gallons.) ▶ *12 bbl. cooking oil*

BBQ See *bar-b-q*.

BBS bulletin board service. (Initialism. A telecommunications system serving as an electronic message center where people can communicate by using a computer modem.) ▶ *Although Chuck was new in town, he made a lot of friends through a local BBS.* ▶ *Marge turned on her computer and called up the BBS to see if she had any e-mail.*

BC before Christ. (Initialism. In the modern calendar system, the years prior to the birth of Christ. Commonly seen abbreviated with periods [B.C.] or in small capitals [BC, B.C.]. Compare with *AD.*) ▶ *The first supernova on record was sighted by the Chinese in 352 BC.* **2.** British Columbia, Canada. (The official two-letter post office abbreviation.) ▶ *Vancouver, BC V6B 1N2*

bc blind copy. (Initialism. Used at the bottom of a letter and followed by a name, indicating that the person noted is to receive a copy of the letter. This is not indicated on the original letter, so that the recipient is not aware that the letter has been sent to someone else. See also *bcc.* Compare with *cc.*) ▶ *bc: Ms. Mary Powell*

bcc blind carbon copy. (Initialism. Used at the bottom of a letter and followed by a name, indicating that the person noted is to receive a copy of the letter. This is not indicated on the original letter, so that the recipient is not aware that the letter has been sent to someone else. The same as *bc.* Compare with *cc.*) ▶ *bcc: David Johnson, Esq.*

BCE before the common era; before the Christian era. (Initialism. Another term for "before Christ." Commonly seen abbreviated with periods [B.C.E.] or in small capitals [BCE, B.C.E.].) ▶ *The Greek poet Homer lived in the eighth century BCE.*

bdrm. See *BR.*

B&E breaking and entering. (Initialism. A criminal charge placed against people who illegally force their way into a building.) ▶ *Joan smashed through a picture window to gain access to the apartment, adding yet another B&E charge to her record.*

Be beryllium. (The chemical symbol for Element 4.)

Benelux Belgium, Netherlands, Luxembourg. (Acronym. Used when referring to these three European nations to-

bet.

gether.) ▶ *The Benelux Economic Union was established in 1948.* ▶ *Smith & Smith, Inc., has several branch offices throughout the Benelux countries and France.*

bet. between. (Used in notes and signs.) ▶ *Closed bet. 12 and 1.* ▶ *War bet. the States—Causes? Results?*

bf boldface. (In typesetting, a type face that is darker and heavier than the regular text type.) ▶ **Hello there** *(bf)*

B.F.A. Bachelor of Fine Arts. (Initialism. A four-year college degree.) ▶ *Thelma received her B.F.A. in musical theater from DePaul University.*

BHA butylated hydroxyanisole. (Initialism. A synthetic food additive used as a preservative in food products containing fat and oil. Found in listings of ingredients on packaging and in nutritional breakdown charts.) ▶ *In an attempt to eat healthfully, Alvin bought organic corn oil without sodium, BHA, or other preservatives.*

BHT butylated hydroxytoluene. (Initialism. A synthetic food additive. Found in listings of ingredients on packaging and in nutritional breakdown charts.) ▶ *The Randolphs forbid their children to eat snacks with BHT, MSG, artificial colors, or high levels of sodium.*

Bi bismuth. (The chemical symbol for Element 83.)

bib. biblical. (Relating to the bible. Found in dictionaries to indicate a word of biblical origin.) ▶ *Ps. (bib.)—Psalms*

Bib. Bible. (The name for the sacred texts of the Judaic and Christian religions.) ▶ *King James Bib.*

b.i.d. *bis in die.* (Initialism. Latin: twice a day. Found in medical prescriptions.) ▶ *Take two tablets b.i.d.*

bio. AND **biol.** biology. (Sometimes a clipping. The study of living organisms.) ▶ *Bio. Dept.* ▶ *"I can't talk to you* *now, I'm late for my bio lab,"* Anne yelled as she ran to class. ▶ *Andrew had a crush on his bio professor.*

biol. See the previous entry.

BIOS Basic Input/Output System. (Acronym. The part of a computer that communicates with the screen, the keyboard, the printers, modems, and other accessories.) ▶ *If you're experiencing trouble with your new computer, please call our BIOS support line at (213) 555-2467.*

Bish. Bishop. (The religious leader of a diocese. In the Roman Catholic religion, a bishop is above a priest and below a cardinal.) ▶ *Bish. Povish celebrated Mass on Easter Sunday at St. Mary's.*

bit binary digit. (Blend. The smallest piece of information recognized by a computer, and the basic unit for storing data.) ▶ *One byte is made up of eight bits.*

Bk berkelium. (The chemical symbol for Element 97.)

bldg. building. ▶ *Bldg. H houses the human resources department.*

BLT bacon, lettuce, and tomato [sandwich]. (Initialism.) ▶ *Warren ordered a BLT and some french fries.*

Blvd. AND **Boul.** Boulevard. (Used in addresses and signs.) ▶ *1950 West Augusta Blvd.* ▶ *Mich. Boul.*

BM bowel movement. (Initialism. Fecal material and the process that expels it from the body. Partly euphemistic.) ▶ *The pediatrician checked the baby's BM for tapeworms.*

BMOC big man on campus. (Initialism. Applied to very popular students, usually male, in high school or college.) ▶ *After Tim scored the winning touchdown, he was suddenly a BMOC.*

BMR

BMR basal metabolism rate. (Initialism. The measure of heat produced by the metabolism of a person at rest.) ▸ *By determining Henry's BMR, the nutritionist devised a diet suited to his needs.*

BMW *Bayerische Motoren Werke.* (Initialism. German: Bavarian Motor Works. A prestigious and expensive car and the company that produces it.) ▸ *Not wanting to arrive at the company's black-tie function in his '82 Chevy, Vernon drove his uncle's BMW.*

BMX bicycle motorcross. (Initialism. The *X* stands for *cross.* This uses a special bicycle designed for rough off-road travel and competition.) ▸ *The potholes of the city streets were so bad that Peter bought a BMX to get around town.*

B&O Baltimore and Ohio. (Initialism. The name of a railroad company, more commonly known as one of the railroads on the Monopoly™ game board.) ▸ *Ellen passed by the hotels on the red color group and landed on B&O Railroad.*

BO **1.** body odor. (Initialism. Sweat, usually with an unpleasant smell.) ▸ *Many deodorants are available to combat BO.* **2.** box office. (Initialism. The area of a theater or auditorium where patrons buy tickets.) ▸ *The BO staff consisted of Amy, Nancy, and Lucille.* **3.** branch office. (Initialism. Auxiliary offices not located at the headquarters of a firm.) ▸ *Smithco, Inc., has BOs in Aurora, Peoria, Moline, and Decatur.*

Boul. See *Blvd.*

bp **1.** AND **bpl.** birthplace. (Found on forms.) ▸ *bp—Atlanta, GA.* **2.** boiling point. (Found in texts, charts, and tables. The temperature at which a liquid boils.) ▸ *bp of water—100°C or 212°F.* **3.** AND **BP** blood pressure. (Initialism. Found on medical charts and in texts.) ▶ *bp—140/80.* ▶ *high BP*

BP See *bp*.

bpl. See *bp*.

bpm beats per minute. (Initialism. A measurement of how fast or slow music is. In reference to classical music, the term is primarily in written form only, but in reference to modern popular music, people such as disc jockeys will use the spoken abbreviated form.) ▶ *Yuri practiced the sonata at 60 bpm until he could play it flawlessly.* ▶ *Eugene arranged all his high-energy dance singles in bpm order from slow to fast.*

BPOE Benevolent and Protective Order of Elks. (Initialism. A national fraternal organization. Usually members are called "Elks" and meet at the "Elk Lodge.") ▶ *The local BPOE sponsored a fund-raiser to assist the families whose homes had been destroyed during the tornado.*

BR AND **bdrm.** bedroom. (Found in house and apartment advertising.) ▶ *Roommate needed to share 2-BR apt. near the university.* ▶ *4-bdrm. 2-BA, 2,500 sf, $195,000.*

br. **1.** branch. (A division of a business, usually located away from the headquarters.) ▶ *Hoboken Br. Office.* ▶ *Post Box Facility—Br. "W"* **2.** branch. (A stream or a section of a river. Found on maps and signs.) ▶ *W. Br. of Grand River* **3.** bridge. (Found on maps and signs.) ▶ *Brooklyn Br.*

Br. **1.** British. ▶ *Br. English* ▶ *Br. History* **2.** AND **Bro.** Brother. (A lay member of a men's religious order.) ▶ *Br. Thomas helped the aging monk up the stairs to the cathedral.* ▶ *Please show your appreciation to the choir, led by Bro. Herbert, after today's service by attending their*

Br

bake sale downstairs. ▸ *Bro. Donatus laboriously copied the ancient scripts onto vellum parchment.*

Br bromine. (The chemical symbol for Element 35.)

Braz. Brazil. (The largest country in South America, comprising much of the eastern part of the continent.) ▸ *São Paulo, Braz.*

Brig. Gen. Brigadier General. (A U.S. military officer ranking below a major general but above a colonel.) ▸ *Brig. Gen. Lee N. Smith*

Brit. 1. Britain. (The island of Great Britain.) ▸ *Gr. Brit.* 2. British. ▸ *Brit. English.* ▸ *Falkland Islands (Brit.)* ▸ *pram (Brit.)*

Brit British; Briton. (Clipping. A person from Great Britain. Sometimes used derisively.) ▸ *"Brits are happy people even though it never gets really hot there," the tourist told her traveling companion.*

Bro. See *Br.*

Bros. 1. brothers. (Used by firms run by brothers.) ▸ *Perkins & Sons Realty was renamed Perkins Bros. Realty after Mr. Perkins, Sr., died.* 2. the plural of *Br.* and *Bro.* See *Br.*

B.S. Bachelor of Science. (Initialism. A four-year college degree.) ▸ *Karen received her B.S. in chemical engineering from Ohio State University.*

BS bullshit. (Initialism. Nonsense; balderdash. Use with caution.) ▸ *"I want you to tell me where you've been, and I don't want to hear any BS," Rebecca told her boyfriend.*

BSA Boy Scouts of America. (Initialism. A national organization for boys that focuses on building character and being charitable to others.)

btu AND **BTU, Btu** British thermal unit. (Initialism. A measurement of heat output. One btu is equal to the amount of heat necessary to raise the temperature of one pound of water 1° Fahrenheit.) ▶ *1 btu is a little more than 250 calories.* ▶ *We could only afford a 6000 btu air conditioner.*

bur. bureau. (A government agency or a division of a government agency.) ▶ *Bur. of Missing Persons*

BVD Bradley, Voorhees & Day. (Initialism. A brand name of underwear, in some instances generalized to all underwear for men.) ▶ *Awakened by the fire alarm, Bill hastily put on his BVDs and a robe, and ran out the door.*

B.V.(M.) *Beate Virgo (Maria);* Blessed Virgin (Mary). (The mother of Jesus. Used in Catholic texts and inscriptions.) ▶ *B.V.M., pray for us.*

b&w See the following entry.

b/w AND **b&w** 1. black and white. (Initialism. A movie or program filmed in black and white. Usually found in reviews and in television program listings.) ▶ *8:00 Leave It To Beaver (b/w)* ▶ *Manhattan (b/w)* 2. black and white [television screen]. (Initialism. Primarily used in advertisements.) ▶ *I don't think I ever saw a b&w T.V.* ▶ *b/w TV, good condition, $25.*

bw birthweight. (Found on medical charts and forms.) ▶ *bw—6 lb., 2 oz.*

B'way Broadway. (A common name for a major urban thoroughfare. In New York City, Broadway is a major street that the theater district is named for.) ▶ *42nd & B'way.* ▶ *4800 N. B'way, Chicago*

BYO bring your own. (Initialism. A party where those invited are expected to bring food and drink.) ▶ *Party— Sat. Nov. 24—BYO*

BYOB bring your own bottle. (Initialism. A party for which food is provided, but those invited are expected to bring any alcohol or other beverage they may wish to drink.) ▶ *The party is BYOB, but Thelma is making her famous guacamole dip.*

BYU Brigham Young University. (Initialism.) ▶ *BYU Cougars*

C

© copyright. (The symbol used for a publication that is copyrighted. The same as *C* and *cop.*) ▸ *©1969*

c. **1.** AND **C.** carat. (A unit of weight for gemstones equal to approximately 200 milligrams. The same as *ct.* Compare with *karat* at *k.*) ▸ *The jeweler placed his favorite 4-c. emerald in the display case.* **2.** catcher. (The baseball position of catcher.) **3.** AND **ca.** *circa.* (Initialism. Latin: near. Denotes an uncertainty about or an approximation of a historical date.) ▸ *The Mongol conqueror Tamerlane was born c. 1336.*

C. Cape. (Land that protrudes into a body of water. Found on maps and signs and in addresses.) ▸ *C. Hatteras* ▸ *C. of Good Hope*

C **1.** a grade indicating average work. (Initialism. In the series *A, B, C, D, E* and *A, B, C, D, F.*) ▸ *Jane Doe received a C for her mediocre paper.* **2.** a musical tone. (Initialism. The first note of the scale of C major.) ▸ *At her first piano lesson, Ellen learned how to find middle C.* **3.** a popular computer language developed by Bell Laboratories. (Initialism.) ▸ *Martha's training involved becoming proficient with Pascal and C.* **4.** carbon. (The chemical symbol for Element 6.) **5.** Celsius. (A unit of degree of temperature. The freezing point of water is 0°C;

c

the boiling point of water is 100°C. Before 1948, the term was *Centigrade*. See also *F.*) **6.** Celtic. (A branch of the Indo-European language, including Gaelic, Welsh, and Breton.) **7.** Centigrade. (See *Celsius* at sense 5.) **8.** cold. (Marked on water faucets and other temperature controls to differentiate between cold and hot.) ▶ *The July heat and humidity was so stifling that Jodie turned the dial on her air conditioner all the way to the C.* **9.** AND **cons.** consonant. (A linguistic symbol for particular speech sounds. The airflow through the mouth during the production of consonants is stopped, limited, or diverted through the nose. See also *V.*) ▶ *C represents any consonant sound, such as p, t, and k.* ▶ *A consonant cluster can be represented as CC (such as st) or CCC (such as str).* ▶ *Examples of words exhibiting a CCVC pattern are* step, prod, frog, *and* clap. **10.** See *cop*. **11.** 100. (A Roman numeral.) ▶ *CCC = 300.*

c 1. the speed of light in a vacuum. (A physics symbol.) ▶ *c = 186,282 miles per hour* **2.** centi- (A prefix meaning 1/100, used with units of measurement.) ▶ *cg (centigram)* ▶ *cm (centimeter)* **3.** cubic. (Of three dimensions. The same as *cu*. Compare with *square*, which indicates two dimensions.) ▶ *cc (cubic centimeter)* **4.** AND **ca.** about.

C.A. Central America. (Initialism. The bridge of land from Mexico to Panama between North and South America. Used in addresses.) ▶ *Trujillo, Colón, Honduras, C.A.*

ca. See *c*.

CA 1. California. (The official two-letter post office abbreviation. See also *Cal.*) ▶ *San Francisco, CA 94101* **2.** chronological age. (Actual age, as opposed to developmental age.) ▶ *Dr. Matthews has been assigned to Betty B. (CA 8) to treat her.* **3.** Confederate Army. (The forces serving the South during the War Between the States.)

Ca calcium. (The chemical symbol for Element 20.)

CAB Civil Aeronautics Board. (Acronym. A government agency from 1940 to 1984 that regulated the airline industry.) ▸ *CAB was dissolved in 1984 following the deregulation of the airlines industry.*

CAD **1.** computer-aided design. (Initialism. A computer system that automates complex and repetitive actions used to assist designers. See also *CAM*.) **2.** coronary artery disease. (Initialism. The medical condition of the narrowing of the arteries leading to the heart.) ▸ *The researcher studied the links between cholesterol intake and CAD.*

CAD-CAM computer-aided design and computer-aided manufacture. (Initialism. Using the computer in automation, design, animation, and imaging.) ▸ *If you want to do CAD-CAM, you need a very fast computer and an enormous amount of RAM.*

CAE **1.** Central African Empire. (Initialism. The name of the Central African Republic from December 4, 1976, to September 20, 1979.) ▸ *Bangui, CAE* **2.** computer-aided engineering. (Initialism. A computer system that automates complex and repetitive actions used to assist engineers.)

CAI computer-assisted instruction. (Initialism. The use of a computer program in teaching and learning.)

Cal a calorie (large). (A unit of energy measurement equal to 1000 small calories, used to determine the amount of energy food can provide. Since most consumers are aware of only large calories, when the abbreviation *cal* is found on packaging, it usually refers to the large calorie even if it is written with a lower case *c*.)

Cal.

Cal. AND **Calif.** California. (See also *CA*.) ▸ *Eureka, Cal.* ▸ *Gov. Pete Jones (Cal.)* ▸ *Santa Barbara, Calif.*

cal. **1.** calendar. (A system used to keep track of time.) ▸ *cal. year* ▸ *Julian Cal.* ▸ *Gregorian Cal.* **2.** calorie. (Often a clipping. The type of calorie familiar to most consumers.) ▸ *1200-cal. diet* ▸ *125 cal. per serving* ▸ *low-cal microwave dinners*

cal a calorie (small). (A unit of energy measurement equal to the energy needed to raise the temperature of one milliliter of water 1° Celsius. This sense of *calorie* is rarely encountered by nonscientists.)

calc. calculus. (Sometimes used as a clipping. A branch of higher mathematics.) ▸ *integral calc.* ▸ *"If I don't get at least a B on the calc exam, I'm going to fail the class," Tom told his parents.*

Calif. See *Cal.*

CAM computer-aided manufacture. (Initialism. A manufacturing system that is guided by computer.)

Can. **1.** Canada. (A country in North America to the north of the contiguous United States.) ▸ *Toronto, Can.* ▸ *Ottawa, Can.* **2.** Canal. (An artificial waterway.) ▸ *Panama Can.* ▸ *Erie Can.*

CAN Cancer. (The astrological abbreviation for the zodiacal constellation of Cancer.) ▸ *CAN (June 21 to July 22)*

canc. canceled. ▸ *canc. check*

cap. **1.** capacity. (The amount necessary to fill a container or room.) ▸ *cap. 100 ml* ▸ *max. cap. 850 people* **2.** capital. (The seat of government.) ▸ *cap. city* ▸ *Cap. building* ▸ *Baton Rouge (cap.)* **3.** capital. (Money, property, and other assets owned by a person or company.) ▸ *cap. expenditure* ▸ *$20,000,000 cap. assets* **4.** capital letter. (Often a clipping. In publishing and printing, an uppercase letter. The plural is **caps**.) ▶ *Please put all the acronyms into caps. this time.*

CAP Capricorn. (The astrological abbreviation for the zodiacal constellation of Capricorn.) ▶ *CAP (December 22 to January 19)*

caplet capsule/tablet. (Blend. A tablet shaped like a capsule designed to prevent tampering with its contents.) ▶ *convenient caplet form*

caps. **1.** capsule. (A tablet-like, dissolvable container containing one dose of medicine.) ▶ *36 caps.* **2.** See *cap.* (sense 4).

Capt. AND **Cpt.** Captain. (The person in charge of a group of people, such as the head of a vessel or team.) ▶ *Capt. Hook* ▶ *Capt. Steubing presided over the wedding ceremony on his ship.* ▶ *Capt. Reynolds guided the DC-10 to the runway safely during the tumultuous storm.* ▶ *Meet the capt. of the football team and all the cheerleaders after today's pep rally in the gym!*

CAR Central African Republic. (Initialism. A nation in Central Africa. From December 4, 1976, to September 20, 1979, this country was known as the Central African Empire.) ▶ *Bambari, CAR*

Card. Cardinal. (A Catholic official appointed by the Pope.) ▶ *Card. Bernardin led a silent prayer for the sick and suffering of the world.*

Card Cardinal. (Clipping. A member of the St. Louis Cardinals baseball team.) ▶ *The Cubs beat the Cards in ten innings.*

CARE Cooperative for American Relief to Everywhere. (Acronym. Founded in 1945, a nonprofit organization that provides food and clothing, health care, programs

cat.

for food production and energy conservation, and emergency assistance throughout the world.) ▸ *The victims of the typhoon welcomed the CARE packages sent to their stricken town.*

cat. catalog. (A list of contents within a library or of products offered by a company.) ▸ *card cat.* ▸ *Sears cat.*

CAT 1. clear air turbulence. (Initialism. An aviation term for air turbulence in the absence of clouds.) ▸ *A pilot has no advance warning before hitting a CAT pocket.* 2. computerized axial tomography. (Acronym. An imaging technique that uses X rays to produce a computer-generated 3-D image.) ▸ *CAT scan* ▸ *No signs of tumors showed up on Mrs. Admundson's CAT scan.*

Cath. Cathedral. (A church that is the head church of a diocese and the headquarters of a bishop.) ▸ *The Holy Name Cath. Choir performance will be shown on Channel 9.*

CATV 1. cable television. (Initialism. A television system in which broadcast signals are transmitted by cable to consumers who subscribe to the service.) ▸ *The Farrells lived in a valley and had poor television reception, so they decided to subscribe to a CATV service.* 2. community antenna television. (An early name for cable television.) ▸ *We had to hook up to the CATV because reception was so poor.*

cauc. caucasian. (Relating to the culture and people of the Caucasus mountains in Asia. More commonly used on government forms and the like as a term for people who are white, as opposed to blacks, Asians, and other people of color.) ▸ *Arnold Abrams, 26, 6' 2", cauc., last seen wearing a blue blazer and black pants.*

caus. causative. (Pertaining to a transitive verb that includes the notion of making something happen. Found in language textbooks and dictionaries.) ▶ *The expectant mother's husband boiled (caus.) the water.*

CB citizens band. (Initialism. A shortwave radio with citizens band frequencies, used by truck drivers to communicate road conditions, and a popular fad of the late 1970s.) ▶ *CB radio.* ▶ *Tim contacted the police by CB after he witnessed the accident.* ▶ *"10-4" is the CB code to signal the end of conversation.*

CBC 1. Canadian Broadcasting Company. (Initialism. A Canadian radio and television network.) ▶ *When Eldon lived in Toledo, he watched the CBC news broadcast from Windsor, Ontario.* 2. complete blood count. (Initialism. A blood test that determines the amount of red and white blood cells in a blood sample, useful in diagnosing many illnesses.) ▶ *The doctor ordered a CBC.* ▶ *The results of the CBC proved the patient to be anemic.*

CBD central business district. (Initialism. The financial and business center of a city.) ▶ *Chicago's CBD has expanded beyond the elevated tracks that were the boundaries of the Loop.*

CBS Columbia Broadcasting System. (Initialism. A radio and television network in the U.S. See also *ABC, NBC.*) ▶ *"Sixty Minutes" is broadcast by CBS.*

cc 1. carbon copy. (Initialism. Usually followed by a name, it indicates that the person noted or mentioned is to receive a copy of something. Often found on the bottom of letters and correspondence.) ▶ *cc: Dr. Velma Ivanev* ▶ *cc: Department of Revenue* ▶ *"Andrea, could you please cc that last letter to Angie and Frank over in accounting?"* 2. cubic centimeter. (Initialism. A unit of volume.) ▶ *The nurse injected 10 cc of serum into the patient.*

CC closed captioned. (Initialism. Television programs that are encoded with captions for the hearing impaired. A special device displays these captions on the screen. Usually found in television programming guides.) ▸ *Murder, She Wrote (CC)* ▸ *60 Minutes (CC)*

C.C.A. Circuit Court of Appeals. (Initialism. A judicial district established to relieve the Supreme Court from reconsidering the decisions of all federal trials. The Circuit Justice of each C.C.A. is a member of the Supreme Court.) ▸ *Justice Kennedy is the Circuit Justice for the 11th C.C.A.* ▸ *The State of California is within the jurisdiction of the 9th C.C.A.*

CCCP (Initialism. The Russian [Cyrillic] spelling for the former USSR. A transliteration of the Russian words is *Soyuz Sovyetskikh Sotsialisticheskikh Respublik*. English speakers sometimes pronounce it "SEE SEE SEE PEE." As Cyrillic characters, *CCCP* should be pronounced "ES ES ES AR" in English. See the comments at *CIS*.) ▸ *Moskva, CCCP*

cckw. AND **ccw.** counterclockwise. (A circular direction, opposite the direction the hands of a clock run. Found in instructions and texts.) ▸ *To remove the screw, turn cckw.*

CCR Commission on Civil Rights. (Initialism. A federal commission that holds hearings on discrimination based on race, color, religion, sex, age, handicap, and national origin, and studies the enforcement of civil rights and equal opportunity laws.) ▸ *The CCR was created by the Civil Rights Act of 1957.*

CCTV closed circuit television. (Initialism. A television system that transmits a program by cable to a limited number of connected receivers.) ▸ *We all watched the boxing match on CCTV.*

CCU coronary care unit. (Initialism. The part of a hospital designated for the care of patients with heart problems.) ▸ *After triple bypass surgery, Mr. Jones stayed in the CCU wing until his condition stabilized.*

ccw. See *cckw.*

CD **1.** Caesarean delivery. (Childbirth in which doctors deliver a baby by surgically opening the abdomen and uterus of the mother and extracting the baby. See also *C section.*) ▸ *Andrew's birth was by CD.* **2.** certificate of deposit. (Initialism. A certification from a financial institution acknowledging money held in a time deposit at a specific interest rate.) ▸ *Jimmy invested the money he received from his grandparents by placing it in a CD account.* **3.** civil defense. (Initialism. A civilian warning system that alerts people to impending natural disasters and enemy attacks, provides emergency services to areas hit by natural disasters and enemy attacks, organizes evacuations, and administers shelters. See also *FEMA.*) ▸ *The basement of City Hall is also a CD shelter in case of tornado or nuclear attack.* **4.** civil disobedience. (Initialism. Protest in the form of deliberate disobeying of a law, usually nonviolently.) ▸ *The activists sponsored a CD workshop prior to the demonstration.* **5.** compact disc. (Initialism. A disc encoded with data that requires a laser beam device to read the encoded information, primarily used for the reproduction of music and the dissemination and storage of information.) ▸ *Audrey bought a CD player because most of the music she listened to wasn't available on records.* ▸ *Erica input all of her writing onto one CD, replacing reams of paper she had kept in her attic for years.*

Cd cadmium. (The chemical symbol for Element 48.)

CDC Centers for Disease Control. (Initialism. Founded in 1946 and now a part of the Department of Health and

Human Services, it protects and promotes health and wellness by overseeing programs for the prevention and control of disease, providing health information, conducting research, and developing immunization programs.) ▶ *Each month the AIDS clinic posted the most recent figures released by the CDC.*

CD-ROM compact disc-read only memory. (Initialism-acronym. Pronounced "SEE DEE RAHM." A compact disc used to store data. The information cannot be altered or deleted. See also *ROM*.) ▶ *The Oxford English Dictionary is now available on CD-ROM.*

CDT Central Daylight Time. (Initialism. The adjusted time in the central United States during early April to late October. It is five hours behind Greenwich Time.) ▶ *3:30 p.m. CDT* ▶ *Bank transactions completed after 2:00 p.m. CDT will be posted on the next business day.*

C.E. 1. AND **Ch.E.** chemical engineer. (A professional title for someone who applies chemistry to industrial situations.) ▶ *David R. Munro, C.E., supervised the cleanup of the hazardous waste site behind the factory.* **2.** civil engineer. (A professional title for someone who designs and constructs city infrastructures such as roadways, sewers, bridges, and tunnels.) ▶ *Gloria Watson, C.E., designed the new bridge to alleviate traffic crossing the river.* **3.** common era; Christian era. (Initialism. The system of numbering years used in most of the world today, commonly known as AD. The approximate birth date of Jesus Christ is used as year 1, C.E. Commonly seen abbreviated with periods [C.E.] or in small capitals [CE, C.E.]. Compare with *BCE*.) ▶ *The Roman Empire reached its greatest extent in the second century C.E.*

Ce cerium. (The chemical symbol for Element 58.)

CERCLA

CEA council of economic advisors. (Initialism. Established in 1946, a three-person group that advises the president on economic policies, current economic conditions, and future economic forecasts.) ▶ *Every person chosen by the president for the CEA must be approved by the Senate.*

Cen. Cenozoic. (The geological time period from roughly 65 million years ago to the present.) ▶ *Cen. Era*

cent. 1. central. ▶ *Cent. Business Dist.* ▶ *Cent. High Senior Prom* 2. century. (A grouping of 100 years. For instance, the first century AD was from AD 1 to AD 100. The nineteenth century was from AD 1801 to AD 1900.) ▶ *20th Cent. technology* ▶ *18th Cent. French literature* 3. centigrade. (The scale for measuring temperature, now known as Celsius. See also C.) ▶ *100° cent. = 212°F*

CENTO Central Treaty Organization. (Acronym. An international military alliance among the United Kingdom, Iran, Pakistan, and Turkey, with the United States as an associate member, formed in 1955.) ▶ *Iran and Pakistan left CENTO in 1979.*

CEO chief executive officer. (Initialism. The highest-ranking executive of a firm or company.) ▶ *John W. Smith, CEO and Treasurer of Smithco-Portland, invites you to a seminar and luncheon on August 3rd.* ▶ *The telemarketer apologized to the CEO for interrupting a meeting.*

CERCLA Comprehensive Environmental Response, Compensation, and Liability Act. (Acronym. Also known as the Superfund. Authorized by Congress in 1980, a program administered by the Environmental Protection Agency to clean up hazardous waste sites.) ▶ *A hazardous waste site is not eligible for CERCLA funds until it is*

cert.

placed on the Environmental Protection Agency's National Priorities List.

cert. AND **ctf.** 1. certificate. (A document attesting that one has met a set of requirements.) ▶ *Wanted: English teacher, with cert.* ▶ *You can't work here without the proper ctf.* 2. certified. (Pertaining to someone or something registered or licensed for some particular purpose.) ▶ *This work is cert. accurate.* ▶ *Are you cert.?*

CETA Comprehensive Employment and Training Act. (Acronym. A government program that provides federal money to states and municipalities for job training and public service jobs for the unemployed.) ▶ *Through CETA, Jackie got a minimum-wage job.*

c.f. center field. (Initialism. A baseball abbreviation for the outfield position of center field.)

cf. *confer.* (Initialism. Latin: compare. Used in cross-referencing to alert the reader to another entry for purposes of comparison.) ▶ cf. *Figure 12-5 and 12-6.*

Cf californium. (The chemical symbol for Element 98.)

CF cystic fibrosis. (Initialism. A hereditary disease in which body organs, especially the lungs and the pancreas, secrete a thick mucus that hinders the function of the organ.) ▶ *Each year, Mr. Jones made donations toward finding a cure for CF.*

CFC chlorofluorocarbon. (Initialism. A class of compounds of carbon, chlorine, fluorine, and hydrogen chiefly used as refrigerants.) ▶ *The entire world is struggling to eliminate CFC emissions into the atmosphere.*

CFTC Commodity Futures Trading Association. (Initialism. Established in 1973 to regulate the trading on United States futures exchanges and the activities of commodity exchange workers and other related fields.) ▶

The CFTC is essential to ensure that futures are traded legally and fairly.

c.g. center of gravity. (The point in a body to which all matter outside of that body is gravitationally attracted.) ▶ *Table 2-5: c.g. by planet.*

C.G. coast guard. (Initialism. An armed services branch that protects life and property on and near water, enforces maritime laws, and is a part of the navy during war.) ▶ *USCG*

cg AND **cgm** centigram. (A unit of weight equal to 1/100 of a gram.) ▶ *100 cg = 1 gram*

cgs centimeter/gram/second. (Initialism. One of two international measurement systems used to measure force, work, energy, and power. The cgs system is for small measurements. Compare with *mks*.) ▶ *The cgs unit for the measurement of force is the dyne.*

Ch. 1. Channel. (The number assigned a television or radio station that corresponds to the frequency band at which the broadcast signal must be transmitted.) ▶ *Ch. 7 News at 11:00* **2.** AND **Chan.** Channel. (A river or stream connecting two larger bodies of water.) ▶ *East Ch.* **3.** AND **Chap.** Chapter. (A division of a book or organization.) ▶ *For Friday, read Chap. 10, 11, and 12.* **4.** church. (The congregation of a religion, as well as the building in which they meet.) ▶ *Ch. of Christ* ▶ *Roman Catholic Ch.* ▶ *St. John the Baptist Ch.*

Chan. See under *Ch*.

Chanc. Chancellor. (An official, as found in some governments and universities.) ▶ *Chanc. Fortini gave the commencement address.*

Chap. See *Ch*.

Chas. Charles. ▸ *Prince Chas.* ▸ *Chas. W. Franklin, proprietor*

Ch.E. See *C.E.*

chem. 1. chemistry. (Sometimes a clipping. The science of the composition, structure, and properties of substances, the changes substances undergo when being produced, and the interactions between substances.) ▸ *Jimmy dropped a vial into a puddle of acid and nearly burned the chem lab down!* ▸ *organic chem.* 2. chemical. (Relating to chemistry.) ▸ *chem. warfare*

chemo chemotherapy. (Clipping. The treatment or control of disease through the use of chemical agents to destroy the tissue or organisms responsible for the disease.) ▸ *The doctor set a schedule for Mrs. Brown's chemo treatments.*

Chgo. [or Chio] Chicago. (The largest city in Illinois; the third largest city in the United States.) ▸ *400 S. State St., Chgo., Ill.* ▸ *Chgo. Public Library*

Chin. Chinese. ▸ *Chin. cuisine* ▸ *Chin. literature*

Chr. 1. Christ Jesus. ▸ *Church of Chr.* 2. Christian. (A follower of Christ or a Christlike attitude.) ▸ *Center for Chr. Studies*

chron. chronology. (A sequential ordering of events from earliest to most recent.) ▸ *reverse chron.*

C.I. 1. Cayman Islands. (Initialism. A British dependent territory located in the Caribbean Sea.) ▸ *Georgetown, C.I.* 2. Channel Islands. (Initialism. A group of islands off the coast of France in the English Channel belonging to the United Kingdom.) ▸ *St. Peter, C.I.*

CIA Central Intelligence Agency. (Initialism. Established in 1947, an American government agency that gathers and disseminates information worldwide and protects national security through many means.) ▶ *The director of the CIA reports to the National Security Council.*

CID Criminal Investigation Department. (Initialism. Commonly referred to as "Scotland Yard." The department of detectives of the London Police.) ▶ *Osric was taken down to the CID for questioning after the bombing incident in the tubes.*

C in C Commander in Chief. (Initialism. The head commander of a nation's or an organization's armed forces.) ▶ *General Sir Patrick Palmer, NATO C in C Allied Forces, Northern Europe*

CIO Congress of Industrial Organizations. (Initialism. A powerful labor organization that merged with the AFL in 1955. See *AFL-CIO*.) ▶ *Hank told his grandchildren about his younger days as a union leader for the newly formed CIO.*

cir. 1. circle. (Found on maps, addresses, and signs.) ▶ *Dupont Cir.* ▶ *421 West End Cir.* ▶ *Arctic Cir.* 2. AND **circ.** circuit. (An electrical term for the path that electrical current flows along.) ▶ *cir. breaker*

circ. 1. circulation. (The number of copies of a magazine, newspaper, or other published periodicals sold.) ▶ *circ. 750,000 readers daily* 2. See *cir.* (sense 2).

circum. circumference. (The line that forms a circle and its measurement.) ▶ *circum. of 2"*

CIS Commonwealth of Independent States. (Initialism. A political entity comprised of eleven of the fifteen former republics of the Union of Soviet Socialist Republics following the breakup of the *USSR* in 1991.) ▶ *The administrative headquarters of the CIS is in Minsk, Belarus.*

CISPES Committee in Solidarity with the People of El Salvador. (Acronym. A grassroots solidarity organization dedicated to ending United States intervention in El Salvador.) ▸ *Members of CISPES sponsored a demonstration to protest U.S. military aid to El Salvador.*

cit. 1. cited. (Quoted previously. Found in articles and dissertations.) 2. citizen. (A resident of a political district.) ▸ *American cit.*

civ. 1. civil. (Relating to citizens and interactions between them.) ▸ *Spanish Civ. War* ▸ *civ. disobedience* 2. civilian. (Someone who is not a member of the military and things relating to such people.) ▸ *civ. clothes*

C.J. Chief Justice. (Initialism. The presiding judge of a court with more than one judge.) ▸ *William H. Rehnquist (C.J., United States Supreme Court)*

Ck. AND **Cr.** Creek. (A small, narrow stream of water. Found on maps, addresses, and signs.) ▸ *Plum Ck.* ▸ *Six Mile Cr. Rd.*

Cl chlorine. (The chemical symbol for Element 17.)

CLEP College Level Examination Program. (Acronym. A program offering achievement exams that test knowledge of general liberal arts or a specific subject area. People who score well on CLEP exams receive college credit.) ▸ *David had pursued interests in chemistry since childhood and had learned enough to pass a CLEP Subject Examination in Chemistry.*

CLI cost of living index. (Initialism. A list published by the American Chamber of Commerce Researchers Association that compares the pretax cost of consumer goods and services in America. Each city's index is expressed as a percentage of the national average of 100.) ▸ *Exorbi-*

tant housing costs in San Diego pushed its composite CLI to 131.4 for the first quarter of 1991.

clm. See *col.*

c.m. **1.** center of mass. (Initialism. The point around which the matter of a body is concentrated.) ▶ *Report 24-1.2: Changes in c.m. as the speed of light is approached.* **2.** circular mail. (Advertisements and similar letters prepared in mass quantity for mass circulation.) **3.** court-martial. (Initialism. The military court system that tries people accused of breaking military law.) ▶ *The C.O. suggested a c.m.*

cm centimeter. (A unit of linear measurement equal to 1/10 of a meter or .3937 inches.) ▶ *Vernon's height in stocking feet is 180 cm.*

CM command module. (Initialism. A spacecraft that houses the control center and living quarters.) ▶ *One astronaut stayed behind in the CM while the rest went out for a space walk.*

Cm curium. (The chemical symbol for Element 96.)

CMA certified medical assistant. (The job title of someone who has been certified by a state medical board to be an aide to a doctor or nurse.) ▶ *Pamela J. Wilson, CMA*

Cmdr. AND **Com., Comdr.** Commander. (A person in authority or a leader. In the United States Navy, an officer of rank.) ▶ *Cmdr. Eagleton discussed the aftermath of the storm with the captain.*

CMEA AND **COMECON** Council for Mutual Economic Assistance. (Initialism AND acronym. An organization of Communist countries that aided the development of the members' technology and economy. CMEA was established in April 1949 and dissolved in June 1991.) ▶ *Al-*

bania left the CMEA in 1961. ▸ *In addition to the East Bloc countries, Mongolia, Vietnam, and Cuba were also members of COMECON.*

CMU Carnegie Mellon University. (Initialism.) ▸ *Jane visited the CMU campus in Pittsburgh.*

CNN Cable News Network. (Initialism. A cable television network that broadcasts news twenty-four hours a day.) ▸ *We watched the first hours of the Persian Gulf War on CNN.*

CNS central nervous system. (Initialism. The brain and the spinal cord.) ▸ *Muscle coordination is controlled by the CNS.*

C.O. conscientious objector. (Initialism. One who refuses to participate in war for moral or religious reasons.) ▸ *The young C.O.'s fled to Canada in droves.*

c/o [in] care of. (Used on envelopes and letters to address correspondence or packages to someone in care of someone else or a firm at that address.) ▸ *Dr. Erich Hahn, c/o The Monopole Hotel* ▸ *Anna Goetz, c/o Mr. & Mrs. Herbert Goetz*

co. **1.** company. (Occasionally pronounced as a clipping, primarily used only in writing. A commercial or industrial firm.) ▸ *Shell Oil Co.* ▸ *Shattered Globe Theatre Co.* ▸ *"Ms. Resnick, please provide me with the full street address of Dow Chemical Co. in Midland, Michigan."* **2.** company. (A military term for a body of troops.) ▸ *The soldiers of Co. B marched through the jungles of Southeast Asia.* **3.** county. (A political division of a state or country.) ▸ *co. clerk* ▸ *Co. Cork, Ireland* ▸ *Cook Co., Illinois* ▸ *Butler Co. Community College*

CO **1.** carbon monoxide. (Initialism. A chemical symbol. A colorless, odorless gas.) ▸ *Running a car in a closed ga-*

rage produces lethal amounts of CO. **2.** Colorado. (The official two-letter post office abbreviation. See also *Colo.*) ▶ *Vail, CO 81657* **3.** commanding officer. (Initialism. The officer in charge of particular divisions of the military.) ▶ *The CO ordered the platoon into battle.*

Co cobalt. (The chemical symbol for Element 27.)

COBOL common business oriented language. (Acronym. A computer language introduced in 1959, used for large-scale data processing.) ▶ *When the president of Iron City Bank decided to automate, he taught himself COBOL so he would know what the programmers were doing.*

COD cash on delivery. (Initialism. A delivery method in which the consumer pays upon receipt of the product. Found in advertising.) ▶ *Save COD charges by sending your check or money order today!* ▶ *Call 1-800-555-CASH to order, $4 COD charge will apply.*

C. of C. Chamber of Commerce. (Initialism. An organization established to promote business within its community.) ▶ *This announcement paid for by the Topeka C. of C.*

C. of E. Church of England. (Initialism. The Anglican church, formed when King Henry VIII broke from the Roman Catholic church.) ▶ *The head of the C. of E. is the reigning monarch of England.*

cog. cognate. (A word stemming from the same source as a word in another language. Often in the plural, indicating two words so related. For example, the English word *ox* and the German word *Ochs* are cognates. Found in language textbooks and dictionaries.) ▶ *Schuh, German —cog. (shoe)*

col. AND **coll.** 1. college. (An institution of higher learning or a division within a university.) ▸ *col. basketball* ▸ *Boston Col.* ▸ *Oberlin Col.* ▸ *Sandy, a sophomore at Michigan State University, switched from the Col. of Education into the Col. of Arts & Letters.* 2. colony. (A region ruled by the government of a distant country.) ▸ *Mass. Col.* ▸ *The capital of Angola (a Portuguese col. until 1973) is Luanda.* 3. AND **clm.** column. (In a statistical table, a vertical series of information.) ▸ *Col. 5 lists the federal taxes paid in 1974, and col. 6 lists the state taxes paid in 1974.* ▸ *You put your name in the wrong clm.*

Col. 1. Colonel. (A military title of rank.) ▸ *Col. and Mrs. Edward H. Yardley request the honor of your presence on January 4th at 5:00 P.M.* 2. Colombia. ▸ *Bogotá, Col.*

COLA AND **cola** cost-of-living adjustment. (Acronym. A change in wages or Social Security benefits determined by changes in the basic cost of living—a figure determined by the U.S. federal government.) ▸ *The colas are what tend to drive the federal budget up every year.*

coll. 1. collection. (An accumulation or compilation.) ▸ *The Definitive Coll. of Emily Dickinson's Writings* 2. See *col.*

colloq. colloquial. (Pertaining to words found in conversational speech but not in standard writing. Found in language textbooks and dictionaries.) ▸ *ain't (colloq.)*

Colo. Colorado. (See also *CO.*) ▸ *Boulder, Colo.* ▸ *Gov. Roy Jones (Colo.)*

com. 1. comedy. (A humorous movie, play, or television show, as opposed to drama. Found in television programming guides, theater and play listings, and the like.) ▸ *All in the Family (com.)* ▸ *You Can't Take It With You (com.)* 2. AND **comm.** commerce. (The buying and selling of products and commodities.) ▶ *Herbert Hoover (Sec. of Com. 1921-1923 under Warren Harding)* **3.** AND **comm.** committee. (An organized group or a subgroup of a larger organization, formed to carry out a particular function.) ▶ *Insurance Com. Report—All policies up to date.* ▶ *This advertisement is paid for by the Com. to Elect Jane Doe for Mayor.* **4.** common. (United or jointly shared.) ▶ *European Com. Market* **5.** common. (Pertaining to a noun that refers to the member of a group or class; the opposite of a proper noun. Found in language textbooks and dictionaries.) ▶ *dog (com.); Fido (prop.)* **6.** common [gender]. (Pertaining to a noun that could refer to either a male or a female. Found in language textbooks and dictionaries.) ▶ *gosling (com.)* ▶ *kid (com.)* **7.** communication. (The exchange of information and the systems by which information is exchanged. A clipping when used as a course of study. Used in combination with other prefixes, especially *telecom.*) ▶ *Since Elizabeth was a com major, she was hired to work at the radio station.* ▶ *Association of Com. Administration* **8.** communist. (Relating to communism, a system of government in which all property is owned in common and is usually controlled by a totalitarian regime.) ▶ *com. regime* ▶ *Gus Hall (Com.)* ▶ *Com. China (People's Rep. of China)*

Com. See *Cmdr.*

comb. **1.** combination. (An ordered sequence.) ▶ *comb. lock* **2.** combined. (Put together; merged.) ▶ *Tanzania (Tanganyika and Zanzibar comb.)* **3.** combustion. (The process of burning.) ▶ *spontaneous comb.*

Comdr. See *Cmdr.*

Comdt. Commandant. (A commanding officer.) ▶ *"Comdt. Weston wants to see you right now," said the cook to the lazy dishwasher.*

COMECON See *CMEA*.

comm. 1. See *com*. 2. commercial. ▶ *Comm. Law League of America* 3. commonwealth. (A political unit.) ▶ *Comm. of Independent States.* ▶ *Comm. of Massachusetts* ▶ *British Comm.*

comp. 1. complimentary. (Sometimes a clipping. Free; usually a gift or token of gratitude.) ▶ *"Everybody gets two comp tickets each month throughout the run of the show," the assistant director informed the cast and crew.* ▶ *Open House 2:00 to 6:00, comp. wine and cheese* 2. complete. (Unabridged, total.) ▶ *Comp. Works of Wm. Shakespeare*

comp compensation. (Clipping. A payment to an employee or employee's dependents upon injury or unemployment.) ▶ *workers' comp* ▶ *Jason's workers' comp ran out six months after he was laid off.*

con. 1. conclusion. (The final segment.) ▶ *Roots, Part X (con.)* 2. See *cont*.

Con. Congo. (A country in west central Africa.) ▶ *Brazzaville, Con.* ▶ *Belg. Con.*

con 1. confidence. (Clipping. First used in *con artist*, then extended to mean "to obtain by deceit.") ▶ *The con artist raked in about $400 a day by running a shell game.* ▶ *The naive tourist was conned out of $50 before he realized what was going on.* 2. convict. (Clipping. A sentenced prisoner convicted of a crime.) ▶ *After a few years of therapy, the ex-con became a contributing member to society.*

cond. 1. condition. (One of the terms of an agreement; stipulation.) ▶ *Cond. #1: No weekend privileges for four weeks.* 2. condition. (A state of being.) ▶ *physical cond. —poor; prognosis—fair* 3. conditional. (Pertaining to a

cong.

sentence or clause that tells the conditions under which a proposition is true. Found in language textbooks and dictionaries.) ▶ *unless (cond. conj.)* ▶ *"If you move one step closer . . . " (cond. clause)* ▶ *"If you move one step closer, I'll break your kneecaps." (cond. sentence)*

Cond. conductor. (The leader of an orchestra or band.) ▶ *Pachelbel's Canon in D (Leonard Bernstein, Cond.)*

Conelrad control of electromagnetic radiation. (Acronym. The system of changing AM radio station frequencies, used in the earlier years of the Cold War to prevent hostile aircraft from using radio signals as a navigational guide.) ▶ *"The radio, in an interval of silence between the local Conelrad broadcasts, suddenly squealed with an alien and powerful carrier wave."* — Pat Frank, Alas, Babylon

conf. **1.** [religious] conference. (An association within a Protestant denomination.) ▶ *Seventh Day Baptist General Conf.* ▶ *Conservative Congregational Christian Conf.* **2.** [sports] conference. (An association of sports teams.) ▶ *The Kansas State Wildcats (Big 8 Conf.) won five games in 1990.* **3.** conference. (A meeting or seminar on a particular topic.) ▶ *Conf. on Holistic Medicine— Room 1200.* **4.** confidential. (Private; secret. Marked on files, envelopes, or correspondence to be kept private between the sender and the recipient.) ▶ *Conf. to: Ms. Gillian Douglas.* ▶ *File #423C012 (conf.)*

Confed. confederate. (Relating to the Confederate States of America, the alliance of states that seceded from the United States of America and fought against the Union during the War Between the States.) ▶ *Confed. flag*

cong. **1.** congregational. (A church with a self-governing congregation; a Protestant denomination.) ▶ *3rd Cong. Church of Albany* **2.** congress. (A formal meeting of dele-

conj.

gates to discuss issues concerning the people they represent.) ▶ *The U.S. Cong.* ▶ *The 102nd Cong. of the U.S.* **3.** congressional. (Relating to a congress.) ▶ *Pictured above is a disabled Vietnam vet receiving a U.S. Cong. Medal of Honor.*

conj. **1.** conjugation. (The paradigm of a verb class that shows the inflectional forms. Found in language textbooks.) ▶ *the Latin second conj.* **2.** conjunction. (A word that joins words, phrases, or clauses. Found in language textbooks and dictionaries.) ▶ *and (conj.)* ▶ *or (conj.)* **3.** conjunction. (In connection with.) ▶ *This program was brought to you by Smithco International in conj. with local broadcasters.*

Conn. Connecticut. (See also *CT*.) ▶ *Hartford, Conn.* ▶ *Gov. John Jones (Conn.)*

cons. **1.** consonant. (A linguistic term for particular speech sounds. The airflow through the mouth during the production of consonants is stopped, limited, or diverted through the nose. The opposite of a consonant is a vowel. See also *C* and *V*.) ▶ *voiced cons.* ▶ *nasal cons.* **2.** constitution. (The written document of a government or organization, outlining its laws and principles.) ▶ *The Bill of Rights consists of the first ten amendments to the U.S. Cons.* **3.** constructed. (Made or fabricated. Used to describe building materials.) ▶ *The Harper house (cons. of brick and fiberglass) was snapped up the moment it was placed on the market.* **4.** construction. (The process of building.) ▶ *The Smith-Jones Building (under cons.) will be the tallest edifice in the county.*

Cons. constable. (A town or village officer whose duties are similar to those of a sheriff. In England, a constable is a police officer.) ▶ *Cons. Warren filed a report on Mrs. Brown's missing cat.*

consol. consolidated. (An organization formed from the merger of two or more entities.) ▶ *The voters of Consol. School District #410 voted against the tax increase.* ▶ *The board of Mayfield-Warrenville Consol. chose a new CEO from an applicant pool of five.*

cont. AND **con., cont., cont'd** continued. (Used in publications at the bottom of a column or page to indicate that the article continues elsewhere.) ▶ *cont. on next page* ▶ *cont'd on page 5, col. 2* ▶ *con. in next month's issue*

contd. See the previous entry.

contemp. contemporary. (Current, up to date.) ▶ *Mus. of Contemp. Art* ▶ *contemp. design*

contrib. **1.** contributor. (In publishing, the writer or supplier of an article or information for an article.) **2.** contributing. (Relating to someone or something that has contributed.) ▶ *contrib. editor*

conv. convention. (An assembly of members from a particular group or organization.) ▶ *Real Estate Conv. Reception—The Grand Suite, Level 2.*

co-op cooperative. (Clipping. A collective enterprise, such as a housing development owned and operated by the people who live there.) ▶ *Elizabeth and Nancy moved off campus and into a nearby co-op.*

cop. AND **C** copyright. (A legal protection granted to the owner of the rights for the reproduction, publication, and sale of written and artistic works. See also ©.) ▶ *cop. 1960* ▶ *C 1978 by Steven King*

Cop. AND **Copt.** Coptic. (A language derived from ancient Egyptian, used in the Coptic church.) ▶ *ancient Copt.*

Copt. See the previous entry.

CORE Congress of Racial Equality. (Acronym. A civil rights group established in 1942 in Chicago.) ▶ *In the early 1960s, CORE sponsored "Freedom Rides" in the South.*

coroll. corollary. (A proposition that is deduced from a proven theorem.)

corp. corporation. (An economic or political organization.) ▶ *International Business Machines Corp.* ▶ *Southwestern Bell Corp.*

corr. correspondent. (A newscaster who provides news and information to a central location from a distant place.) ▶ *War Corr. Arthur Kent*

cos cosine. (Clipping. A trigonometric function. For a given acute angle in a right triangle, the cosine is the ratio of the adjacent side of the acute angle to the hypotenuse.) ▶ $cos(x + y) = cosx\ cosy - sinx\ siny$

cot cotangent. (A trigonometric function. For a given acute angle in a right triangle, the cotangent is the ratio of the adjacent side of the acute angle to the opposite side, or the inverse of the tangent.) ▶ $cotx = 1/tanx$

CP 1. cerebral palsy. (Initialism. A disability caused by damage to the central nervous system during birth.) ▶ *The Johnsons adopted the baby born with CP because its biological parents knew they wouldn't be able to provide proper care.* 2. command post. (Initialism. The field headquarters of a commander.) ▶ *Billy rode his horse at breakneck speed to deliver news of the armistice to the remote CP.* 3. Communist Party. (Initialism. The political party whose ideology is based on the Communist Manifesto, written by Karl Marx and Friedrich Engels.) ▶ *Gus Hall (CP)*

CPA 1. Certified Public Accountant. (Initialism. An accountant who has met requirements as determined by the examining board of a particular state.) ▶ *The Offices of Evangeline Murotti, CPA* ▶ *The current recession left several newly trained CPAs scrambling for few openings.* 2. critical path analysis. (Initialism. A system of planning and maintaining intricate operations by using a computer to show all connections and relations of all aspects of the operation and selecting the most efficient option.) ▶ *The personnel at the nuclear reactor relied on CPA to ensure that all safety precautions were integrated with every step of energy production.*

CPB Corporation for Public Broadcasting. (Initialism. A private, not-for-profit organization established by Congress in 1967 funded by government grants to support public television and radio.) ▶ *Most educational television on PBS is funded in part by the CPB.*

CPI consumer price index. (Initialism. An economic gauge of inflation that measures the average change in prices of basic goods and services over a particular period of time.) ▶ *The CPI report indicated that $100 of medical costs in 1984 cost over $160 in 1990.* ▶ *The Monthly Labor Review and CPI Detailed Report is published by the U.S. Bureau of Labor Statistics.*

Cpl. Corporal. (A position of rank in the military.) ▶ *The troops all respected Cpl. Jones.*

cpm cycles per minute. (Initialism. The number of revolutions an object makes in one minute.) ▶ *It was turning at 14 cpm.*

CPO chief petty officer. (Initialism. A position of rank in the United States Navy.) ▶ *The CPO in the ship was very efficent.*

CPR cardiopulmonary resuscitation. (Initialism. A first-aid technique performed on a person whose heart has stopped, involving mouth-to-mouth resuscitation and cardiac compression by pressing down on the sternum.) ▸ *The public service announcement urged everyone to take a CPR class.* ▸ *Tom performed CPR on the waiter who collapsed.*

cps **1.** characters per second. (Initialism. The number of characters that are typed or printed in one second.) ▸ *The company bought a new laser printer that operated at 120 cps.* **2.** cycles per second. (Initialism. The number of complete cycles of motion made in one second. See also Hz.) ▸ *The frequency of the sound was 200 cps.*

CPSC Consumer Product Safety Commission. (Initialism. A government agency that evaluates and enforces safety standards for consumer products.) ▸ *The toy industry must follow several guidelines enacted by the CPSC.*

Cpt. See *Capt*.

CPU central processing unit. (Initialism. The circuits in a computer that run the entire system.) ▸ *The CPU is responsible for reading and running computer programs.*

C.R. Costa Rica. (Initialism. A country in Central America.) ▸ *San José, C.R.*

Cr. See *Ck*.

cr. **1.** AND **CR** credit. (An amount paid toward a debt. *CR* is used on receipts to show credit.) ▸ *The accountant added a figure to the cr. column.* ▸ *$1.50CR* **2.** credit. (A unit of class hours in colleges.) ▸ *Eng. 202 (3 cr.)* ▸ *Students taking 12 cr. hours and above are eligible for this scholarship.*

CR **1.** conditioned reflex; conditioned response. (A response to a secondary stimulus normally associated with another stimulus.) ▸ *Pavlov's CR experiments showed that when a dog was fed each time a bell was rung, the dog salivated when the bell rang even if no food were present.* **2.** carriage return. (Initialism. A key on a computer keyboard that starts a new line.) ▸ *Enter D: and then press CR.*

Cr chromium. (The chemical symbol for Element 24.)

CRC **1.** camera-ready copy. (Initialism. In publishing, advertisement copy that is already set to go to the printer and requires no work by the printer or publisher.) ▸ *Betty found that CRC ads were much cheaper to buy than having the publisher do the layout.* **2.** Civil Rights Commission. (Initialism. An government agency formed in 1957 to ensure the civil rights of women and non-whites in voting, education, housing, employment, and other areas. Also referred to as the Commission on Civil Rights.) ▸ *The CRC sent decoys to real estate offices to determine how often home buyers of different races were steered to different neighborhoods.*

cresc. crescendo. (A musical direction: Gradually louder.)

crit. **1.** critic. (A person who analyzes and judges theater, motion pictures, art, literary works, television, etc.) ▸ *Roger Ebert—Film Crit., Chicago Sun-Times* **2.** criticism. (Used as a clipping in the phrase *Theory and Crit*, a discipline within the study of theater or art.) ▸ *Suzy skipped her Theory and Crit class in order to finish the costumes for the upcoming dress rehearsal.*

CRT cathode-ray tube. (Initialism. A television screen or computer monitor.) ▸ *The service technician replaced a broken CRT, and Lee's TV was as good as new.*

CS Christian Science. (A Christian religion that promotes the use of Scriptures to overcome disease and death.) ▸ *CS Reading Room Hours 9-5:30*

CSA Confederate States of America. (Initialism. The confederacy of the secessionist states that fought against the Union during the War Between the States.) ▶ *The CSA was established on February 8, 1861, with Jefferson Davis as president.*

csc cosecant. (A trigonometric function. For an acute angle in a right triangle, the ratio between the length of the adjacent side to the length of the opposite side, or the reciprocal of the sine.) ▶ *cscx = 1/sinx*

C section Caesarean section. (Childbirth in which doctors deliver a baby by surgically opening the abdomen and uterus of the mother and extracting the baby. The same thing as Caesarean delivery. See *CD*.) ▶ *Judy had a C section with her last child.*

CSF cerebrospinal fluid. (Initialism. The liquid surrounding the brain and spinal cord.) ▶ *A spinal tap involves removing CSF from the body for testing.*

CST 1. central standard time. (Initialism. The standard time in the central United States from late October to early April. It is six hours behind Greenwich Time.) ▶ *3:30 p.m. CST* ▶ *This offer expires December 31, 1991, at 5:00 p.m. CST.* **2.** convulsive shock treatment. (Initialism. A therapy method for patients with mental disorders. It uses electroshock to the brain to induce convulsions.) ▶ *Sam still suffered side effects from CST sessions administered in the 1960s.*

Ct. 1. count. (A title for certain Europeans of nobility.) ▶ *Ct. Dracula* **2.** Court. (Used on maps and signs and in addresses.) ▶ *1411 Everly Ct.*

ct. 1. AND **Ct.** carat. (A unit of weight for gemstones equal to approximately 200 milligrams. The same as *c*. Compare with *karat* at *k*.) ▶ *Sharon's grandfather gave her a 2-ct. ruby for her sixteenth birthday.* **2.** cent. (1/100 of a unit of currency; one penny.) ▸ *Maxine's 99-ct. breakfast special appealed to the impoverished in her neighborhood.* **3.** count. (On packaging, the amount of the product inside the packaging.) ▸ *chocolate peanut clusters—24 ct.—$3.29 on sale with coupon*

CT **1.** Connecticut. (The official two-letter post office abbreviation. See also *Conn.*) ▸ *New Haven, CT 06501* **2.** Central Time. (Initialism. The time in the central United States.) ▸ *The president's speech will be carried live, 9:00 ET/8:00 CT.* ▸ *Chicago (CT)*

ctf. See *cert.*

ctn. carton. ▸ *paper clips—12 ctn.* ▸ *cigarettes by the pack or ctn.*

CTOL conventional takeoff and landing. (Partial acronym. Pronounced "SEE-tol." Describing the takeoff and landing of regular aircraft. Compare with *VTOL*.) ▸ *We can only land at a CTOL airport.*

ctr. center. (An office, building, or area that caters to a specific interest.) ▸ *Ctr. for Performing Arts* ▸ *Registration begins at noon at the Student Ctr.*

cu. cubic. (Of three dimensions. The same as *c*. Compare with *sq.*, which indicates two dimensions.) ▸ *cu. centimeter* ▸ *cu. inch*

Cu copper. (The chemical symbol for Element 29. The symbol is derived from Latin *cuprum*.)

cur. currency. (A country's paper and coin money in circulation.) ▸ *foreign cur.* ▸ *Cur. Exchange*

CV cardiovascular. (Initialism. Relating to the heart and blood vessels. Used in medical circumstances.) ▸ *CV exercises*

C&W country & western. (Initialism. A popular music format with roots in Southern folk music.) ▶ *While driving through Iowa, we listened to Country Joe's C&W Show.* ▶ *After basing record popularity on sales instead of airplay, many C&W performers worked their way up the pop charts.*

cw. clockwise. (In the direction of the hands of a clock.) ▶ *To open, push down and turn cw.*

cwt. hundredweight. (A unit of measurement equal to 100 pounds [in the United States] or 112 pounds [in Great Britain.] From the Latin word for hundred, *centum*.) ▶ *5 cwt. sugar*

cyl. cylinder. (A container with a cylindrical shape.) ▶ *graduated cyl.* ▶ *8-cyl. engine.*

CZ Canal Zone. (The official two-letter post office abbreviation for the ten-mile-wide strip of land along the Panama Canal, governed by the United States until 1977 and administered by the United States until 1997.) ▶ *Balboa, CZ*

Czech. Czechoslovakia. (A landlocked country of eastern Europe.) ▶ *Prague, Czech.*

D

D. AND **Du.** Duchy. (Land ruled by a duke, as in the feudal days of Europe. Used on maps.) ▶ *D. of Württemberg* ▶ *D. of Luxembourg*

d. died. ▶ *George Washington (d. 1797) was the first president of the United States.*

D **1.** a grade indicating below-average work, but not failure. (Initialism. In the series *A, B, C, D, E* and *A, B, C, D, F.*) ▶ *Shannon's parents grounded him because he received a D in algebra.* **2.** a musical tone. (Initialism. The second note of the scale of C major.) ▶ *Angie wrote a moving ballad in the key of D minor.* **3.** December. (Often used in graph columns or rows to chart the month-by-month progress of something. See also *Dec.*) ▶ *Finals week—D 5-11.* **4.** AND **Dem.** Democrat. (A member of the Democratic Party, one of the two primary United States political parties.) ▶ *Paul Simon—D, Illinois* **5.** dime. (One-tenth of a dollar or 10¢. Used as a column heading to keep track of loose change, as in a cash register, for instance.) **6.** dimension. (Initialism. The length, width, and depth of an object.) ▶ *3-D glasses.* **7.** drive. (Initialism. Found on gearshifts, it indicates that the automatic transmission of a vehicle is in "drive.") **8.** 500. (A Roman numeral.) ▶ *Be prepared for a quiz on Sections CDXCV through D of the text.*

d 1. day. (A 24-hour period.) ▸ *The winner of the grueling transcontinental auto race (5 d 12 h 32 m) dedicated the trophy to all of the participants.* **2.** deci- (A prefix meaning one-tenth, used with units of measurements.) ▸ *dl (deciliter)* ▸ *dm (decimeter)* ▸ *dB (decibel)*

D.A. district attorney. (Initialism. A prosecuting lawyer for city, state, or federal government.) ▸ *The defendant's lawyer tried to negotiate with the D.A., but to no avail.*

D/A digital to analog. (Initialism. A conversion that changes digital data to analog data. Compare with *A/D*.) ▸ *A lot of fidelity was lost in the D/A conversion.*

DA 1. deposit account. (Initialism. A banking account, usually for a business or company, into which daily or frequent deposits are made.) ▸ *Jane emptied the cash register, placed the money in her bank's DA envelope, and put it in the night depository on the way home.* **2.** duck's ass [haircut]. (Initialism. A hairstyle of the late fifties in which the greased hair in back flipped up, resembling the tail of a duck.) ▸ *The army cut off Earl's DA the day he enlisted.*

da deca-; deka- (A prefix meaning 10, used with units of measurement.) ▸ *dag (dekagram)* ▸ *dal (decaliter)*

dag dekagram. (10 grams.) ▸ *Sally measured 1 dag of the purplish substance and placed it in her petri dish.*

DAR Daughters of the American Revolution. (Initialism. An organization of women whose ancestors aided the cause of the American Revolution.) ▸ *Catherine Anne, a prominent society figure and a member of DAR, was doted on by the East Coast media at her daughter's debutante ball.*

DARE Dictionary of American Regional English. (Acronym. A four-volume publication detailing regional

D&C

speech and its variations throughout the United States.) ▶ *The library's copy of the DARE was dog-eared from constant use.*

dat. dative. (The grammatical case applied to the English indirect object, grammatically denoting the receiver of something. Used in language textbooks and dictionaries.) ▶ *German test on acc. and dat. prepositions tomorrow.*

DAT digital audio tape. (Acronym and sometimes an initialism. A sound reproduction format that digitally records sound onto a special audiocassette tape, resulting in playback free of distortion.) ▶ *Keeping up with the latest in technology, Joan bought a DAT player.*

DAV Disabled American Veterans. (Initialism. An organization of American veterans who became disabled in the line of duty during war.) ▶ *The DAV raises money to provide for adequate care for disabled American veterans.*

db AND **dB** decibel. (A unit of loudness.) ▶ *Exposure to sound greater than 120 db can impair hearing.*

d/b/a doing business as. (A common business and legal abbreviation.) ▶ *The Tenant is Eloise F. Caparelli d/b/a Ellie's Pasta Emporium.*

dbl. 1. double. (Twice the amount.) ▶ *dbl. capacity front loader* 2. double. (A baseball term for a player reaching second base on a base hit.) ▶ *Sam hit a dbl. just before it started to rain.*

DBMS data base management system. (Initialism. Computer software designed to establish and maintain a data base.) ▶ *The company hired a computer consulting firm to install a customized DBMS.*

D&C 1. dilation and curettage. (Initialism. The dilation of the uterus and scraping of the lining of the uterus. Also used as a means of terminating a pregnancy.) ▶ *Mary is*

D.C.

scheduled for a D&C tomorrow. **2.** drugs and cosmetics. (Initialism. A Food and Drug Administration designation for a dye or coloring that has been approved for use in drugs and cosmetics, but not food. Found on packaging and labeling. Compare with *FD&C*.) ▸ *The ingredients of the deodorant stick included D&C Orange No. 4 and D&C Green No. 5.*

D.C. **1.** da capo. (Initialism. Italian: from the beginning. A musical direction: Repeat a section of music from the beginning.) ▸ *Harry faked his way through the sixteen bars prior to the D.C. al fine.* **2.** District of Columbia. (Initialism. See also *DC*.) ▸ *Washington, D.C.*

DC **1.** direct current. (Initialism. Electrical current with a constant magnitude and whose direction does not change.) ▸ *In some countries, they still use DC.* **2.** District of Columbia. (The official two-letter post office abbreviation. See also *D.C.*) ▸ *Washington, DC 20002*

DCM Distinguished Conduct Medal. (Initialism. A British military medal given to those who displayed distinguished conduct in the field against the enemy.) ▸ *Receiving the DCM was the proudest moment of Michaelson's life.*

D.D. Dishonorable Discharge. (Removal from the armed forces for a disreputable action.)

DDD direct distance dialing. (Initialism. A telephone network that allows a customer to place a call without operator assistance.) ▸ *If you have any questions concerning DDD, please contact your phone representative.* ▸ *The International DDD prefix is 011.*

DDE dichlorodiphenyldichloroethylene. (Initialism. A by-product of DDT that is stored in animal tissues.) ▸ *Eggs laid by birds poisoned with DDE have very fragile shells that break when incubated.*

DDR *Deutsche Demokratik Republik.* (Initialism. German: German Democratic Republic. The German name for what was East Germany prior to unification in 1990. See *GDR.*) ▸ *Hermann, a soldier for the DDR, stood watch at the Brandenburg Gate.* ▸ *Karl-Marx-Stadt, DDR*

D.D.S. Doctor of Dental Surgery. (Initialism. The medical degree awarded to dentists and oral surgeons.) ▸ *The Dental Offices of Virginia C. Mahler, D.D.S.*

DDT dichlorodiphenyltrichloroethane. (Initialism. A powerful insecticide hazardous to the environment.) ▸ *The DDT sprayed on the crops ran off into the creek, entering the food chain.*

DE Delaware. (The official two-letter post office abbreviation. See also *Del.*) ▸ *Newark, DE 19711*

dec. deceased. (Indicates that a person mentioned has died.) ▸ *The founders of Smithco are Christopher Smith, Mr. and Mrs. Arnold Smith, and Mrs. Eugenie Smith-Clark (dec.).*

Dec. December. (See also *D.*) ▸ *Christmas—Dec. 25*

decl. declension. (A paradigm of a particular class of nouns, pronouns, or adjectives.) ▸ *In Latin, 1st decl. nouns end in -a in the nom. sing.*

DEFCON Defense Readiness Condition. (Acronym. A stage of defensive preparedness at military bases.) ▸ *Large video monitors alerted personnel of the present DEFCON stage.*

deg. **1.** degree. (A title conferred upon a student by an institution of learning for completing a proscribed course of study.) ▸ *bach. deg.* **2.** degree. (A unit for measurement of angles and arcs, equal to 1/360th the circumference of a circle.) ▸ *deg. mark (°)*

Del. Delaware. (See also *DE*.) ▸ *Dover, Del.* ▸ *Gov. Michael Brown (Del.)*

Del delete. (A key on a computer keyboard that deletes or erases characters.) ▸ *After I pressed Del, the letter disappeared from the screen.*

dely. delivery. ▸ *Free dely. with $20 order!*

Dem. AND **Dem** 1. Democrat. (Often a clipping. A member of the Democratic Party, one of the two major parties of the U.S. Compare with *Rep*. See also *D*.) ▸ *Sam Nunn—Dem. (Georgia)* 2. Democratic. (Often a clipping. Pertaining to the Democratic Party.) ▸ *Dem. Party.*

dem. See *demon*.

demon. AND **dem.** demonstrative. (The pronouns *that, this, these,* and *those*. When used as an adjective, the demonstrative pronouns modify a specific noun. Found in language textbooks and dictionaries.) ▸ *demon. pronoun*

Den. Denmark. (A Scandinavian country of Northern Europe.) ▸ *Copenhagen, Den.*

denom. 1. denomination. (A church division within a religion. Found on forms and in advertising.) ▸ *interdenom. services* 2. denomination. (The monetary value of a bill, coin, or stamp.) ▸ *$20 denom.*

dent. dental. (Relating to teeth.) ▸ *dent. school* ▸ *dent. hygiene*

Dep. deputy. (An appointed assistant to an authority figure.) ▸ *Jeremy Smith, Dane Cty. Dep. Sheriff*

dep. 1. departure. (Found on transportation schedules at airports, train stations, bus terminals, etc., to indicate the time of departure of particular planes, trains, buses, etc. Compare with *arr*. See also *ETD*.) ▸ *Flight 425—Fort Worth/dep. 4:35* 2. deponent. (A type of verb in ancient

Greek and Latin that has a passive form but an active meaning. Found in language textbooks and dictionaries.) ▶ *dep. construction* ▶ *abritror, -ari, -atus sum (dep.)* **3.** deposit. (Money paid on an item that is repaid if the product is returned undamaged or if the container is returned for recycling and money paid as a down payment.) ▶ *No dep., no return* ▶ *5¢ dep. in IA, ME, CT* ▶ *Floor Sander Rental: $75/day, $300 dep.*

dept. AND **dpt.** department. (A division of a government, company, school, or other entity. A section of a department store that stocks specific items.) ▶ *Human Resources Dept.* ▶ *Dept. of History* ▶ *Cookware Dpt.*

Des. Desert. (An arid, barren land. An abbreviation found on maps.) ▶ *Sahara Des.* ▶ *Mojave Des.*

DES diethylstilbestrol. (Initialism. A synthetic, carcinogenic estrogen.) ▶ *The daughters of women who took DES during pregnancy to combat morning sickness run a high risk of contracting vaginal cancer.* ▶ *DES was used to fatten cattle until the Food and Drug Administration banned it.*

DFC Distinguished Flying Cross. (Initialism. A United States medal granted for extraordinary achievement while in flight. Also a British medal granted for extraordinary achievement while flying in combat.) ▶ *The media snapped pictures as the young air officer was awarded a DFC for heroic efforts during battle.* ▶ *The BBC interviewed three brave pilots who had earned DFCs.*

dg decigram. (1/10 of a gram.) ▶ *10 dg = 1 g* ▶ *Julia boiled 1 dg of the solvent before adding it to the beaker.*

D.H. Doctor of Humanities. (Initialism. The highest degree awarded by a university for research in the area of humanities.)

DH   designated hitter. (Initialism. A baseball term. In the American League, the pitcher does not bat; instead, a designated hitter, who does not play in the field, completes the batting lineup.) ▸ *Reggie Jackson (DH) scored the winning run of the game.*

dia. AND **diam.**   diameter. (The length of a line segment intersecting the circle's center between two points on the circle.) ▸ *6-inch dia.*

diag.   **1.** diagonal. (On a slant; not straight up and down nor side to side. Running on an angle.) ▸ *diag. line* **2.** diagram. (A figure or sketch used to illustrate or explain something by outlining its parts and the parts' relationship to each other.) ▸ *See diag. 4.10—Skeletal System of Birds.*

dial.   **1.** dialect. (A variant of a language understood by most speakers of the language. Found in language textbooks and in dictionaries.) ▸ *British dial.* ▸ *fixin' to (Southern U.S. dial.)* **2.** dialogue. (Verbal discourse between two or more people.) ▸ *Under the dial., the curtain closes and the footlights reveal the Hero.*

diam.   See *dia.*

dict.   dictionary. (An alphabetized collection of words or terms and their meanings.) ▸ *Dict. of Grammar Terminology* ▸ *Dict. of American Regional English*

diff AND **dif**   difference. (Clipping. Slang, as found in the phrase *no diff*, meaning any of the options proposed are equally acceptable. Also in the phrase *same diff*, meaning "either way," "whichever," or the fact that two options offered are equally favorable or equally repellent.) ▸ *When offered a choice between going to the movies or out to the bar, Nina responded "Makes no diff to me."*

diff. AND **dif.** 1. difference. (The result of one quantity subtracted from another.) ▶ *4 is the diff. of 5 subtracted from 9.* 2. difference. (A factor of variance.) ▶ *Tonight's Lecture: Diff. between North African and sub-Saharan cultures.*

dim. 1. dimension. (The length, width, and depth of an object.) ▶ *3rd. dim.* 2. diminutive. (A form of a word that denotes smallness or youth.) ▶ *cat—kitty (dim.)* ▶ *kitchen—kitchenette (dim.)* ▶ *Elizabeth—Lizzie (dim.)* 3. AND **dimin.** diminuendo. (A musical direction: Gradual softening.)

dimin. See *dim.*

dip. diploma. (A certificate evidencing graduation from an educational institution.) ▶ *high school dip.*

dipl. 1. diplomat. (An official representing the national government to some other national government; an ambassador.) ▶ *Shown above is the only dipl. present at the peace conference.* 2. diplomatic. (Relating to diplomacy or to pragmatic, tactful behavior.) ▶ *dipl. relations*

dir. 1. director. (The head of a department or institution.) ▶ *Dir. of Human Resources* 2. director. (The person who directs a play or movie.) ▶ *Best Dir., 1980—Warren Beatty for* Reds.

disc. discount. (Found in sales advertising and merchandise on sale.) ▶ *25% disc. w/ coupon*

dist. 1. district. (A part of a city, country, or other governmental unit.) ▶ *business dist.* ▶ *red-light dist.* ▶ *Dist. of Columbia* ▶ *The delegates from Dist. 14 voted against the candidate.* 2. distance. ▶ *What is the dist. to the next town?*

div. 1. division. (A separate political, economic, administrative, or military unit within a larger entity.) ▶ *Copy-*

right by Simon & Schuster, a Div. of Gulf & Western Corp. **2.** dividend. (Money split among a company's stockholders.) ▸ *1st quarter div.—$1.45 per share* **3.** divorced. (Pertaining to someone or a couple whose marriage has been legally dissolved. Found on forms and in texts. Also used in family trees and histories to indicate divorced family members.) ▸ *Ronald Reagan & Jane Wyman (mar. 1940, div. 1948)*

D.J. district judge. (Initialism. A judge presiding over a district court.) ▸ *The Honorable Robert Cahill (D.J.)*

DJ disc jockey. (Initialism. A person who chooses and plays records for a radio station or nightclub.) ▸ *Sally tipped the DJ $5 for playing her favorite dance song.* ▸ *Ed switched radio stations because the DJ was talking too much.*

DJIA Dow-Jones Industrial Average. (Initialism. It occurs more in print than spoken, often referred to as "The Dow." An index of the stock price performance of thirty well-known and well-run companies. It is used as an overall indication of the strength of the stock market.) ▸ *The companies represented by the DJIA are chosen by the editors of the* Wall Street Journal.

dm decimeter. (1/10 of a meter, slightly less than 4 inches.) ▸ *4 dm × 5 dm rectangle*

DM Deutsche mark. (Initialism. The unit of German currency.) ▸ *Today's exchange rate: 1.71 DM per $1.*

DMSO dimethyl sulfoxide. (Initialism. A colorless liquid that rapidly passes through skin, used experimentally in medicine to relieve pain and also as an industrial solvent.) ▸ *Having tried everything else, Dr. Wettig prescribed DMSO for Elsa's swollen joints.*

dol.

DMZ demilitarized zone. (Initialism. Neutral territory between two warring states or factions.) ▶ *The pilot was shot down while flying over the Korean DMZ.*

DOA dead on arrival. (Initialism. Used to describe a person who dies before getting to a hospital.) ▶ *The gunshot victim arrived at the hospital DOA.*

DOB date of birth. (Commonly found on forms.) ▶ *DOB 9/14/41* ▶ *Men whose DOB is 3/1/60 or after must register for the draft.*

doc. document. (Written material that can be presented as proof of something.) ▶ *Stella requested Doc. #89-LR01298 from the court librarian.* ▶ *Place doc. along the guide strip and close cover before copying.*

Doc Doctor. (Clipping. The formal abbreviation is *Dr.*) ▶ *"Tell me, Doc," the cowboy whispered weakly, "will I die?"* ▶ *"What's up, Doc?" Bugs Bunny asked of Elmer Fudd.*

DOD Department of Defense. (Initialism. The executive department of the U.S. government in charge of the military forces for war and security.) ▶ *The DOD is headquartered at the Pentagon.* ▶ *The DOD issued a media blackout to protect the secrecy of the mission.*

DOE Department of Energy. (Initialism. The executive department of the U.S. government in charge of the administration of the nation's energy policies, including research and development, conservation, regulation, and nuclear arms.) ▶ *The Federal Energy Regulatory Commission is an administrative division within the DOE.*

dol. dollar. (A unit of currency in many countries, including the United States. Also represented by the symbol "$.") ▶ *a 5-dol. bill (a $5 bill)*

Dom. Dominican. (A member of the religious order founded by St. Dominic.) ▶ *Dom. abbey*

dom. dominion. (A country or territory.) ▶ *Dom. of Canada*

Dom. Rep. Dominican Republic. (An island in the Caribbean.) ▶ *Santo Domingo, Dom. Rep.*

DOS disk-operating system. (Acronym. Rhymes with "floss." Software that directs the flow of data between disk drives and a computer.) ▶ *Tim had to learn DOS before he could use his new word processing software.*

DOT Ddepartment of Transportation. (Initialism. The executive department of the U.S. government that administers policies relating to highways, waterways, mass transit, rail, and air traffic. Individual states also have DOTs, which are often pronounced as acronyms; for instance, the Michigan Department of Transportation [MDOT] is pronounced as "EM-dot," and so on.) ▶ *The United States Coast Guard is one of nine administrative divisions within the DOT.*

doz. dozen. (Twelve.) ▶ *2 doz. roses* ▶ *6 doz. donuts*

DP **1.** data processing. (Initialism. The process of inputting, storing, and manipulating large amounts of information, using a computer.) ▶ *Wanted: Systems Mgr. with 5 years exp. in DP.* ▶ *The delivery clerk carried the computer hardware to the DP Department.* **2.** dew point. (Initialism. The temperature at which a vapor condenses into liquid. Compare with "melting point" at *MP*.) ▶ *Jim's research included a chart on the DP of several liquids, including water, ammonia, and methane, and their roles in the formation of planets.* **3.** double play. (Initialism. A baseball term for a play that results in two outs.) ▶ *The Tigers made 5 DP's against the Brewers, but still lost the game.*

DPH Department of Public Health. (Initialism. A state or municipal agency that administers the health care system of its jurisdiction.) ▶ *The DPH reported a severe outbreak of chicken pox at several local grade schools.*

dpt. See *dept.*

DPT diphtheria, pertussis, tetanus (vaccine). (Initialism. A vaccine given to small children to prevent diphtheria, pertussis [whooping cough], and tetanus.) ▶ *Volunteers provided free DPT and polio shots throughout the poorer sections of the city.*

DPW Department of Public Works. (Initialism. A municipal government agency in charge of infrastructures that service the public, such as roadways, sewers, sanitation, etc.) ▶ *The DPW received numerous complaints from Albany Park residents concerning cavernous potholes in their neighborhood.*

DR AND **dr** dining room. (Found in advertisements.) ▶ *For rent, 2-BR w/ fully-furnished DR and kitchen, $900.*

dr. **1.** dram. (A unit of apothecaries' weight equal to 1/8 of an ounce.) ▶ *The pharmacist weighed out 4 dr. of the grayish powder for Mrs. Davis.* **2.** dram. (A unit of avoirdupois weight equal to 1/16 of an ounce.) ▶ *6 oz. 8 dr.*

Dr. Doctor. (The title for someone who has received a doctoral degree.) ▶ *Dr. Marcus Welby.* ▶ *Dr. Ellis made a presentation to the high school class about careers in the medical field.* ▶ *History of Chinese Literature will be taught next semester by Dr. Qi Xiao.*

dram. **1.** dramatic. (Relating to drama, such as a play or movie. Serious, as opposed to comedic.) ▶ The Glass Menagerie *(dram.)* **2.** dramatist. (A playwright.)

D.S. *dal segno.* (Italian: From the sign. A musical direction: Repeat a section of music starting at the sign.) ▶

DSC

Sam faked his way through the sixteen bars prior to the D.S. al fine.

DSC Distinguished Service Cross. (Initialism. A United States army medal awarded for extraordinary heroism in combat. Also a British military medal awarded for outstanding service in wartime.) ▶ *Pvt. Washington received a DSC after single-handedly holding back the enemy and saving the lives of hundreds of soldiers.* ▶ *Jean placed her father's DSC on the mantelpiece next to his picture.*

DSM Distinguished Service Medal. (Initialism. A United States military medal awarded for meritorious service in a wartime duty of great responsibility. Also a British military medal awarded for distinguished conduct during wartime) ▶ *After the war, Roger was decorated with a DSM for having cracked the enemy code that had baffled cryptologists.* ▶ *The young widow clutched her slain husband's posthumously awarded DSM.*

DSO Distinguished Service Order. (Initialism. A British military medal awarded for special service in action.) ▶ *The Manchester newspaper proudly listed all of its citizens who had received DSOs.*

d.s.p *decessit sine prole*. (Initialism. Latin: died without issue. Used in legal, medical, and scholarly documents to refer to people who died without ever having children. See also *s.p.* and *s.p.s.*) ▶ *The Estate of Agnes Millhew* (d.s.p.) *is now in probate.*

DST daylight saving time. (Initialism. The period of time between early April and late October when clocks in most of the United States are set an hour ahead, providing an extra hour of light in the evening.) ▶ *DST ends on the last Saturday of October.*

DT daylight time. (Initialism. See *DST*. Used with the names of time zones—Eastern, Central, Mountain, Pacific—to form the abbreviations for daylight time zones. See *EDT, CDT, MDT,* and *PDT.*)

DT's delirium tremens. (Initialism. Violent shaking and tremors due to excessive use of alcohol or drugs.) ▸ *Chris stepped over the drunk who was having DT's in the middle of the stairs.*

Du. 1. Dutch. (Pertaining to the people or the language of the Netherlands.) ▸ *cookie < Du. koekje, little cake* ▸ *Du. East Indies* 2. See *D.*

DUI driving under the influence. (Initialism. The charge applied to people arrested for driving while drunk. Compare with *DWI.*) ▸ *After his third DUI, Jerry had his license suspended for one year.*

dup. duplicate. (A replica or copy. Used in correspondence and filing. Sometimes a clipping.) ▸ *Memo of 4/12/83 (dup.)* ▸ *Send a dup of this right down to billing.*

D.V. *Deo volente.* (Initialism. Latin: God willing. Popular expression in the early part of the twentieth century.) ▸ *"Sarah will go to Vassar, D.V.," Selma said, knocking on wood.*

DVA Department of Veterans Affairs. (Initialism. The Executive Department of the U.S. government in charge of benefit programs for veterans and their families.) ▸ *In 1990, the DVA spent almost half a billion dollars for education programs.*

D.V.M. Doctor of Veterinary Medicine. (Initialism. See also *V.M.D.*) ▸ *The sign said D.V.M., so we dragged the cat in for treatment.*

DWI driving while intoxicated. (Initialism. The charge applied to people arrested for driving while drunk. Compare with *DUI.*) ▸ *She got her second DWI charge in two weeks.*

dwt.

dwt. pennyweight. (A unit of weight equal to 1/20 troy ounce or 1.55 grams. The *d* comes from the Latin *denarius*, meaning penny.) ▸ *The 3 dwt. gemstone cost more than Brian could afford.*

dy dyne. (The unit of measurement of force. One dyne is equal to the force needed to accelerate a one-gram mass one centimeter per second each second.)

Dy dysprosium. (The chemical symbol for Element 66.)

E

e The mathematical symbol for the base number for natural logarithms, approximately equal to 2.7183. ▶ *A natural logarithm is a logarithm to the base e.*

E 1. a grade indicating failure. (Initialism. In the series *A, B, C, D, E.*) ▶ *Selena never went to class, and so she got an E.* 2. a musical tone. (Initialism. The third note of the scale of C major.) ▶ *Brett tried to reach the high E, but always ended flat.* 3. Earth. (The planet we live on.) 4. AND **E.** east. (A compass direction. Found on maps and signs and in addresses. See also *N, S, W.*) ▶ *Winds E, 15mph* ▶ *E. St. Louis, Illinois* ▶ *505 E. Court Street* 5. ecstasy. (Initialism. A drug. See *MDMA*. The same as *X.*) 6. empty. (Initialism. Found on gauges indicating something, such as a gas tank, is empty.) ▶ *"You'd better get gas soon because we're riding on E," Joan told Gabriel as they cruised down the tollway.* 7. energy. (Initialism. The physics symbol that denotes energy.) ▶ $E = mc^2$ 8. error. (Initialism. A baseball term denoting a play that should have resulted in an out but was mishandled, allowing a runner to advance a base. The example is to be interpreted as 12 hits, 5 runs, 3 errors.) ▶ *Tigers: 12H 5R 3E*

e electron. (A subatomic particle with a negative charge that spins around the nucleus of the atom.)

E = mc² Energy equals mass times the speed of light squared. (Initialism. Einstein's theory of relativity.)

ea. each. (Used on signs and in advertising.) ▸ *Apples, 65 cents ea.*

Ec. Ecuador. (A country on the Pacific coast of South America, straddling the equator.) ▸ *Quito, Ec.*

EC European Community. (Initialism. An umbrella organization for the European Economic Community, the European Coal and Steel Community, and the European Atomic Energy Community. See *EEC, ECSC, Euratom*. The EC implements economic policies and treaties through which economic unification of Western Europe can be attained.) ▸ *One goal of the EC is to eliminate trade barriers between member countries.*

eccl. ecclesiastical. (Relating to the church and its clergy.) ▸ *Eccl. Latin*

Eccles. Ecclesiastes. (A book of the Bible.) ▸ *Eccles. 2:1*

ECG electrocardiogram. (Initialism. The graph produced by a machine that measures the changes in the electrical force causing the heartbeat. The same as *EKG*.) ▸ *An ECG readout is a diagnostic tool used to detect heart disease.*

ECM European Common Market. (Initialism. The European Economic Community. Sometimes referred to as the Common Market. See *EEC*.)

ecol. ecology. (The study of the relationship between organisms and their environment.) ▸ *Ecol. 103 meets in Room 215 in Science Hall.*

econ. economics. (Often a clipping. The study of finance.) ▸ *Adele only dated econ majors until she met Harry, a rebellious musician.* ▸ *Econ. Dept.*

ECSC European Coal and Steel Community. (Initialism. A common market for coal and steel among [then West] Germany, France, the Netherlands, Belgium, Luxembourg, and Italy.) ▶ *As part of the treaty that established the ECSC, government subsidies for coal and steel were eliminated.*

ECU AND **ecu** European Currency Unit. (Acronym. The currency unit of the European Community in the attempt by Western Europe, except for the United Kingdom, to attain economic unification. See *EC*.) ▶ *The term ECU is influenced by the name for an old French currency, the écu.*

ed. **1.** editor. (The head of a newspaper or publishing department who edits and compiles manuscripts and submissions.) **2.** AND **educ.** education. (The process of imparting knowledge or skills.) ▶ *Dept. of Ed.* ▶ *secondary educ.* ▶ *The school district offered different special ed. courses depending on the particular student's needs.* ▶ *Jane skipped phys. ed. until she was in danger of flunking the course.* **3.** edition. (A published work or a version of a published work.) ▶ *We are bringing out a new ed. next year.* ▶ *The final ed. of the newpaper appeared late in the evening.*

EDA Economic Development Administration. (Initialism. An agency within the Department of Commerce that protects jobs and encourages economic growth in low-income areas.) ▶ *The run-down neighborhood received aid from the EDA to stimulate business growth.*

EDP electronic data processing. (Initialism. The collection and management of information by electronic means.) ▶ *The company's new EDP system allowed Ted to receive on-line reports from Dun and Bradstreet.*

EDT Eastern Daylight Time. (Initialism. The adjusted time in the easternmost time zone of the United States from early April to late October. It is four hours behind Greenwich Time.) ▸ *3:30 p.m. EDT*

educ. See *ed.*

E.E. electrical engineer. (Initialism. A professional title for someone who applies the use of electricity to industrial situations.) ▸ *Derek Frazier, E.E., was called in to redesign the building's electrical system to prevent the elevators from overloading the circuits.*

EEC European Economic Community. (Initialism. Also known as the Common Market. An organization within the European Community established in the 1950s to eradicate tariffs and trade barriers and to integrate economic policies. See *EC* and *ECM*.) ▸ *West Germany, France, the Netherlands, Belgium, Luxembourg, and Italy were the original six members of the EEC.* ▸ *Sally could not understand how the televangelist linked the EEC with the Apocalypse.*

EEG electroencephalogram. (Initialism. A printout of brain waves.) ▸ *The EEG indicated the patient was in a coma.*

EEOC Equal Employment Opportunity Commission. (Initialism. A government agency that handles discrimination complaints in employment situations.) ▸ *When men with far less seniority were being promoted over Jane, she threatened to report the company to the EEOC.*

EFT electronic funds transfer. (Initialism. A financial system for handling many transactions electronically through automatic teller machines, wire deposits, and other electronic means.) ▸ *The bank embraced the EFT system in order to reduce the handling of currency.* ▸ *The company issued its payroll by EFT.*

EFTA European Free Trade Association. (Acronym. A European economic organization devised by the United Kingdom in 1959 that set aside trade barriers for nonfarm products among member nations.) ▸ *The United Kingdom left EFTA in 1973 to become a part of the European Community.*

e.g. *exempli gratia.* (Initialism. Latin: for example. Used before a list of examples.) ▸ *Religion 401 will discuss the major tenets of several religions, e.g., Christianity, Judaism, Islam, Buddhism, and Janism.*

Eg. Egypt. (A country in northeast Africa on the Sinai Peninsula.) ▸ *Alexandria, Eg.*

EGA enhanced graphics adapter; enhanced graphics adapter [monitor]. (A type of computer graphics circuit board that drives a computer monitor with high resolution, but not as high as a video graphics array monitor, or the monitor itself. See *VGA*.) ▸ *EGA monitor* ▸ *A new EGA board.*

EHF extremely high frequency. (Initialism. A radio frequency between 30,000 MHz and 300,000 MHz.)

EKG electrocardiogram. (The abbreviation is from the German *Electrokardiogramme*. The graph produced by a machine that measures the changes in the electrical force causing the heartbeat. The same as *ECG*.) ▸ *An EKG readout is a diagnostic tool used to detect heart disease.*

el. AND **elev.** elevation. (The height of land, measured in terms of sea level.) ▸ *Mt. Kilimanjaro (el. 19,340 feet)* ▸ *Mt. McKinley (elev. 20,320 feet)*

el elevated [train]. (Clipping. A train that runs aboveground on an elevated track so that it has an unimpeded

elec.

right of way.) ▶ *Every time Brian rode the el it seemed that token prices had gone up.*

elec. electric; electricity. (Creating electricity; pertaining to electricity.) ▶ *elec. bill* ▶ *the cost of elec.* ▶ *elec. eel* ▶ *elec. typewriter*

elem. 1. elementary. (Basic or introductory.) ▶ *Elem. Physics is a prerequisite for Adv. Physics.* 2. elementary. (A school for grades kindergarten through fifth, sixth, or eighth, depending on the structure of the school system.) ▶ *Gaines Elem. School*

elev. See *el.*

ELF extremely low frequency. (Acronym. A radio frequency from 30 to 300 Hz.) ▶ *Many people oppose the military's ELF project in Michigan's Upper Peninsula.*

e-mail electronic mail. (Initialism-*mail*. A communication that is posted by computer onto an electronic bulletin board that can be accessed by other computers.) ▶ *"You can use the computer as soon as I read my e-mail," Lance told his roommate.*

emf electromotive force. (Initialism. Electric force that causes current to flow in a circuit equal to the difference between the terminals.) ▶ *The volt is the unit of emf measurement.*

EMT emergency medical technician. (Initialism. A paramedic.) ▶ *The EMT applied mouth-to-mouth resuscitation to the drowning victim.*

enc. AND **encl.** 1. enclosed. (Indicates that one or more items are enclosed within a package or envelope.) ▶ *I am responding to your letter of January 5 (copy enc.) in which you called me a liar.* 2. enclosure; enclosures. (Placed at the bottom of a letter to indicate one or more enclosures are accompanying the letter.) ▶ *Watch for 3 enc.*

encl. See the previous entry.

encyc. AND **encycl.** encyclopedia. (A compendium of articles of information and knowledge listed alphabetically.) ▶ *World Book Encyc.* ▶ *Collier's Encycl.*

encycl. See the previous entry.

ENE east-northeast. (A compass direction halfway between northeast and due east.) ▶ *The enemy target was 10 miles ENE of the pilot.*

eng. 1. engineer. (Someone trained in engineering. See *engin.*) ▶ *civil eng.* ▶ *Wanted: Mech. Eng. w/ 5 years experience.* 2. engineer. (A train operator.) ▶ *Occupation: locomotive eng.*

Eng. 1. England. (A part of the United Kingdom, occupying most of the southern portion of the island of Great Britain.) ▶ *London, Eng.* 2. English. ▶ *Eng. History* ▶ *Eng. language*

engin. engineering. (The application of scientific knowledge to practical use.) ▶ *chemical engin.*

ENIAC Electronic Numerical Integrator and Computer. (Acronym. An early computer of the 1940s designed to calculate trajectories.) ▶ *The ENIAC, which performed simple calculations in comparison to today's supercomputers, weighed over 50 tons and took up 2,000 square feet.*

Ens. Ensign. (In the U.S. Navy, the lowest rank of commissioned officer.) ▶ *Ens. Fuller reported to the deck.*

e.o. *ex officio.* (Initialism. Latin: by virtue of office. Perks and benefits resulting from holding a particular job or position.) ▸ *Walter attended the meeting e.o.* ▸ *Walter Ryan (e.o.)*

EOE equal opportunity employer. (Initialism. Used in help wanted ads to indicate that the employer does not discriminate or is legally prohibited from discriminating on the basis of race, sex, creed, physical handicap, or as otherwise mandated.) ▸ *Wanted: Press Operator. 555-3982. EOE.*

EP extended play. (Initialism. A type of record or tape cassette that is longer than normal; for instance, a song on an EP single will be longer than the album version, and the EP single may feature different variations of the song.) ▸ *Eugene bought a few new EPs especially for his party on Friday.*

EPA Environmental Protection Agency. (Initialism. A government agency established in 1970 to protect the environment by controlling pollution and regulating disposal of waste.) ▸ *Neighbors of the toxic waste dump contacted the EPA to have the site shut down and cleaned up.*

EPCOT experimental prototype community of tomorrow. (Acronym. The EPCOT Center is a Disney attraction in Orlando, Florida, featuring exhibits on science, health, and foreign lands and cultures.) ▸ *Jane rode the monorail between the Magic Kingdom and the EPCOT Center.* ▸ *The grade-school students each wrote an essay on their trip to EPCOT.*

Epis. AND **Episc.** **1.** Episcopal. (A Protestant denomination.) ▸ *St. John's Epis. Church* **2.** Epistle. (In the Christian Bible, an apostolic letter.) ▸ *The 2nd Epis. of St. Peter*

eq. **1.** equal. ▸ *= (eq. sign)* **2.** equation. (A mathematical statement expressing the equality of two quantities on opposite sides of an equal sign.) ▸ *Eq. 6 holds true by the reflexive property.*

equip. equipment. (Items or supplies necessary for or accompanying something.) ▶ *Bring your own baseball equip. (bats, balls, bases).*

equiv. 1. equivalent. (Of equal value.) ▶ *Twenty ounces of silver or cash equiv.* 2. equivalent. (A geometry term. The relationship between two different shapes or forms that have an equal area or volume.) ▶ *ABC is equiv. to DEF.*

ER emergency room. (Initialism. The part of a hospital that provides immediate care.) ▶ *The gunshot victim died in the ER.*

Er erbium. (The chemical symbol for Element 68.)

ERA 1. earned run average. (Initialism. A baseball term. For every nine innings pitched, the average number of earned runs scored by batters against a particular pitcher.) ▶ *Ed Walsh holds the record for the lowest ERA at 1.82.* 2. equal rights amendment. (Initialism. A proposed and defeated amendment to the U.S. Constitution that would have strengthened the constitution's prohibitions against discrimination on the basis of sex.) ▶ *Despite intense lobbying efforts by several women's rights groups, the ERA was defeated in 1982.*

ERDA Energy Research and Development Administration. (Acronym. A government agency from 1974 to 1977 that administered the research and development of energy-related concerns.) ▶ *ERDA researched methods of producing energy from both fossil fuels and solar power.* ▶ *Upon its establishment in 1977, the Department of Energy subsumed the duties of ERDA.*

Es einsteinium. (The chemical symbol for element 99.)

Esc escape. (A key on a computer keyboard.) ▶ *Press Esc to cancel the most recently executed command.*

ESE east-southeast. (A compass direction halfway between east and southeast.) ▶ *Winds from the ESE at 24 miles per hour.* ▶ *Lansing, Michigan, is approximately 60 miles ESE of Grand Rapids.*

ESL English as a second language. (Initialism. Referring to the English language as taught to nonnative speakers.) ▶ *The school district offered ESL classes to the newly arrived boat people.*

ESOL English for speakers of other languages. (Acronym. "E-sol." English courses for people whose native language is not English.) ▶ *The ESOL program at the city college taught English for speakers of Spanish, Polish, Vietnamese, and Hmong.*

ESOP Employee Stock Ownership Plan. (Acronym. "E-sop." A system that encourages company employees to own company stock.) ▶ *When contracts were being renegotiated, management wasn't in a position to offer large raises, but they did offer some lucrative ESOPs.*

esp. especially. (Used in notes for emphasis.) ▶ *Study chap. 12, esp. pgs. 245 thru 269.*

ESP extrasensory perception. (Initialism. The "sixth sense," a paranormal ability associated with mind reading and predicting the future.) ▶ *If Lauren didn't have ESP, she was at least highly intuitive.* ▶ *The young seer used ESP to predict correctly each card as it was turned over from the deck.*

Esq. Esquire. (An honorary title appended to the name of a male or to the name of a lawyer, either male and female. Not used in conjunction with another title [Miss, Ms., Mrs., Mr., Dr., etc.] before the name.) ▶ *Warren D. Smith, Esq.* ▶ *Alicia A. Benson, Esq.*

est. **1.** estimated. (An approximation.) ▸ *est. viewing distance—6 miles* ▸ *est. mileage—25 mpg (city), 32 mpg (highway)* **2.** established. (Marked on storefronts and other items associated with a company, indicating the year the company was formed.) ▸ *est. 1945*

Est. Estonia. (A nation on the Baltic Sea, a republic of the U.S.S.R. until 1991.) ▸ *Tallinn, Est.*

EST Eastern Standard Time. (Initialism. The time in the eastern quarter of the United States from the last weekend in October to the last weekend in April. It is five hours behind Greenwich Time.) ▸ *4:30 P.M. EST* ▸ *Funds must be remitted by 1:00 p.m. EST, or an additional day's interest will accrue.*

ET **1.** Eastern Time. (Initialism. The time in the eastern quarter of the United States.) ▸ *New York City (ET)* ▸ *5:00 ET/4:00 CT* **2.** extraterrestrial. (A being from outer space. The term was popularized by the Steven Spielberg movie of the same name.) ▸ *The intrepid reporter followed up on every lead concerning UFOs and ETs.* ▸ *The baby-sitter took a nap while little Lisabeth watched* ET *on the VCR.*

ETA **1.** estimated time of arrival. (Initialism. Used at airports and other transportation terminals.) ▸ *Due to the snowstorm, the ETA for Flight 803 is now 2:45 p.m.* **2.** Euzkadi ta Azakatasuna. (Initialism. Basque: Basque Nation and Liberty. A separatist group that demands the formation of a Basque nation in northern Spain and southwestern France.) ▸ *The ETA claimed responsibility for kidnapping the official's children.*

et al. *et alii.* (Latin: and others. Used to shorten lists and series of names, such as in law firms.) ▸ *Valerie works for the law firm of Vaid, Finley, Hughes, et al.* ▸ *Maroon, crimson, cherry, brick, et al.*

etc. *et cetera.* (Latin: and so forth.) ▸ *Smithco expects all employees to be courteous, punctual, orderly, etc.* ▸ *Washington, Adams, Jefferson, Madison, Monroe, etc.*

ETD estimated time of departure. (Initialism. Used at airports and other transportation terminals.) ▸ *Since the plane for Flight 103 is late coming in from Denver, we regret to inform you that the ETD has been moved up to 5:30 p.m.* ▸ *5:30 p.m. (ETD)*

Eth. Ethiopia. (A country in eastern Africa on the Red Sea.) ▸ *Addis Ababa, Eth.*

ETV educational television. (Initialism. Television programming used for instruction.) ▸ *The Public Broadcasting System offers several hours of ETV each week.*

etym. etymology. (The study of word origins and development.) ▸ *etym. unknown*

Eu europium. (The chemical symbol for Element 63.)

Eur. **1.** Europe. (One of seven continents of the earth. Found on maps and in texts.) ▸ *Will you go to Eur. or S.A.?* **2.** European. ▸ *Eur. Studies* ▸ *Eur. History*

Euratom European Atomic Energy Community. (Acronym. A European treaty that sought to develop nuclear energy for peaceful purposes among West Germany, France, the Netherlands, Belgium, Luxembourg, and Italy. *Euratom* became a part of the European Community in 1967. See *EC*.) ▸ *Since its inception, Denmark, Ireland, the United Kingdom, Greece, Portugal, and Spain have joined Euratom.*

eV electron volt. (A unit of electrical energy equal to -.0000000000016 erg.)

ex. **1.** example. (An item shown as an instance of something discussed. See also *e.g.*) ▸ *Write a five to seven page*

exec.

essay about a South American country (ex. Chile or Argentina), detailing its political structure and election methods, if any. ▶ *Do the following addition problems. Ex.: 2 + 5 = 7* **2.** AND **exc.** except. (Exclude, omit. The same as *exc.*) ▶ *Tomorrow's Assignment: Pg. 43, odd problems ex. 7 and 13.* **3.** AND **exc.** exception. (A departure from standard procedure.) ▶ *Absolutely NO classes are to be skipped. (ONLY ex.: Doctor's written excuse.)* **4.** See *exec.* **5.** See *exp.* (sense 1). **6.** See *ext.*

exam examination. (Clipping. A comprehensive test.) ▶ *Final exams are next week.* ▶ *Grandpa scheduled an eye exam because he's been getting headaches from reading the newspaper.*

exc. **1.** excellent. (Of superior quality. Used as a rating.) ▶ *For each appliance, mark exc., good, fair, or poor to describe its condition.* **2.** See *ex.* (senses 2 and 3).

Exc. Excellency. (An title of honor applied to important, high-ranking individuals.) ▶ *I thank Your Exc. for taking the time to respond to this written plea for assistance.*

exch. **1.** exchange. (Pertaining to the act of giving something and taking an equivalent thing in return.) ▶ *exch. rate: $.75 (Canadian) to $1 (U.S.)* **2.** exchange. (A location or office where transactions or exchanges take place.) ▶ *Retail Exch. Dept. 2nd Floor* ▶ *LaSalle/Chicago Currency Exch. Open 24 Hours!*

excl. exclamation. (A sharp and sudden outburst.) ▶ *"!" (excl. point)*

exec. **1.** AND **ex.** executive. (An officer or official of a company or an organization. Informally used as a clipping, as in gossip columns.) ▶ *Exec. Vice President of Human Relations* ▶ *Exec. Committee Meeting* **2.** executor. (The person in charge of carrying out the particulars of a last will and testament.) ▶ *Todd Willis, exec.*

exp. **1.** AND **ex.** express. (Nonstop, usually related to transportation.) ▸ *Flight 401, Ex. Service to New York La Guardia* ▸ *exp. lanes closed* ▸ *exp. lanes—minimum of 2 passengers per car* ▸ *Reverse Commuter Exp. Train Schedule* **2.** experiment. (A scientific procedure that tests a theory or hypothesis.) ▸ *Exp. 2-13 details the effects of ultraviolet rays on unprotected skin.* **3.** expires. (Found on packaging to indicate the final date the product is guaranteed to be fresh; found in documents to indicate the final date the terms of that document apply.) ▸ *exp. 10/30/95.* ▸ *Letter of Credit #104-2903-32C, exp. 4/15/90.* **4.** expiration. ▸ *(exp. date 10/90)* **5.** exponential. (A mathematical term. Involving the operation of raising a number to a certain power. For instance, $2^3 = 8$ is an exponential equation.) ▸ *exp. function.* **6.** expenses. (Costs.) ▸ *$35.00 for exp.*

EXP natural logarithm. (Initialism. An alternative way to express *e*, the mathematical symbol for the base number for natural logarithms: 2.7183.) ▸ $EXP(x) = e^x$

expy expressway. (A limited-access divided highway; a freeway.) ▸ *Kennedy Expy* ▸ *Expy Next Right—Toll Road Next Left*

ext. **1.** extension. (One of two or more telephone instruments assigned to a specific telephone line.) ▸ *Sally's assistant is at ext. 250.* **2.** external. (On the outside.) ▸ *ext. injuries* ▸ *ext. affairs* **3.** extinct. (Pertaining to a species that has died out.) ▸ *The dodo bird (ext.) had wings but could not fly.* **4.** extract. (A concentrate of a substance. Used in medicine and on packaging.) ▸ *pure vanilla ext.* **5.** exterior. (On the outside.) ▸ *ext. house paint* ▸ *ext. view of the house* ▸ *ceramic ext.* **6.** extended. (Used in reference to sales, plays, concerts, contracts, and similar events whose end date has been postponed.) ▸ *White Sale ext. through January 15 for extra savings!* ▸

Springfield Community Theatre's South Pacific *now ext. thru March.* ▶ *Loan Commitment ext. to 3/15/85* **7.** AND **ex.** extra. ▶ *popcorn with butter $2.00. (ex. butter 50¢)* ▶ *It costs $.25 ext.*

EZ easy. (Initialism. Found frequently in advertising and as part of the name of a product or company.) ▶ *EZ does it!* ▶ *EZ-Slim Weight Loss Diet Plan*

F

F **1.** a grade indicating failure. (Initialism. In the series *A, B, C, D, F.*) ▸ *Chris received an F in biology and had to take the course over again.* **2.** a musical tone. (Initialism. The fourth note of the scale of C major.) ▸ *To play an F on a trombone, the slide is placed in first position.* **3.** Fahrenheit. (A unit of degree of temperature. The freezing point of water is 32° F; the boiling point of water is 212° F. See also *C.*) **4.** false. (Initialism. Used in logic and in true and false tests. See also *T.*) ▸ *T or F? The capital of Sudan is Khartoum.* **5.** February. (Often used in graph columns or rows to chart the month-by-month progress of something. See also *Feb.*) **6.** female. (Found on forms, classified ads, and other printed material to indicate the person being described is female. See also *f* and *fem.* Compare with male at *M.*) ▸ *Check M or F.* ▸ *Roommate wanted (F only, no smokers) 555-2356* **7.** fighter. (Initialism. Used as a prefix in front of certain military aircraft.) ▸ *F-105* ▸ *The F-16 was shot down by enemy aircraft.* **8.** fluorine. (The chemical symbol for Element 9.) **9.** Friday. (A day of the week. In the series *S, M, T, W, T, F, S* or *Su, M, Tu, W, Th, F, Sa.* See also *Fr.* and *Fri.*) ▸ *Piano lessons are M, W, F at 2:30.* **10.** full. (Initialism. Found on gauges to indicate that something, such as a gas tank, is full.) ▸ *"I filled the tank up to two notches below the F," Gail told her father.* **11.** function [key]. (Initialism. A computer

fac.

keyboard abbreviation.) ▸ *If you need help, push F1.* **12.** French. (Used in dictionaries to show the etymology of a word. The same as *Fr.*) ▸ *parfait < F parfait, something perfect*

f **1.** focal length; focal distance. (Distance from the optical center of a lens to the point where light rays from a distant object converge. See also *FD, FL.*) **2.** forte. (A musical direction: Loud.) **3.** feminine. (A grammatical subclass in languages where nouns are inflected for gender. The biological sex [if any] of the object represented by the noun is irrelevant. Found in language textbooks and dictionaries. See also *fem.* Compare with *m, n.*) ▸ *die Pflanze (f)* ▸ *la abuela (f)* **4.** feminine. (Pertaining to nouns and pronouns that refer to females. Found in language textbooks and dictionaries. Compare with *m.*) ▸ *executrix (f)* ▸ *waitress (f)* ▸ *her (f)*

F.A. fine arts. (Initialism. Aesthetic art forms, including drawing, painting, sculpture, music, drama, and dancing. Used in combination with Bachelors and Masters Degrees. See *BFA* and *MFA*.) ▸ *Sue was in F.A. for a while and then shifted to liberal arts.*

FAA Federal Aviation Administration. (Initialism. An agency within the Department of Transportation that oversees policies regarding air traffic, airspace, and other aviation matters.) ▸ *The residents of the neighborhoods surrounding the airport persuaded the FAA to develop ways to reduce the noise pollution.*

fac. **1.** facsimile. (A replica or copy. See *fax* for the definition of facsimile as a telecopier.) **2.** faculty. (The teaching staff of a school or other educational institution.) ▸ *Fac. Lounge*

Fahr. Fahrenheit. (A scale used to measure temperature; the unit used to represent degrees on the Fahrenheit scale. The same as *F.*) ▸ *10° Fahr.*

FALN *Fuerzas Armadas de Liberación Nacional.* (Acronym. Spanish: Armed Forces of National Liberation. A Puerto Rican organization supporting Puerto Rican independence from the United States.) ▸ *FALN supporters passed out pro-independence literature at the Puerto Rican festival.*

F.A.M. Free and Accepted Masons. (Initialism. An international secret society.) ▸ *Father McCarthy threatened to excommunicate Uncle Mike if he were to join the F.A.M.*

fam. 1. familiar. (A form of the word *you* used in languages that distinguish between a polite *you* and a familiar *you*. The familiar form is usually used in addressing close relatives, friends, and children. Found in language textbooks and dictionaries. See also *pol.*) ▸ *Spanish: tu (fam. sing.), Usted (pol. sing.), vosotros (fam. plur.), Ustedes (fam. plur.)* **2.** family. (A biological term. A category in plant and animal classification. Orders are split into families, which in turn are made up of genera.) ▸ Homo sapiens *(fam: Hominidae)*

FAO Food and Agriculture Organization. (Initialism. An independent international organization associated with the United Nations. It was established to increase production from farms, forests, and fisheries.) ▸ *Member nations of the FAO donate food and services to the World Food Program for global emergencies.*

fath. AND **fth.** fathom. (The unit used to measure the depth of water or the length of rope, equal to six feet.) ▸ *2 fath. = 12 feet* ▸ *10 fth. deep*

fax 1. facsimile. (Clipping. A machine that electronically transmits and reproduces copies of written materials over telephone lines; a telecopier.) ▸ *"Jane, place a service call. The fax is on the fritz again!"* ▸ *Please do not place coffee cups on the fax machine!* **2.** papers transmitted by a fax machine. ▸ *"I'm missing the last page of the fax you just sent me. Could you resend it?"* ▸ *"You just got a fax. I put it on your desk," the receptionist told Jeff.* **3.** to send documents by fax. ▸ *"I'll fax you the figures right now," the sales agent told the prospective buyer.* ▸ *Nathan faxed the press release to all East Coast news stations.* ▸ *Faxing one-page letters is less expensive than the price of a first-class postage stamp.* **4.** placed before a telephone number to indicate it is a fax number. ▸ *(FAX) 301-555-2932*

FB fullback. (In football, the offensive running back stationed behind the quarterback and farthest from the line of scrimmage.) ▸ *Alan Ameche (FB) of the University of Wisconsin won the Heisman Trophy in 1954.*

FBI Federal Bureau of Investigation. (Initialism. A branch of the U.S. Department of Justice that investigates violations of federal laws.) ▸ *Anna contacted the FBI when she received death threats in the mail.*

fc AND **ft-c** foot-candle. (A unit of illumination equal to the illumination produced by a source of one candle at a distance of one foot.) ▸ *6 fc*

FCA Farm Credit Administration. (Initialism. A government agency that regulates organizations providing credit to farmers, ranchers, farm-equipment producers, and agricultural associations.) ▸ *During the drought, the FCA monitored the assistance provided to the farming communities that were hardest hit.*

FCC Federal Communications Commission. (Initialism. An agency that regulates telephone, television, radio,

FD

and satellite communications.) ▸ *The FCC levied a heavy fine against the disc jockey.*

FD **1.** fire department. (A group of fire fighters, professional or volunteer, who put out fires and inspect buildings to prevent the occurrence of fires.) ▸ *Thetford Twp. FD* **2.** focal distance. (Distance from the optical center of a lens to the point where light rays from a distant object converge. Also known as *focal length*.)

FDA Food and Drug Administration. (Initialism. A government agency within the Department of Health and Human Services that monitors the purity and safety of food, cosmetics, and drugs; truth in packaging and labeling information; and sanitary practices in restaurants and other food-handling establishments.) ▸ *The FDA can take many years to approve a drug.*

FD&C food, drugs, and cosmetics. (Initialism. A Food and Drug Administration designation for a dye or coloring that has been approved for use in food, drugs, and cosmetics. Found on packaging and labeling. Compare with *D&C*.) ▸ *The ingredients included FD&C Yellow No. 6.*

FDIC Federal Deposit Insurance Corporation. (Initialism. Established in 1933 to insure deposits of state banks that do not belong to the Federal Reserve System.) ▸ *Is this account insured by the FDIC?*

FDR Franklin Delano Roosevelt. (Initialism. The thirty-second president of the United States, in office from 1933 until his death in 1945.) ▸ *FDR met with Churchill and Stalin at the Yalta Conference shortly before the end of World War II.*

Fe iron. (The chemical symbol for Element 26. The symbol is derived from Latin *ferrum*.)

FEA Federal Energy Administration. (Initialism. A government agency from 1974 to 1977 that allocated fuel, regulated pricing, and researched energy conservation.) ▸ *The FEA analyzed new sources of energy production.*

Feb. February. (See also *F.*) ▸ *Valentine's Day—Feb. 14*

FEC Federal Election Commission. (Initialism. A watchdog group that monitors the campaigning practices of presidential and congressional candidates, their sources of income, the uses of these funds, and the activities of Political Action Committees.) ▸ *FEC Report on Financial Activity* ▸ *The FEC tracks the amount of money spent by candidates on campaign finances.*

Fed AND **FRS** Federal Reserve System. (Clipping AND initialism. Usually referred to as "the Fed." The United States centralized banking system created to monitor the economy by regulating the money supply.) ▸ *The Fed lowered the discount rate during 1991 in order to stimulate the economy.* ▸ *There are twelve regional Fed banks across the United States.*

fed. **1.** federal. (Referring to the central government; the system of government whereby states in a federation cede their individual power over certain matters to a central government.) ▸ *Fed. Bureau of Investigation* ▸ *Fed. Rep. of Germany* ▸ *fed. gov't* **2.** federation. (A union of states or other political units that cede their individual power to a central organization.) ▸ *American Fed. of Labor*

fed a federal agent. (Clipping. A slang term.) ▸ *Once Henry crossed the state line with the stolen goods, the feds got involved.*

fem. **1.** female. (Found on forms and other printed material to indicate that the person or creature being described is female. See also *F* and *f.*) ▸ *Lost, fem. white cat,*

FEMA

answers to "Sparkle." **2.** feminine. (A grammatical subclass in languages where nouns are inflected for gender. The biological sex [if any] of the entity represented by the noun is irrelevant. Found in language textbooks and dictionaries. Compare with *masc., neut.*) ▶ *die Katze (fem.)* ▶ *la cama (fem.)* **3.** feminine. (A noun or pronoun that refers to females. Found in language textbooks and dictionaries. Compare with *m.*) ▶ *aviatrix (fem.)* ▶ *waitress (fem.)* ▶ *she (fem.)*

FEMA Federal Emergency Management Agency. (Acronym. An American governmental agency that coordinates civilian preparedness for enemy attacks and peacetime disasters, operates fallout shelters, and coordinates relief funds to presidentially declared disaster areas.) ▶ *After the devastating earthquake, the Red Cross and the FEMA officials were the first to arrive on the scene.*

FF fast forward. (The marking on a console or remote control for the button that fast forwards through a video tape or audio tape.) ▶ *You can find the place you want on the tape if you press the FF button.*

ff fortissimo. (A musical direction: Very loud.)

FHA Federal Housing Administration. (Initialism. A division within the Department of Housing and Urban Development that insures mortgages.) ▶ *The FHA does not place mortgages, but only insures them.*

FHLMC Federal Home Loan Mortgage Corporation. (Initialism. Called "Freddie Mac." A government-sponsored agency that buys mortgages and sells securities backed by those mortgages.) ▶ *FHLMC securities*

FICA Federal Insurance Contributions Act. (Acronym. Pronounced "FI-kah." The legislation that withholds money from income to go toward Social Security. Found on paycheck stubs.) ▸ *FICA $102.23* ▸ *Federal and state taxes, union dues, and FICA ate over 35 percent of Harry's paycheck.*

fict. fiction. (A book, article, story, or other narrative that is made up, as opposed to nonfiction.) ▸ *Rabbit at Rest—John Updike (fict.)*

FIFO first in, first out. (Acronym. Pronounced "FI-foe." An accounting term. A method of allocating costs between inventory and sales. See also *LIFO*.) ▸ *With FIFO, sold items are valued as if they were sold in order of acquisition.*

fig. figure. (Referring to a chart or table within a text.) ▸ *Fig. 12-4 shows the upper respiratory system.*

fin. 1. financial. (Relating to money matters.) ▸ *fin. district* 2. finished. (Indicates completion; for instance, marked on a tally sheet upon completion of the tasks listed.) ▸ *shopping, fin.; trip to bank, fin.*

Fin. Finland. (A country in northern Europe.) ▸ *Helsinki, Fin.*

fl. floor. (A level of a building. The first floor is at ground level.) ▸ *pediatrics, 4th fl.* ▸ *women's clothing—8th fl.*

FL 1. Florida. (The official two-letter post office abbreviation. See also *Fla.*) ▸ *Orlando, FL 32801* 2. focal length. (Distance from the optical center of a lens to the point where light rays from a distant object converge. Also known as *focal distance, FD*.)

Fla. AND **Flor.** Florida. (See also *FL*.) ▸ *Tallahassee, Fla.* ▸ *Miami, Flor.*

fl. dr. fluid dram. (A unit of liquid measure equal to 1/8 of a fluid ounce or approximately 3.7 milliliters.) ▸ *Net weight: 20 fl. dr.*

Flor. See *Fla.*

fl. oz. fluid ounce. (A unit of liquid measure equal to 1/32 of a quart or approximately 29.6 milliliters. Often found on packaging and labeling.) ▶ *250 fl. oz.*

FLRA Federal Labor Relations Authority. (Initialism. Established in 1979 to protect the labor rights of federal employees and supervise the obligations of federal employees and their labor organizations.)

fm. AND **fr.** from. (Used in note taking or advertisements.) ▶ *Get notes fm. Prof. Stanley today.* ▶ *cheese comes fr. milk*

Fm fermium. (The chemical symbol for Element 100.)

FM frequency modulation. (Initialism. A system of radio broadcasting by varying the modulation of the radio carrier wave, the opposite of *AM*.) ▶ *FM Stereo* ▶ *WXRT—FM 93.1* ▶ *Halfway across Nebraska, Danny realized the U-Haul did not have an FM radio.*

FMLN *Farabundo Martí Liberación Nacional.* (Initialism. Spanish: Farabundo Martí National Liberation Front. The El Salvadoran political organization in opposition to the formal government from 1980 to 1992.) ▶ *The El Salvadoran government signed a peace treaty with the FMLN in 1992.*

fn. footnote. (A reference at the bottom of a page of text providing additional comment on, or source material for, information within the text.) ▶ *Check source material in fn. 12.*

FNMA Federal National Mortgage Association. (Initialism. Pronounced and often referred to as "Fannie Mae." A government lending agency that buys and sells federally insured mortgages.) ▶ *Peter thought he could get a*

for.

better deal through the FNMA, but he hadn't counted on bureaucratic red tape.

f.o.b. AND **FOB** free on board. (Initialism. Free delivery from point of origin to the buyer by any means of transportation.) ▸ *An f.o.b. shipment of brick and lumber enabled the contractor to landscape the grounds with the money saved.*

FOE Fraternal Order of Eagles. (Initialism. A national fraternal society.) ▸ *The local FOE chapter helped the school district raise money for band uniforms.*

FOIA Freedom of Information Act. (Initialism. A federal law that allows anyone to see records documenting the activities of any executive branch agency by providing a written request asking for specific documents. Exceptions under the law include documents concerning personnel files of government employees, matters relating to national security, criminal investigation records, patent applications, and other private business-related documents.) ▸ *The FOIA provides legislation by which someone can challenge the federal government in court for not supplying documentation upon request.*

fol. **1.** folio. (A sheet folded once that forms four pages for a manuscript. Also, a large book made from pages formed this way.) **2.** following. (Used parenthetically to refer to items about to be mentioned.) ▸ *The great ocelot (see fol.) is a member of the cat family.*

for. **1.** foreign. (Not native or indigenous to a particular culture or area.) ▸ *for. origin.* **2.** forest. (A large area of trees. Also used in the names of cities and towns.) ▸ *Sherwood For.* ▸ *Lake For., Ill.* **3.** forestry. (The science of managing forests.) ▸ *Dept. of For.*

fort. fortified. (Enriched. Common abbreviation found on nutritional panels of food packaging.) ▸ *Breakfast Sugar Crunchies—fort. with vitamins and minerals!*

FORTRAN formula translation. (Acronym. A scientific and business-oriented computer language that uses algebraic formulas.) ▸ *In her second year of computer studies, Kim took advanced courses in FORTRAN.*

4-H head, heart, hands, and health. (Pronounced "FOR-AITCH." A program for children run by the U.S. Department of Agriculture. Its goal is to improve the four H's listed above by providing classes in agriculture, conservation, home economics, etc.) ▸ *Paul and Jane attended 4-H Club meetings twice a week.* ▸ *Jimmy's prize-winning pumpkin was the centerpiece of the 4-H booth at the county fair.*

4WD four-wheel drive. (A vehicle with four wheels all directly powered by the engine, used primarily for off-road traveling.) ▸ *4WD pickup truck* ▸ *Pull up on the lever to engage 4WD.*

fp 1. freezing point. (The temperature at which a liquid becomes solid. See also *MP.*) ▸ *The fp of water = 0° Celsius.* 2. forte piano. (A musical direction: Loud, then soft.)

fpm feet per minute. (Initialism. A measurement of velocity determined by the distance traveled in feet in one minute.) ▸ *60 mph = 5,280 fpm*

FPO Fleet Post Office; Field Post Office. (Initialism. Part of an address to a military unit stationed outside the U.S.) ▸ *Camp Butler, Okinawa, FPO Seattle 98773*

fps 1. feet per second. (Initialism. A measurement of velocity determined by the distance traveled in feet in one second.) ▸ *60 mph = 88 fps* 2. frames per second. (In film, the number of frames projected every second.) ▶ *Modern films operate at 24 fps.*

Fr. 1. Father. (Form of address for a priest.) ▶ *Mass was celebrated by Fr. Franklin.* 2. France. (A country of Western Europe.) ▶ *Paris, Fr.* 3. French. ▶ *Fr. Fries* ▶ *Fr. wine* 4. Friar. (Form of address for a monk.) ▶ *Fr. Tuck* 5. Friday. (See also *F* and *Fri.*) ▶ *Fr. Apr. 23*

fr. See *fm*.

Fr 1. francium. (The chemical symbol for Element 87.) 2. French. (The French language. Used in dictionaries to show the etymology of a word. See also *F.*) ▶ *parfait <Fr parfait, something perfect.*

FRB Federal Reserve Board. (Initialism. The policy-making body of the Federal Reserve System. See *FRS*.) ▶ *Members of the FRB serve fourteen-year terms.* ▶ *The FRB Discount Rate*

Freon fluorine + refrigerant + the suffix *-on*. (The trademarked name of a gaseous inert chlorofluorocarbon used in refrigerants, aerosol propellants, and plastic foams. See *CFC*.) ▶ *Freon is being phased out around the world.*

freq. frequency. (Used in notes, texts, and charts.) ▶ *statistical freq.* ▶ *freq. modulation*

FRG Federal Republic of Germany. (Initialism. The full English name for Germany and the full English name for West Germany prior to unification in November 1990.) ▶ *Bonn, FRG*

Fri. Friday. (See also *F* and *Fr.*) ▶ *Fri., April 23*

FRS See *Fed*.

FSH follicle-stimulating hormone. (Initialism. A hormone secreted by the anterior pituitary gland that stimulates the development of follicles in the ova of women and of sperm in men.) ▸ *The biology teacher stressed the role of FSH in reproduction.*

FSLIC Federal Savings and Loan Insurance Corporation. (Initialism. The government agency that insured the deposits of member savings and loan institutions until 1989, when it went broke.) ▸ *The FSLIC became insolvent.*

ft. foot; feet. (A unit of linear measurement, equal to 12 inches or .0305 meter.) ▸ *The house for sale featured 14-ft. cathedral ceilings.* ▸ *First 25 ft. of insulation now 50% off the regular price.*

Ft. Fort. (A permanent army base, fortified for military defense, also used in cities named for forts. Used on maps and signs and in addresses.) ▸ *Ft. Sheridan* ▸ *Ft. Knox* ▸ *Ft. Lauderdale, Florida* ▸ *Ft. Collins, Colorado*

FT **1.** free throw. (Initialism. A basketball term for the opportunity to shoot a basket from the free-throw line without interference following a violation or foul by the opposing team. A successful free throw scores one point. Used primarily in written form in statistical tables, newspaper articles, sports programs, and the like.) ▸ *FT attempts* **2.** full-time. (Initialism. Employment of at least 37.5 to 40 hours a week. Used in classified advertisements and in employment descriptions. Compare with part-time at *PT*.) ▸ *Now hiring FT sales clerks. 555-1022.*

ft-c See *fc*.

FTC Federal Trade Commission. (Initialism. Established in 1914 to promote competition and free enterprise by breaking up monopolies and to prevent trade restraints and unfair trading practices.) ▸ *The FTC hit the false advertiser with a charge of fraud.*

fth. See *fath*.

ftl faster than light. (Initialism. The term for the theoretical concept of objects that travel faster than light.) ▶ *A tachyon is an ftl particle.*

ft-lb foot-pound. (A unit of energy equal to the work required to lift a one-pound object one foot.) ▶ *1 kilowatt = 737.25 ft-lb/sec.* ▶ *1 ft-lb = 1,356 joules*

FUBAR fouled up beyond all recognition. (Acronym. Probably of military origin, describing a situation where everything went wrong that could possibly happen. Note: The military version of this and similar acronyms used the taboo word *fucked* rather than *fouled*. See also *SNAFU.*) ▶ *"Everything went FUBAR," Jeff explained. "I ran out of gas on the interstate, and my car phone died."*

fur. furlong. (A unit of measurement equal to 1/8 of a mile or 660 feet.) ▶ *8 fur. = 1 mile*

furn. furnished. (Found in apartment ads to describe an apartment or house that comes with furniture.) ▶ *2-BR. 2-BA., furn. No pets.*

fut. future. (A grammatical tense expressing action to be begun or completed at some time in the future. Found in language textbooks and dictionaries.) ▶ *fut. progressive* ▶ *fut. perfect.* ▶ *Latin:* portabo, portabis, portabit, portabimus, portabitis, portabunt *(fut. indicative)*

fwd. **1.** forward. (The marking on a console or remote control for the button that plays a videotape or audiotape.) ▶ *Press fwd. to start the tape.* **2.** forward. (A position in various sports, including football and basketball.) ▶ *James Edgar, fwd.*

FWD front-wheel drive. (A vehicle in which only the front wheels are powered by the engine.) ▶ *For sale: Ford 2-door (FWD, AC) good cond. 555-3323.*

FX 1. foreign exchange. (The process of settling debts between people in different countries.) **2.** effects. (Initialism. A motion picture term, referring to special effects.) ▸ *Special FX*

FY fiscal year. (Initialism. The twelve-month period over which a company or organization measures its business. At the end of each fiscal year, financial accounts are settled. Found on financial forms, in column headings, etc.) ▸ *FY ending May 31, 1985*

FYI for your information. (Initialism. Uttered or written about a piece of information that may be of interest to others.) ▸ *FYI—The mayor will be making a speech tonight at City Hall.*

G

g AND **gm** gram. (The basic unit of weight in the metric system, defined as the mass of 1 cubic milliliter of water at 4°C [39°F].) ▶ *1,000 g = 1 kg* ▶ *1 oz. = 28.35 gm*

G **1.** a musical tone. (Initialism. The fifth note of the scale of C major.) **2.** game. (Used in sports statistical charts as a column or row heading to indicate the number of games played. The example is to be interpreted to mean 14 games; 10 wins; 4 losses.) ▶ *G 14 (10 W/4 L)* **3.** general admission. (Initialism. A motion picture rating in the series G, PG, PG-13, R, NC-17, X. It indicates that the movie is suitable for all audiences.) ▶ *101 Dalmatians (G)* ▶ *For her daughter's birthday, Emma bought some classic G-rated Disney cartoons.* **4.** German. (The German language, used in dictionaries to show the etymology of a word.) ▶ *sauerkraut G sauer (sour) + kraut (cabbage).* **5.** giga- (A prefix meaning 1,000,000,000 [one billion], used with units of measurement.) ▶ *Gw (gigawatt)* ▶ *GHz (gigahertz)* **6.** gigabyte. (Initialism. A computer term denoting one billion bytes or 1,000 megabytes of information or storage space.) ▶ *This supercomputer has a 10G hard drive.* **7.** goal; goals. (In hockey or soccer, the number of goals scored in a game or season by a player or a team. Found in sports statistical charts as a column or row heading.) **8.** grand. (Initialism. A slang term for

Ga.

$1,000.) ▸ *The gangster demanded the 12 G's that was owed him.* **9.** gravitational constant. (Initialism. The symbol used in physics to represent the constant ratio of gravitational force between two objects.) **10.** guard. (The offensive football positions to the right and left of the center or the defensive position in front of the offensive center; the offensive basketball positions at the back of the court when the team is in possession of the ball.) ▸ *Mohammed Elewonibi (G) of Brigham Young University was awarded the 1989 Outland Trophy as the outstanding interior lineman of the season.* ▸ *Kenny Anderson (G), New Jersey Nets* **11.** Gulf. (A part of an ocean or sea extending into the land.) ▸ *G. of Fonseca* ▸ *G. of Mexico.*

Ga. Georgia. (See also *GA*.) ▸ *Atlanta, Ga.* ▸ *Gov. Tom Taylor (Ga.)*

GA 1. General Assembly. (One of the principal components of the United Nations, consisting of all member nations, that discusses major world issues and crises. The United Nations does not have the authority to enforce the resolutions voted on by the General Assembly. Also the name of the legislative assembly in some states.) ▸ *The Illinois GA will reconvene next week.* **2.** Georgia. (The official two-letter post office abbreviation. See also *Ga.*) ▸ *Macon, GA 31201*

Ga gallium. (The chemical symbol for Element 31.)

GAAP generally accepted accounting principles. (Initialism. An accounting term referring to formally recognized accounting principles. Accompanies financial reports.) ▸ *This report has been filed with the Department of Revenue according to GAAP.*

gal. gallon. (A unit of liquid measurement equal to four quarts. Found on packaging and labels.) ▸ *2 gal.* ▸ *12-gal. gas tank*

Gam. The Republic of The Gambia. (A country in Western Africa along the Gambia River with a small Atlantic Ocean coastline and surrounded on three sides by Senegal.) ▸ *Banjul, Gam.*

GAO General Accounting Office. (Initialism. The office of the legislative branch of the federal government that provides legal, accounting, and auditing services for the United States Congress.) ▸ *The GAO was established in 1921 by the Budget and Accounting Act.*

GAR Grand Army of the Republic. (Initialism. Established in 1866, the association of Civil War veterans who fought for the Union.) ▸ *The last member of the GAR died in 1956.*

GATT General Agreement on Tariffs and Trade. (Acronym. An independent organization associated with the United Nations. Its member nations attempt to liberalize trade among themselves by reducing trade barriers and mediating trade disputes.) ▸ *Member nations of GATT account for 85 percent of global trade.*

GB AND **Gr. Brit., Gt. Brit.** Great Britain. (The island in the North Sea comprised of England, Wales, and Scotland.) ▸ *This toffee is from GB.* ▸ *She stayed in Gr. Brit. for over 2 mos.*

gcd AND **GCD** greatest common divisor. (Initialism. The largest number that can evenly divide each number in a given set of numbers. Also called "greatest common factor," see *gcf*.) ▸ *The gcd of 12, 18, and 24 is 6.*

gcf AND **GCF** greatest common factor. (Initialism. The largest number that is a factor of each number in a given set of numbers. Also called "greatest common divisor," see *gcd*.) ▸ *The gcf of 12, 15, and 24 is 3.*

Gd gadolinium. (The chemical symbol for Element 64.)

GDP gross domestic product. (Initialism. A measure of economic welfare determined by the total value of a country's output of goods and services produced within the borders of the country.) ▸ *Unlike the GNP, the GDP does not reflect earnings from income acquired abroad.*

GDR German Democratic Republic. (Initialism. The English translation of the German *Deutsche Demokratik Republik*, the official name of East Germany prior to German reunification. See *DDR*.) ▸ *Leipzig, GDR*

GE General Electric. (Initialism. A major United States corporation best known for electrical devices and appliances.) ▸ *GE soft white light bulb*

Ge germanium. (The chemical symbol for Element 32.)

GED general equivalency diploma. (Initialism. A diploma awarded to someone who has met all the requirements for a high school diploma.) ▸ *Five years after dropping out of school, Sam took night classes and earned his GED.*

GEM Gemini. (The astrological abbreviation for the zodiacal constellation of Gemini.) ▸ *GEM (May 21 to June 20)*

gen. 1. gender. (The linguistic term for a paradigm of inflections for a group of nouns and their modifiers. The most common genders are masculine [*m.* and *masc.*], feminine [*f.* and *fem.*] and neuter [*n.* and *neut.*]. The biological sex [if any] of the object represented by the noun is irrelevant. Found in language textbooks and dictionaries.) 2. AND **genl.** general. (Common; widespread; overall.) ▸ *gen. admission* ▸ *gen. education requirements* 3. AND **genit.** genitive. (The linguistic term for the grammatical case expressing possession and ownership. Found in language textbooks and dictionaries.) ▸ *obj. gen.* ▸ patria *(nom.),* patriae *(gen.)* ▸ *'s (genit. marker)* 4. genus. (In the biological classification of plants and ani-

gi.

mals, the division of families. *Genera* [the plural of *genus*] are divided into species, and each species of life is indicated by its genus and species.) ▶ *Humans: gen. Homo* ▶ *Fruit flies: gen. Drosophila*

Gen. 1. General. (A military officer ranking above a colonel.) ▶ *Maj. Gen.* ▶ *Gen. Norman A. Schwarzkopf* 2. Genesis. (The first book of the Old Testament.) ▶ *Gen. 1:1—In the beginning God created heaven and earth.*

genit. See *gen.* (sense 3).

genl. See *gen.* (sense 2).

geog. geography. (The science that deals with the surface of the earth; its geopolitical divisions; and the physical features, plant and animal life, and culture of those divisions.) ▶ *Dept. of Geog.* ▶ *Geog. 121: Latin America and Its Cultures*

geol. geology. (The science that deals with the history of the earth.) ▶ *Dept. of Geol.*

geom. geometry. (The study of the properties of and relations between points, lines, and planes.) ▶ *plane geom.* ▶ *solid geom.*

Ger. AND **Germ.** 1. German. ▶ *Ger. shepherd* ▶ *Germ. reunification* 2. Germany. (A country of central Europe.) ▶ *Duisburg, Germ.*

ger. gerund. (The present participle of a verb that functions as a noun. In English, all gerunds end in *-ing*. Found in language textbooks and dictionaries.) ▶ *ringing (ger.)*

gi. gill; gills. (A unit of liquid measure equal to 1/4 of a pint.) ▶ *4 gi. = 1 pt.*

GI 1. galvanized iron. (Initialism. Iron coated with zinc.) ▶ *GI can* ▶ *GI trash receptacle* 2. an enlisted soldier of the United States Army. (Initialism. Informal military slang probably originally derived from sense 1. Later assumed to have come from "government issue.") ▶ *The GI's crouched in a trench somewhere in France.* 3. relating to enlisted soldiers. (Initialism.) ▶ *GI haircut* 4. strict observance of military regulation. (Initialism.) ▶ *The soldiers avoided the GI drill sergeant when they spotted him in town.* 5. to make ready for official inspection. ▶ *The soldier GI'd his shoes with a toothbrush.* 6. gastrointestinal. (Initialism. Relating to the stomach and the intestines.) ▶ *Dr. Smith was the head GI surgeon.* 7. Government Issue. (Initialism. Supplies issued to military personnel.) ▶ *The new recruit's GI pants were two sizes too large.*

Gib. AND **Gibr.** Gibraltar. (A two-square-mile peninsula under British control. It is connected to Spain by a narrow isthmus.) ▶ *Col. of Gib.*

GIGO garbage in, garbage out. (Acronym. Pronounced "GUY-go" and "GEE-go." Slang term expressing that computers run according to how they are programmed. Inputing garbage will produce garbage.) ▶ *Well, you know, GIGO.*

gliss. glissando. (A musical direction: Glide up or down a scale quickly.)

GM 1. General Motors. (Initialism. The largest automotive manufacturer in the United States.) ▶ *Willie had worked at the GM plant for fifteen years when he was laid off in 1980.* ▶ *The economies of several Michigan communities are dependent on GM, Ford, and Chrysler.* 2. Grand Master. (The head of a fraternal lodge or similar society.) ▶ *After the dinner, the GM personally presented the scholarship to the selected student.*

gm See *g*.

GMAC General Motors Acceptance Corporation. (Initialism. A subsidiary of General Motors that provides financing for purchase of General Motors vehicles. Commonly seen in advertising.) ▶ *GMAC financing available.*

GMAT Graduate Management Admission Test. (Partial acronym. Pronounced "GEE-mat." A standardized test required for admission to most graduate schools offering graduate degrees in business administration.) ▶ *Michael hoped to do well enough on the GMAT to get into graduate school.*

GMT Greenwich Mean Time. (Initialism. See comments at *UT*. This is the standard time of the meridian that passes through Greenwich, England, and serves as the basis for global time.) ▶ *The eclipse begins at 4:14 pm GMT.*

GNMA Government National Mortgage Association. (Initialism. Usually referred to as and pronounced "Ginnie Mae." The government agency that purchases mortgages and sells interest in securities backed by these mortgages to the public.) ▶ *GNMA securities*

GNP gross national product. (Initialism. A measure of economic welfare determined by the total value of a country's output of goods and services.) ▶ *Japan's 1988 GNP was almost $2 billion.* ▶ *The United States 1970 GNP was $977 million.*

GO general order. (Initialism. A military order, announcement, or directive, numbered serially.) ▶ *The colonel read the latest GO and threw it on top of the growing pile of papers on his desk.*

GOP Grand Old Party. (Initialism. The Republican Party of the United States.) ▶ *George Bush, the GOP candidate for president in 1988, won the election.*

Goth. 1. Gothic. (An East Germanic language spoken by the Goths in the third through fifth centuries A.D.) 2. Gothic. (A style of west European architecture developed between the twelfth and sixteenth centuries A.D.) ▶ *Goth. arch* 3. Gothic. (A genre of mystery novel with gloomy settings.) ▶ *Goth. romance*

Gov. governor. (The elected head of each state of the United States. A clipping when used informally. Sometimes spelled *Guv.*) ▶ *Gov. James Smith* ▶ *Gov. of Delaware* ▶ *"Did you catch the Gov on the news last night?"*

gov. See *govt.*

govt. AND **gov't, gov.** government. (The authority ruling over a state, organization, etc.) ▶ *property of the U.S. Govt.* ▶ *govt. regulated* ▶ *gov. inspected*

GP general practitioner. (Initialism. A physician or veterinarian whose practice is not limited to one specialized field of medicine.) ▶ *The GP advised Aunt Emma to see an osteopathic surgeon.* ▶ *When the only GP in Summerboro retired, the residents had to travel twenty miles to the county hospital to see a doctor.*

GPA grade point average. (Initialism. A numerical conversion of letter grades used to rank students. An *A* is usually either 4.0 or 5.0, depending on the scale. A GPA figure is often followed by the value of an *A*. Often found on resumés and college entrance applications.) ▶ *3.5/4.0 GPA.* ▶ *4.25/5.0 GPA.* ▶ *With a 1.85 GPA for the winter semester, Chris was put on probation.*

GPO 1. general post office. (Initialism. A postal abbreviation.) ▶ *GPO mail truck* 2. government printing office. (Initialism. A printing office operated by the U.S. government for the production of government publications.) ▶ *A GPO copy editor proofread Sheryl's article on the United States patent system.*

Gr AND **Gk** (The Greek language. Used in dictionaries to show the etymologies of words.) ▶ *agoraphobia < Gr fear of the marketplace* ▶ *a Gk word*

gr. **1.** grade. (A rank, degree, or classification.) ▶ *Six dozen Gr. A eggs* ▶ *Gr. III(c)* **2.** grain. (A unit of measure equal to 1/7,000 of one pound avoirdupois or 1/5,760 of one pound troy.) ▶ *36-gr. gemstone* **3.** AND **gt.** great. (Larger than similar items. Found on maps and applied to geophysical features of very large size.) ▶ *Gr. Barrier Reef* ▶ *Gr. Wall of China* ▶ *Gt. Slave Lake* ▶ *Gt. Salt Lake* **4.** gross. (A dozen dozen; 144.) ▶ *2 doz. paddles and 1 gr. Ping-Pong balls.* **5.** gross. (In totality or entirety; the opposite of *net*.) ▶ *gr. income* ▶ *gr. weight*

Gr. **1.** Greece. (A country in southeast Europe on the Mediterranean Sea.) ▶ *Athens, Gr.* **2.** Greek. (Relating to the people and the language of Greece.) ▶ *Homeric Gr.* ▶ *Modern Gr.*

grad. **1.** graduate. (Often a clipping. Someone who has received an undergraduate degree or diploma from a school or college.) ▶ *The grad student decided to pursue a Ph.D.* ▶ *Office of Grad. Studies* **2.** graduated. (Marked to show the units of measure.) ▶ *grad. cylinder*

gram. **1.** grammar. (The study of word structure, word arrangement, language sounds, and word meanings.) ▶ *English gram.* **2.** grammar. (An elementary school, usually through grade 8.) ▶ *Maria attended Pritzker Gram. School.*

GRAS generally regarded as safe. (Acronym. Term used by the Food and Drug Administration applied to substances that are not known to cause harm when used as directed.) ▶ *With the exception of a few files marked GRAS, the biochemist's desk was cluttered with descriptions of toxic substances.*

Gr. Brit. See *GB*.

GRE Graduate Record Examination. (Initialism. A placement test required for entrance to many graduate-level schools that covers verbal, math, and logic skills.) ▸ *Jane scored in the top percent of all three areas on the GRE and was able to attend the school of her choosing.*

gr. wt. gross weight. (The entire weight of a product, including its container. Found on packaging and labeling.) ▸ *gr. wt. 1 lb. 6 oz.*

GS ground speed. (Initialism. An aircraft's velocity in relation to the ground it passes over.) ▸ *GS 780 mph*

GSA 1. General Services Administration. (Initialism. A government agency established in 1949 to maintain and manage government property, records, and services.) ▸ *After 25 years at the GSA, Jerry worked his way from mail clerk to an executive position.* **2.** Girl Scouts of America. (Initialism. An organization founded by Juliette Low in 1912 that provides character-building activities for girls and young women.) ▸ *Americans buy millions of boxes of cookies from the GSA each year.*

GST Greenwich Standard Time. (Initialism. The standard time zone of the longitudinal meridian that passes through Greenwich, England. See *GMT*.) ▸ *The flight departed from Heathrow at 2:30 PM GST.*

gt. See *gr.*

GT gross ton. (Also called a "long ton." The British ton equal to 2,240 pounds, 240 pounds more than a United States ton.) ▸ *12 GT capacity*

Gt. Brit. See *GB*.

gtd. AND **guar.** guaranteed. (Promised or pledged, usually in writing. Frequently used in advertising.) ▶ *Gtd. to last forever or your money back!*

GU 1. Guam. (The official two-letter post office abbreviation.) ▶ *Agana, GU 96910* 2. genito-urinary. (Initialism. Referring to both the genitalia and the urinary tract.) ▶ *This problem is some sort of GU disorder. You will have to go to a specialist.*

Guad. Guadelupe. (A Caribbean island.) ▶ *Basse-Terre, Guad.*

guar. 1. guarantee. (A promise or pledge, usually in writing.) ▶ *4-year guar. for all parts and labor.* 2. See *gtd*.

Guat. Guatemala. (A country in Central America.) ▶ *Quezaltenango, Guat.*

Guin. Guinea. (A country on the Atlantic Ocean in northwestern Africa.) ▶ *Conakry, Guin.*

Guy. Guyana. (A country on the Atlantic Ocean in northern South America.) ▶ *Georgetown, Guy.*

GWU George Washington University. (Initialism. A university in Washington, D.C.) ▶ *Sue attended GWU for two yrs.*

gym 1. gymnasium. (Clipping. The room in which sporting activities are held.) ▶ *The crowd filled the gym to capacity half an hour before the championship game began.* ▶ *We played kickball in the gym today.* 2. physical education class. (Abbreviation from a clipping of gymnasium, the room in which such classes are generally held.) ▶ *We played kickball in gym today.*

gyn. 1. gynecology. (The medical practice specializing in the treatment and prevention of disease in women, especially concerning the reproductive system of women.) ▶ *ob.-gyn.* 2. gynecologist. (A medical doctor specializing in gynecology.) ▶ *gyn. appt. 2:30 pm*

H

h 1. hecto- (A prefix meaning 100, used with units of measurements. The "o" is dropped before a unit, such as the *are*, that begins with a vowel.) ▶ *hm (hectometer)* ▶ *ha (hectare)* 2. hour. (A unit of time equal to 60 minutes. See also hr.) ▶ *6h 53m 32s (six hours, fifty-three minutes, thirty-two seconds)* 3. Planck's constant. (A symbol in physics. A universal constant. The energy of an electromagnetic wave is equal to Planck's constant multiplied by the frequency of the wave.) ▶ $h = 6.6262 \times 10(-34)$ *joules/hertz*

H 1. heroin. (Initialism. A slang term. A very addictive narcotic.) 2. high. (Initialism. Found on control panels that have different speed settings, high being the fastest.) ▶ *The eggs started to burn, so Henry turned on the fan above the stove to H.* 3. hit. (A baseball term. A play in baseball where the batter hits the ball and reaches a base or home plate without being tagged out. Found on statistical charts and summaries. The example is to be interpreted to mean five hits, four runs, two errors.) ▶ *5H 4R 2E* 4. hot. (Marked on water faucets and other temperature controls to differentiate between cold and hot.) ▶ *Allie slid the lever to H to warm up the car before she started her trip.* 5. hydrogen. (The chemical symbol for Element 1.)

Ha. Hawaii. (See also *HI*.) ▸ *Hilo, Ha.* ▸ *Gov. John Davis (Ha.)*

Ha hahnium. (The chemical symbol for Element 105.)

ha hectare. (A metric unit of land measurement, equal to 100 square meters or roughly 2.5 acres.) ▸ *If Farmer Jones can plow 10 ha in 4 hours, and Farmer Brown can plow 15 ha in 4.5 hours, how long will it take for them to plow a 20-ha plot?*

hab. corp. *habeas corpus.* (Latin: you should have the body. A legal term for a writ mandating that a person being held must be brought before the court to determine the legality of the imprisonment or holding.) ▸ *writ of hab. corp.*

HB halfback. (A football position. One of two offensive players on either side of the fullback.) ▸ *The 1961 NFL Player of the Year was the Green Bay Packers' Paul Hornung (HB).*

Hb hemoglobin. (The component of blood that carries oxygen and carbon dioxide between the lungs and body tissues.) ▸ *1 pint Hb*

H-bomb hydrogen bomb. (Initialism-*bomb*. A highly explosive atomic weapon.) ▸ *As the civil defense sirens pierced the air, Sally crouched under her desk, worrying about the onslaught of H-bombs.*

HBP hit by pitch. (Initialism. A baseball term for when the pitcher hits the batter with the baseball. The batter then gets to go to first base. Used in statistical charts and baseball notation.)

H.C. **1.** Holy Communion. (A Christian sacrament involving the taking of bread and wine in remembrance of Christ's Last Supper.) **2.** House of Commons. (Initialism.

Hf

The lower chambers of the British and Canadian parliaments.)

hdqrs. headquarters. (The central office or control center of an organization or military unit. See also *HQ*.) ▶ *After completing the assignment, Agent 99 returned to hdqrs.*

H.E. **1.** His Eminence; Her Eminence. (A title for a person of high rank in the government or religion.) ▶ *"I needn't remind you," Jenkins wrote to the steward, "that you will promptly obey whatever command H.E. issues."* **2.** His Excellency; Her Excellency. (A title for a person of high rank in the government or religion.) ▶ *"Further," Jenkins continued, "remember the proper procedures upon meeting H.E., the Queen."*

He helium. (The chemical symbol for Element 2.)

Heb Hebrew. (The ancient Semitic language of the Israelites and its modern form, which is the state language of Israel. Used in dictionaries to show the etymology of a word.) ▶ *shibboleth < Heb. shibolet*

HEW Department of Health, Education and Welfare. (Initialism. An executive department of the United States government that administered health, education, and social service programs. HEW was established in 1953. In 1979 it was split into the Department of Health and Human Services and the Department of Education.) ▶ *Joseph A. Califano, Jr. (Secretary of HEW under Jimmy Carter)*

hex hexagon. (A six-sided polygon. Used as a clipping in the term *hex nut*, a type of tightener used on bolts and screws.) ▶ *"Hand me that bag of hex nuts, will you?" Uncle Arthur shouted as he balanced on the top of the ladder.*

Hf hafnium. (The chemical symbol for Element 72.)

hf high frequency. (A radio frequency with a range of 3 to 30 megahertz.)

HG High German. (The modern German dialect spoken in central and southern Germany, also known as *Hochdeutsch*. This is the standard dialect of German used in literature. Linguistically, it is called New High German to differentiate it from its older forms. Compare with Low German at *LG*.) ▶ *I am fluent in Russian, Polish, German (HG), and English (UK).*

Hg mercury. (The chemical symbol for Element 80. The symbol is derived from Latin *hydragyrum*.)

hgt. See *ht*.

H.H. 1. His Highness; Her Highness. (A title for a person of high rank in the government or religion.) 2. His Holiness. (A title for the Roman Catholic pope.) ▶ *H.H. Pope John Paul II*

HHS Department of Health and Human Services. (Initialism. The executive department of the United States government in charge of public health and welfare policies. The HHS administration includes the Social Security Administration and the Public Health Service. See *SSA, PHS*.) ▶ *In 1979, the duties of the Department of Health, Education, and Welfare were split between the newly created HHS and DOE.*

H.I. Hawaiian Islands. ▶ *Hilo, H.I.*

HI Hawaii. (The official two-letter post office abbreviation. See also *Ha*.) ▶ *Honolulu, HI 96801*

hi fi high fidelity. (Acronym. The reproduction of sound with a high degree of faithfulness to the original.) ▶ *The CD player is to the nineties what the hi fi stereo was to the seventies.*

Hind. 1. Hindi. (An official language of India.) ▶ *She speaks Hind. and Eng.* 2. Hindu. (An adherent of the Hindu religion.) ▶ *He practices the Hind. religion.*

hist. 1. history. (A systematic account of the past.) ▶ *Amer. Hist.* ▶ *Hist. of SE Asia* 2. historical. (Established by history.) ▶ *Chicago Hist. Society*

HIV human immunodeficiency virus. (Initialism. One of several retroviruses believed to cause, or to be a cofactor in, the development of AIDS. See also *AIDS.*) ▶ *The scientific community has not reached a consensus whether HIV infection is the sole cause of AIDS.* ▶ *HIV positive* ▶ *HIV negative*

H.M. His Majesty; Her Majesty. (Initialism. A title of respect for a monarch.) ▶ *H.M. the Queen of England* ▶ *H.M. the Prince of Wales*

HMO health maintenance organization. (Initialism. A prepaid health care plan that employs a diverse medical staff to offer a comprehensive array of health services.) ▶ *Smithco Corporation's benefits package offers a choice of three different HMO plans.*

H.M.S His Majesty's Ship; Her Majesty's Ship. (Initialism. A ship of the British navy.) ▶ *H.M.S Pinafore.*

HNS Holy Name Society. (Initialism. An association of Roman Catholic laymen directed by the Dominican Order, established in the thirteenth century to counteract blasphemy and profanity.) ▶ *The HNS promotes the reverence of Jesus' name.*

Ho holmium. (The chemical symbol for Element 67.)

Hon. 1. Honorable. (A title for various high-ranking officials, including judges.) ▶ *The Hon. Ralph Lee Preston, III* 2. AND **Hond.** Honduras. (A country on the Caribbean Sea in Central America.) ▶ *Trujillo, Hond.*

Hond. See the previous entry.

HOPE Health Opportunity for People Everywhere. (Acronym. A project operated by the People-to-People Health Foundation, Inc., that teaches modern medicine to health professionals in developing nations.) ► *Project HOPE is made possible by private contributions.*

hor. horizontal. (Parallel to the horizon; side to side. Commonly used on television sets for the knob that controls the horizontal hold.) ► *hor. hold*

hort. **1.** horticulture. (The science of growing plants.) ► *Dept. of Hort.* **2.** horticultural. (Relating to horticulture.) ► *Hort. Gardens*

hosp. hospital. (An institution providing medical and surgical testing and treatment.) ► *St. Joseph's Hosp.* ► *Our Lady of the Lake Hosp.*

HP **1.** horsepower. (Initialism. A unit of amount of power exerted equal to 746 watts or the amount of force required to raise 33,000 pounds one foot in one minute. Name derives from when horses were used as an energy source; horsepower was the weight a horse could pull.) ► *250 HP* **2.** Hewlett Packard. (Initialism. A manufacturer of technical calculators and computer-related items.) ► *The meticulously designed program was printed up on an HP compatible laser printer.* ► *Martin's professor taught him how to use an HP calculator.*

HQ headquarters. (Initialism. The central office or control center of an organization or military unit. The same as *hdqrs.*) ► *McCoy met the Chief of Police at District HQ.*

hr. **1.** hour. (A unit of time equal to 60 minutes. See also *h.*) ► *2-hr. seminar* **2.** hour. (A session or period of time, not necessarily 60 minutes in length.) ► *4th hr. Biology 101 meets in Lab #2.* ► *Happy hr. starts at 5:00 pm.*

HR 1. home run. (In baseball, when the batter makes a hit, is able to round all the bases, and make it to home plate, thereby scoring a run. Found in statistical charts as a column or row heading.) ▸ *Jackie Robinson—137 HRs.* 2. Home Rule. (The self-government of a local district, colony, or municipality, granted by the ruling governmental authority.) 3. House of Representatives. (Initialism. One branch of the United States Congress. Its 435 members are elected every two years. The districts each member represents are determined by population, but each state has at least one representative. The government of each state also has a House of Representatives, except for Nebraska.) ▸ *HR Bill 4099*

H.R.E. Holy Roman Empire. (A political entity existing in Europe from 962 to 1806.) ▸ *History 301: H.R.E. (AD 900–1200.)*

H. Res. House Resolution. (A formal piece of legislation adopted by the House of Representatives.) ▸ *H. Res. 1022*

H.R.H His Royal Highness; Her Royal Highness. (Initialism. A title for a monarch.) ▸ *H.R.H. Queen Elizabeth II*

HS high school. (Initialism. A secondary school comprised of grades 9 through 12 or 10 through 12.) ▸ *Northern HS routinely beat Central HS in basketball.*

HST Hawaiian-Aleutian Standard Time. (Initialism. The standard time in the Hawaiian and Aleutian Islands. It is ten hours behind Greenwich Time and two hours behind Pacific Standard Time.) ▸ *The solar eclipse can be seen from the Hawaiian Islands, with the total phase beginning at 3:03 pm HST.*

ht. AND **hgt.** height. (The linear measurement of an object from top to bottom.) ▸ *hgt. × wdth. = area* ▸ *Platform X —ht. = 42″*

HTLV human T-cell leukemia virus. (Initialism. Any of several retroviruses that infect T-cells, causing a rare strain of leukemia to develop.) ▶ *HTLV-1, HTLV-3*

Hts. heights. (Indicating higher land than the surrounding area, used as a feature in naming cities and suburbs.) ▶ *Shaker Hts.* ▶ *Glen Avon Hts., California*

HUD Housing and Urban Development. (Acronym. An executive department of the United States government in charge of administering mortgage programs to enable people to own homes, aiding in construction and renovation of housing, aiding low-income families who cannot afford rent, and working to abolish discrimination in housing.) ▶ *Max Ryan, Secretary of HUD.*

Hung. Hungary. (A landlocked country of eastern Europe.) ▶ *Budapest, Hung.*

HV high voltage. (Initialism. Marked on wires carrying a high load of electricity to indicate danger of electrocution.) ▶ *Danger: HV wires!*

HWM high-water mark. (The highest point reached by water in a tide or flood as well as the mark left by water after the tide or flood has ebbed.) ▶ *HWM 16 feet*

hwy. highway. (A main road, usually better maintained than secondary roads. Used in addresses and signs.) ▶ *Pan American Hwy.* ▶ *U.S. Hwy. 12*

hyp. hypotenuse. (The side of a right triangle opposite the right angle.)

hypoth. hypothesis. (A premise or proposition used as a basis for further investigation.)

Hz hertz. (The unit of frequency equal to one cycle per second.) ▶ *The electric drill operated on 60 Hz of power.*

I

i imaginary number. (A mathematical term; *i* is equal to the square root of -1.)

I. AND **Is., Isl.** island; isle. (Land surrounded by a body of water. Found on maps and signs and in addresses.) ▶ *Easter I.* ▶ *Ellis I.* ▶ *I. of Man* ▶ *I. Royale Nat'l Park* ▶ *Mackinac Is., Mich.* ▶ *Kodiak Is., Alas.* ▶ *Is. of Wight* ▶ *Long Isl., N.Y.* ▶ *San Clemente Isl., California* ▶ *Isl. of Hope, Georgia*

i **1.** interest. (An amount paid in return for using money. Usually in *p & i.*) ▶ *The monthly p & i payment on the mortgage for the condo wiped out Sam's paycheck.* **2.** AND **intr.** intransitive. (Pertaining to a verb that does not have a direct object, such as *die.* See also *vi.*) ▶ *run, (i)* ▶ *die, intr.*

I **1.** the physics symbol for electric flow in amperes. (The example formula means that power in watts equals electrical flow in amperes times the potential electrical energy in volts.) ▶ $P \times I = E$ **2.** Independent. (A voter or politician who is not a follower of any particular political party.) ▶ *Lowell P. Weicker (I) was elected as governor in Connecticut in 1990.* **3.** iodine. (The chemical symbol for Element 53.) **4.** 1. (A Roman numeral.) ▶ *I. Introduction*

Ia.

and Meeting Overview ▶ *Queen Elizabeth I* ▶ *Queen Elizabeth II*

Ia. Iowa. (See also *IA.*) ▶ *Des Moines, Ia.* ▶ *Gov. Terry Kelly (Ia.)*

IA Iowa. (The official two-letter post office abbreviation. See also *Ia.*) ▶ *Davenport, IA 52801*

IAEA International Atomic Energy Agency. (Initialism. A self-governing, independent organization that reports to the General Assembly of the United Nations. Responsible for the development of nonhostile uses of atomic energy, the dissemination of atomic technology, and setting standards for environmental protection and safety.) ▶ *The IAEA was established in 1957.*

ibid. *ibidem.* (From Latin: in the same place. Refers to the source most recently cited. Found in footnotes and text of dissertations, theses, papers, and the like.) ▶ *Ibid., 34-6.*

IBM International Business Machines. (Initialism. A major industrial corporation whose products include office equipment, computers, and computer technology.) ▶ *In 1981, IBM released its first personal computer, setting the industry standard.* ▶ *"My dad worked at IBM back when they programmed computers with punch cards," Jane told her instructor.*

IC integrated circuit. (Initialism. An electronic circuit with numerous interconnected elements on a single silicon chip. These fully-integrated components cannot be rearranged without changing the electronic function of the chip.) ▶ *Deep in the heart of the Silicon Valley, Ned meticulously perfected the design layout of the IC circuitry.* ▶ *IC technology*

Id.

ICBM intercontinental ballistic missile. (Initialism. A land-based nuclear strategic missile with a large enough trajectory to go from one continent to another.) ▸ *Minuteman ICBM* ▸ *Peacekeeper ICBM* ▸ *George Bush and Boris Yeltsin pledged to decrease the number of ICBMs in their arsenals.*

ICC Interstate Commerce Commission. (Initialism. A government agency that regulates commerce across state lines.) ▸ *Thomas informed the ICC of the error.*

Ice. Iceland. (An island country between the northern Atlantic Ocean and the Norwegian Sea off the coast of Europe.) ▸ *Reykjavik, Ice.*

ICPO AND **INTERPOL** International Criminal Police Organization. (Initialism AND clippings. Established in 1923 to ensure and promote the widest possible mutual assistance between all criminal police authorities within the limits of the laws in the different countries.) ▸ *ICPO found the drug baron hiding in a small shack outside Lucerne.*

ICU Intensive Care Unit. (Initialism. The section of a hospital where critically ill patients are monitored around the clock.) ▸ *The nurse at the front desk directed the families of the crash victims to the ICU ward on the fourth floor.*

i.d. inner diameter. (Initialism. The distance from the center of the opening of a tube to the inside edge of the material the tube is made from.) ▸ *"I need a foot-long piece of copper tubing with a half-inch i.d.," Sam told the hardware store clerk.*

Id. AND **Ida.** Idaho. (See also *ID*.) ▸ *Moscow, Id.* ▸ *Sen. Paul Jones (Ida.)*

137

id.

id. *idem.* (From Latin: the same, the same as has been mentioned.)

ID **1.** Idaho. (The official two-letter post office abbreviation. See also *Id.*) ► *Pocatello, ID 83201* **2.** identification. (Initialism. Proof of one's identity.) ► *To enter the bar, you must show three forms of ID, and one must have your picture.* ► *Sally flashed her ID card, and the guard admitted her into the high-security area.*

Ida. See *Id.*

IDP integrated data processing. (Initialism. The reduction or elimination of redundant data-processing procedures to improve efficiency and accuracy.) ► *The firm hired an IDP consultant who pointed out that several different departments were independently doing identical tasks.*

IDU injection drug user. (Initialism. Someone who uses drugs that are injected into the body.) ► *IDUs are at high risk for a number of serious diseases.*

i.e. *id est.* (Initialism. Latin: that is. Used to clarify or restate what has been said or written.) ► *Today we're going to discuss the primary colors; i.e., red, blue, and yellow.* ► *At the intersection go west, i.e., left.*

I.E. Industrial Engineer. (Initialism. A title for someone who applies the sciences to industry.) ► *The directors contracted for Eduardo Jimenez, I.E., to overhaul the deteriorating industrial complex at one of their suburban sites.*

IF interferon. (Initialism. A protein produced by the body to counteract a viral infection by slowing or stopping the virus from replicating.) ► *George studied the different applications of IF treatments.*

iff if and only if. (In logic and geometry, used in proofs, statements, theorems, and equations.) ▶ *A triangle is a right triangle iff one of the angles is a right angle.*

IL Illinois. (The official two-letter post office abbreviation. See also *Ill.*) ▶ *Chicago, IL 60622*

ILGWU International Ladies' Garment Workers' Union. (Initialism. A women's clothing workers union and member of the AFL-CIO.) ▶ *Strikes led by the ILGWU in 1909 and 1910 resulted in improved working conditions, higher wages, and fewer hours of work per week.*

ill. AND **illus.** illustrated. (Used to describe a publication that has pictures or illustrations.) ▶ *The Complete Works of Beatrix Potter (ill.)* ▶ *Charles Dickens'* A Christmas Carol *(illus.)*

Ill. Illinois. (See also *IL.*) ▶ *Lincolnwood, Ill.* ▶ *Gov. Jim Jones (Ill.)*

illus. See *ill.*

ILO International Labor Organization. (Initialism. An international agency established to promote employment, raise standards of living, create global standards of labor, and improve working conditions.) ▶ *The ILO helped the industrially developing nations develop guidelines for occupational safety.*

IMF International Monetary Fund. (Initialism. An independent organization established in 1945 within the United Nations. It provides financing and economic management assistance for member countries.) ▶ *With the help of the IMF, the struggling developing country was able to become a regional leader.*

immunol. immunology. (The science of antigens and antibodies and their role in immune mechanisms and infection.) ▶ *immunol. lab*

imp. **1.** important. (Used in notes and signs for emphasis of a statement.) ▸ *Imp.—pick up Ed at work today!* **2.** import; imported. (Often used in statistical charts, food labels, and on imported products.) ▸ *1970 imp. = $800,000 (in 1970 U.S. dollars)* ▸ *Imp. from Spain* **3.** imperative. (A grammatical label for an order or a command. Found in language textbooks.) ▸ *imp. mood* ▸ *Take a hike! (imp. sentence)* **4.** imperfect. (A grammar term for a verb construction consisting of an auxiliary and a verb in the progressive tense, indicating that the action of the verb will continue without ending; for example: "will be playing" and "was thinking." Found in language textbooks.) ▸ *imp. tense* ▸ *imp. aspect*

in. inch. (A unit of linear measurement, equal to 1/12 foot or 2.54 centimeters. The plural is **ins.**) ▸ *6-in. wood fitting* ▸ *6 in. × 6 in. floor tile* ▸ *3-in.-thick insulation*

IN Indiana. (The official two-letter post office abbreviation. See also *Ind.*) ▸ *South Bend, IN 46601*

In indium. (The chemical symbol for Element 49.)

inc. **1.** income. (Used on financial reports and tables.) ▸ *Net inc.—1961-1965, by year* **2.** incorporated. (A company set up as a legal organization. Often pronounced "INK" when spoken.) ▸ *Smith & Smith Cobblers, Inc.* ▸ *Velma had no time to organize the reception, so she called Food & Fun, Inc., a local caterer.*

incl. including. (Used in notes and advertising.) ▸ *Ms. Frisch is entitled to the house, incl. the estate grounds.* ▸ *1-BR apt. for rent, incl. porch & patio.*

ind. **1.** independence. (The state of being self-governing.) ▸ *Ind. Day* ▸ *Declaration of Ind.* **2.** independent. (A country that is self-governing.) ▸ *Zaire (ind. 1960)* **3.** AND **indus.** industrial. (Relating to industry.) ▸ *Ind. Revolution* ▸ *ind. park* ▸ *Walden Pond Ind. Park—Office Space*

Still Available! **4.** AND **indus.** industry. (The part of the economy dealing with manufacturing and production.) ▸ *Mus. of Science and Ind.*

Ind. **1.** India. ▸ *New Delhi, Ind.* ▸ *East Ind. Tea Company* **2.** Indian. (Relating to the cultures, peoples, and land of India.) ▸ *Ind. Ambassador to the U.S.* ▸ *Ind. Ocean* **3.** Indian. (A person whose ancestry is indigenous to that particular land he or she lives in.) ▸ *Native Am. Ind.* **4.** Indian. (The adjectival form of Indian.) ▸ *Ind. corn* ▸ *Ind. summer* ▸ *Ind. headdress* **5.** Indiana. (See also *IN*.) ▸ *Vincennes, Ind.* ▸ *Gov. Ed Davis (Ind.)* **6.** Indies. (The West Indies are the islands in the Caribbean that comprise the Greater Antilles, the Lesser Antilles, and the Bahamas. The East Indies are the islands of Indonesia, also known as the Malay Archipelago.) ▸ *W. Ind.* ▸ *E. Ind.* **7.** Independent. (A politician not affiliated with democrats, republicans, or any other established party. See also *I*.) ▸ *Richard Ryan—Ind., was elected as governor in Connecticut last year.*

indic. indicative. (Pertaining to a sentence that states a fact or makes an assertion. Found in language textbooks and dictionaries.) ▸ *indic. sentence* ▸ *Jill slapped Jack. (indic.)*

indus. See *ind.*

inf. infinitive. (A verb preceded by *to;* not limited by tense, person, or number; and that functions as a noun. Found in language textbooks and dictionaries.) ▸ *to die (inf.)* ▸ *inf. phrase.*

INRI *Iesus Nazarenus Rex Iudaeorum.* (Initialism. Latin: Jesus of Nazareth, King of the Jews. INRI was the inscription placed on the cross above Christ during the crucifixion.)

ins. insurance. (A system that guarantees payment for medical treatments or specified losses—fire, death, theft, accidents, etc.—in exchange for regular payments of a predetermined fee.) ▸ *health ins.* ▸ *New England Mutual Life Ins. Co.*

INS Immigration and Naturalization Service. (Initialism. A bureau within the United States Department of Justice responsible for monitoring immigration into the U.S.) ▸ *The sheriff reported the illegal aliens to the INS for deportation.*

Insp. Inspector. (An official examiner; a rank in police forces and fire departments.) ▸ *Insp. O'Reilly made sure that all fire extinguishers were in working order.*

inst. 1. instant. (Immediately; without delay. Often used to describe freeze-dried or dehydrated food.) ▸ *inst. coffee* ▸ *inst. milk* 2. institute. (A school, university, or museum specializing in a particular subject.) ▸ *Inst. of Museum Services* ▸ *Mass. Inst. of Technology* ▸ *Detroit Inst. of Arts* 3. institution. (A public service organization, such as a hospital or a bank.) ▸ *mental inst.* ▸ *banking inst.*

instr. 1. instrumental. (A grammatical case that expresses the way in which something was done. In English, this is expressed with the words *by* and *with*. Found in language textbooks and dictionaries.) 2. instrumental. (A music term. Usually found in theater programs and on recorded music packaging to indicate that a particular track or song is not accompanied with voice but is merely instrumental.) ▸ *Don't Cry for Me Argentina (instr.)* 3. instructor. (A teacher; a professor.) ▸ *Biology 301—Instr.: Dr. Williams.* 4. instructions. (Documentation; a description of how to use or operate something.) ▸ *instr. incl.*

INTELSAT International Telecommunications Satellite. (Acronym. An international organization established in 1973 to develop, launch, and operate the global communication satellite network.) ▶ *INTELSAT provides two-thirds of the world's telephone, television, telex, and fax transmissions.*

interj. interjection. (A word or expression of emotion inserted into a stream of speech. Found in language textbooks and dictionaries.) ▶ *Oh! (interj.)* ▶ *Yikes! (interj.)*

INTERPOL See *ICPO.*

interrog. interrogative. (Pertaining to a word or sentence that asks a question. Found in language textbooks and dictionaries.) ▶ *interrog. pronoun* ▶ *interrog. sentence* ▶ *"What did you drag in from outside?" (interrog.)*

int'l. AND **intl.** international. (Relating to more than one nation. Often used in the titles of corporations, organizations, etc.) ▶ *Bishop Intl. Airport* ▶ *Rockwell Intl.* ▶ *Int'l. Conference on Aging.*

intr. AND **intrans.** intransitive. (Pertaining to a verb with no direct object. See also *vi = intransitive verb.* Found in language textbooks and dictionaries.) ▶ *Mice squeak. (intr.)* ▶ *intrans. verb.*

intro. introduction. (Sometimes a clipping. The beginning of something.) ▶ *I got a B in my Intro to Algebra class!* ▶ *8:00—Intro. and Meeting Overview*

IOOF International Order of Odd Fellows. (Initialism. A secret benevolent fraternal order that assists members and families of members in time of need.) ▶ *The American IOOF split in 1843 from England and later merged with lodges in Canada.*

IOU I owe you. (Initialism. The letters *I, O, U* sound like the words "I owe you." An IOU is a signed note given to

IPA

someone who is owed something as an acknowledgement of debt.) ▸ *After Pete won the lottery, he paid off all of his IOUs.* ▸ *The diner had to wash dishes for three hours because the manager would not accept his IOU.*

IPA 1. International Phonetic Alphabet. (Initialism. A phonetic alphabet in which each symbol stands for only one sound or point of articulation.) ▸ *Tony wanted a German dictionary that provided an IPA transcription of each word.* ▸ *Although the English alphabet has only twenty-six letters, well over forty IPA symbols are needed to represent all of the sounds made in English.* 2. International Phonetic Association. (Initialism. An organization founded in 1886 to develop a standard phonetic alphabet for languages.) ▸ *The IPA developed the International Phonetic Alphabet to provide a key to pronouncing languages unfamiliar to the speaker.*

i.p.s. inches per second. (Initialism. A unit of measurement for measuring the speed of an object.) ▸ *The cockroach scampered across the lab table at 2 i.p.s.*

IQ Intelligence Quotient. (Initialism. A relative measure of intelligence determined by mental age multiplied by 100 and divided by the chronological age.) ▸ *A genius is someone with an IQ of 140 or more.* ▸ *The school psychologist administered an IQ test to the young prodigy.*

Ir iridium. (The chemical symbol for Element 77.)

IRA 1. individual retirement account. (Initialism and acronym. A retirement plan that allows a certain portion of one's annual income to be placed in a special account. No taxes are due on the earnings until retirement.) ▸ *Jamie didn't think Social Security would still be in existence by the time he turned sixty-five, so she opened an IRA.* ▸ *On the advice of his accountant, Herb sought out an IRA with an attractive return.* 2. Irish Republican Army. (Initialism. An Irish nationalist organization whose goal is the reunification of Ireland and Northern Ireland.) ▶ *The IRA claimed responsibility for the bomb blast in the London subway.*

Ire. Ireland. (An island to the east of Great Britain comprised of the Republic of Ireland as well as Northern Ireland, which is a part of the United Kingdom.) ▶ *Dublin, Ire.*

irid. iridescent. (Used to describe objects such as prisms that show the shifting colors of the rainbow when seen from different angles.) ▶ *irid. crystal*

irreg. 1. irregular. (Pertaining to words that do not fit ordinary patterns; exceptions to linguistic rules. Found in language textbooks and dictionaries.) ▶ *drink (irreg. verb)* ▶ *to be (irreg.)* 2. irregular. (A term describing uneven or flawed fabric.) ▶ *irreg. bolts of cloth, 25% off*

IRS Internal Revenue Service. (Initialism. The office within the Department of the Treasury that collects federal taxes as well as social and retirement insurance payments.) ▶ *After years of hiding from the IRS, Monty decided to make good and consulted a lawyer about the years of back taxes he owed.* ▶ *On April 14, the IRS office was flooded with calls from frantic taxpayers requesting assistance.*

Is. See *I*.

ISBN International Standard Book Number. (Initialism. A number assigned to books to make it easier to order them and for identification purposes.) ▶ Foucault's Pendulum, *by Umberto Eco, ISBN 0-345-36875-4*

Isl. See *I*.

Isr. Israel. (A country on the east bank of the Mediterranean Sea.) ▶ *Tel Aviv, Isr.*

ISSN International Standard Serial Number. (Initialism. A number assigned to periodical publications for identification purposes.) ▶ Ebony—*ISSN 0012-9011*

isth. isthmus. (A geographical term for a narrow stretch of land connecting two larger masses of land. Found on maps and in texts.) ▶ *Isth. of Panama.*

It. **1.** Italy. (A country in southern Europe between the Tyrrhenian, Adriatic, Ionian, and Mediterranean Seas.) ▶ *Venice, It.* **2.** AND **Ital.** Italian. ▶ *It. classical music.* ▶ *house salad w/ Ital. dressing*

Ital. **1.** Italic. (A branch of the Indo-European language family, including old Latin, Oscan, Umbrian, French, Italian, Spanish, Portuguese, Romanian, and other modern Romance languages.) **2.** See *It.*

ital. **1.** italic; italics. (A printing font *that looks like this*, used to set off emphasized text from standard text. Used by editors and proofreaders to denote that a font should be italic.) **2.** italicize. (To use italic fonts.) ▶ *"Please ital. every mention of the president," the editor wrote to the assistant.*

ITU International Telecommunication Union. (Initialism. An international agency that regulates global radio, telegraph, telephone, and space radio communication procedures.) ▶ *The ITU is responsible for apportioning radio frequencies among the nations of the world.*

I.U. international unit. (An expression of potency for fat-soluble vitamins—Vitamin A, Vitamin D, and Vitamin E—found on the nutritional breakdown charts.) ▶ *Vitamin A—5000 I.U.*

IUD intrauterine device. (Initialism. A birth control device consisting of a plastic coil placed in the uterus to prevent conception.) ▸ *An improperly fitted IUD can cause uterine bleeding.*

IV intravenous. (Initialism. Directly into a vein. Used in medicine to describe treatments and procedures that involve direct injection into a vein.) ▸ *IV drug user* ▸ *The nurses prepared the patient for an IV injection.*

IWW Industrial Workers of the World. (Initialism. A radical socialist labor organization established in 1905 in opposition to the American Federation of Labor and capitalism. Its workers were referred to as "Wobblies.") ▸ *The goal of the IWW was the total dismantling of capitalism.*

J

J. judge; justice. (An elected or appointed official whose duty is to hear and decide cases in a court of law.) ► *J. Elzerman found the defendant guilty.*

J **1.** Jack. (Used on playing cards. In the series *J, Q, K, A*.) ► *J♦ was all that stood between Mr. van Hoeven and a $10,000 jackpot.* **2.** January. (Often used in graph columns or rows to chart the month-by-month progress of something. See also *Jan.*) ► *J 4-10* **3.** joule. (A unit of energy equal to the work done when one newton of force moves an object one meter.) ► *1 Cal = 4,184 J* ► *1 J = 10,000,000 ergs* **4.** June; July. (Often used in graph columns or rows to chart the month-by-month progress of something. If the context does not distinguish June from July, some other abbreviation should be used.)

J/A joint account. (Initialism. A bank account issued to two or more people. Any of the parties can deposit or withdraw money.) ► *J/A 239-00129-28192, assigned to William J. Ryerson and Jane A. Ilford.*

JA Junior Achievement. (Initialism. A program sponsored by businesses and firms to provide students the chance to see how the American business system works.) ► *Students in Central High's JA program who ran and* *operated the school store were advised by the president of the local Chamber of Commerce.*

Jam. Jamaica. (An island nation in the Caribbean Sea.) ▶ *Port au Prince, Jam.*

Jan. January. (See also *J.*) ▶ *Macy's White Sale—Jan. 2 through Jan. 10*

Jap. AND **Jpn.** Japan. (An island nation off the west coast of Asia.) ▶ *Tokyo, Jap.*

Jap Japanese. (Clipping. A derogatory term for a Japanese. ▶ *The teacher punished Mike and made him apologize for calling Takeo a Jap.*

JAP Jewish American Princess; Jewish American Prince. (Acronym. A slang, derogatory term for pampered children of rich Jewish parents.) ▶ *Esther slapped Mike when he told a JAP joke in front of her parents.*

J.C. Jesus Christ. (Initialism. The founder of Christianity. Found on prayer cards and other religious texts.) ▶ *J.C., Son of God, pray for us.*

JC junior college. (A two-year college that awards associates degrees.) ▶ *After graduating from the local JC, Anne transferred to a state university forty miles away.* ▶ *Jones County JC, Ellisville, Miss.*

JCC Jewish Community Center (Initialism. An organization providing recreational and educational services to Jewish people. It largely replaces the *YMHA* and *YWHA.*) ▶ *I had swimming lessons every week at the JCC.*

J.C.D. 1. *Juris Canonici Doctor.* (Initialism. Latin: doctor of canon law. The highest graduate degree awarded for study in matters relating to the laws governing Christian churches.) ▶ *The opening prayer will be offered by*

JCS

Rev. Gabriel Collins, J.C.D. **2.** *Juris Civilis Doctor.* (Initialism. Latin: Doctor of Civil Law. The highest graduate degree awarded for study in codified civil law.) ▸ *Judge Miriam L. Argonne, J.C.D., ruled against the plaintiff after five hours of deliberation.*

JCS Joint Chiefs of Staff. (Initialism. The organization within the Department of Defense consisting of the heads of the different branches of the military and a chairman. They inform and advise the president and the defense secretary about military matters.) ▸ *General Colin L. Powell, JCS Chairman.*

jct. AND **junc.** junction. (An intersection where two or more paths cross or join. Found on roadside signs to show the junction of two county, state, or interstate roadways. Also the place name of certain towns, usually a town at the intersection of a railway line.) ▸ *Jct. I-75/I-69* ▸ *Petticoat Junc.—10 miles*

J.D. *Jurum Doctor.* (Initialism. Latin: Doctor of Laws. The highest graduate degree awarded in the study of law; the degree most lawyers hold.) ▸ *Irving received his J.D. from Harvard.* ▸ *Irving D. Edison, J.D.*

JD 1. Jack Daniels. (Initialism. A brand name of whiskey.) ▸ *The travelers passed a bottle of JD around the campfire.* **2.** juvenile delinquent. (Initialism. Someone under the age of eighteen whose actions are in violation of the law. Used as a generic term for any young person who appears to be lawless or rebellious.) ▸ *The cop picked up the JD for loitering and threw him into a detention cell.*

JFK 1. John Fitzgerald Kennedy. (Initialism. The thirty-fifth president of the United States.) ▸ *JFK was assassinated in Dallas, Texas.* **2.** John F. Kennedy International Airport. (Initialism. A busy airport servicing the metropolitan New York City area.) ▶ *Sally flew in to JFK, but Jane had gone to LaGuardia to pick her up.*

Jos. Joseph. ▶ *Jos. A. Jones*

jour. journal. (A newspaper or periodical.) ▶ *The Wall Street Jour.* ▶ *British Jour. of Sociology*

JP justice of the peace. (Initialism. A public officer authorized to administer law in minor civil and criminal cases, advance a case to trial by a higher court, and perform marriages.) ▶ *Phil and Wendy said their wedding vows before the local JP because they couldn't afford a fancy ceremony.*

Jpn. See *Jap.*

jr. AND **jun.** 1. junior. (The third year of high school or college.) ▶ *History 301—jr. level.* 2. junior. (Of a lower status or level.) ▶ *jr. member* ▶ *jr. varsity*

Jr. Junior. (Part of the name of a son named for his father.) ▶ *Dr. Martin Luther King, Jr.*

Jul. July. (See also *J.*) ▶ *Freedom Sale—Jul. 1 to Jul. 5.*

Jun. June. (See also *J.*) ▶ *Jun. 6, 1951*

jun. See *jr.*

junc. See *jct.*

juv. juvenile. (A minor; someone who has not reached the age of majority.) ▶ *Juv. Court* ▶ *Juv. delinquent*

JV junior varsity. (Initialism. Freshman and sophomore level sports teams.) ▶ *The JV basketball game starts at 6:30.*

K

K **1.** Kelvin. (Initialism. A scale for measuring temperature with 0°K being absolute zero [-273.15°C or -459.7°F]. One Kelvin degree is equal to one Celsius degree. The Kelvin scale is used primarily in science.) ▸ *Water freezes at 273.15°K, 32°F, and 0°C.* ▸ *Water boils at 373.15°K, 212°F, and 100°C.* **2.** kilobyte. (Initialism. A computer term denoting 1,024 bytes of information or storage space.) ▸ *Suzanne's term paper was 12K long.* ▸ *Jason marveled that his father's early computer had only 32K of memory.* **3.** kilogram. (Initialism. A slang term for one kilogram of an illegal substance, usually drugs.) ▸ *The feds pulled in 10K of heroin in the most recent drug bust off the coast of Miami.* **4.** kindergarten. (Initialism. A school grade before first grade for 4- and 5-year-olds.) ▸ *Main Street Elementary School provides a basic education for grades K through 5.* ▸ *Mrs. Jones is qualified to teach grades K-8.* **5.** king. (Used on playing cards. In the series *J, Q, K, A.*) ▸ *If Michael drew K♥, he would win the game of rummy.* **6.** king. (A game piece in chess.) **7.** potassium. (The chemical symbol for Element 19. The symbol is derived from Latin *Kalium*.) **8.** strikeout. (The baseball symbol for a strikeout, which occurs when a batter is out after making three strikes. Used in statistical tables as a row or column heading.)

k **1.** AND **kt.** karat. (A measure of the purity of gold. One karat is 1/24 of total purity. Compare with *c*.) ▸ *24-k gold is 100% pure.* ▸ *Pete presented his betrothed with a 14-k gold ring.* **2.** kilo- (A prefix meaning 1,000, used with units of measurements. See also the use under *K*.) ▸ *kg (kilogram)* ▸ *km (kilometer)* ▸ *kw (kilowatt)*

Kan. Kansas. (See also *KS*.) ▸ *Topeka, Kan.* ▸ *Gov. Joan Smith (Ky.)*

KC **1.** Kansas City. (Initialism. An important midwestern city at the junction of the Kansas and Missouri rivers.) ▸ *Scott moved to KC to work at the Nelson-Atkins Museum of Art.* ▸ *KC, Missouri* **2.** See *K of C*.

kc kilocycle. (One thousand cycles per second. The old name for kilohertz. See *kHz*.)

Kcal kilocalorie. (1,000 small calories [*cal*] or one large calorie [*Cal*]. This is a scientific unit of energy required to burn off consumed food. The type of calories familiar to most consumers, such as those found on packaging, are the same as kilocalories, but are called calories.) ▸ *1 Kcal = 1 Cal = 1,000 cal*

Ken. AND **Ky.** Kentucky. (See also *KY*.) ▸ *Frankfort, Ken.* ▸ *Gov. Walter Smith (Ky.)*

kg kilogram. (A measurement of weight equal to 1,000 grams.) ▸ *Determine the relative velocity of a 10-kg object accelerating at 25 m/sec^2 at 100 m.* ▸ *1 kg = 2.205 pounds.*

KGB *Komitet Gosudarstvennoi Bezopasnosti.* (Initialism. Russian: State Security Committee. The state police of the Union of Soviet Socialist Republics.) ▸ *The KGB arrested the young protester and exiled him to Siberia.*

kHz kilohertz. (A unit of frequency equal to 1,000 hertz, or 1,000 cycles per second. Found on AM radio tuners.) ▶ *WJR-AM operates on 760 kHz.*

KIA killed in action. (Initialism. A military term applied to personnel who die in combat.) ▶ *Pvt. A. S. Wilson (KIA, Vietnam Conflict)*

KISS keep it simple, stupid. (Acronym. A slang expression. Originally military.) ▶ *Before the examination, the professor wrote KISS in large letters on the board, explaining that he refused to read rambling essay answers.*

KJV King James Version. (Initialism. The revised English translation of the Bible under the authorization of King James I of England in 1611.) ▶ *The biblical scholar compared the newly discovered Dead Sea Scrolls with the translations found in the KJV.*

KKK Ku Klux Klan. (Initialism. An organization of white supremacists who use terrorist tactics against Americans of African descent.) ▶ *Ten white-hooded members of the KKK ignited a fourteen-foot cross in the yard.*

km kilometer. (1,000 meters, or roughly 5/8 of a mile. Found on signs.) ▶ *10-km road race* ▶ *Paris (35 km)*

kmph AND **kph** kilometers per hour. (A metric measure of velocity or speed determined by the distance in kilometers covered in one hour.) ▶ *The Johnsons traveled at a leisurely 90 kmph across Ontario.*

kmps kilometers per second. (A metric measure of velocity or speed determined by the distance traveled in kilometers covered in one second.) ▶ *Light travels through a vacuum at 299,792.458 kmps.*

KO to knockout. (Initialism. In boxing, to strike a blow that knocks one's opponent out. See also *TKO*. By extension, any blow that has a severe impact.) ▸ *The rookie boxer KO'd the champion in a stunning upset.* ▸ *The new monthly mortgage payment KO'd Keith's paycheck.*

K of C AND **KC** Knights of Columbus. (Initialism. A Roman Catholic fraternal organization.) ▸ *The proceeds from the K of C bake sale went toward the fund to carpet the activities room at the church.* ▸ *St. Rita's K of C is sponsoring a teen dance Saturday night at 8:00.* ▸ *St. Mary's KC meets every Thursday at 7:00.*

Kor. Korea. (A peninsula in east Asia between the Sea of Japan and the Yellow Sea, home of North Korea and South Korea.) ▸ *Seoul, S. Kor.* ▸ *Pyongyang, N. Kor.*

KP kitchen police. (Initialism. Soldiers assigned to work in an army kitchen. Also, to be assigned to do work in an army kitchen.) ▸ *Sarge assigned Benson and Cooper to KP.*

kph See *kmph*.

Kr krypton. (The chemical symbol for Element 36.)

KS 1. Kansas. (The official two-letter post office abbreviation. See also *Kan.*) ▸ *Wichita, KS 67201* 2. Kaposi's Sarcoma. (A rare skin cancer and an opportunistic disease that strikes people with AIDS.) ▸ *Danny informed his doctor that KS lesions were forming on his body.*

kt. See *k*.

Kuw. Kuwait. (A country on the northwestern shore of the Persian Gulf.) ▸ *Al-Kuwait, Kuw.*

kw kilowatt. (A unit of electrical power equal to 1,000 watts.) ▸ *1 kw = 1.34 horsepower*

kwh AND **kwhr** kilowatt-hour. (A unit of measure equal to 1,000 watts of power over the period of an hour. Used on electricity bills to show the amount of electricity consumed over a period of time.) ▶ *187 kwh used* ▶ *A state tax of .3¢ per kwh is levied.*

Ky. See *Ken.*

KY Kentucky. (The official two-letter post office abbreviation. See also *Ken.*) ▶ *Frankfort, KY 40601*

L

L. AND **Lk.** lake. (A large body of fresh water, also found in names of cities and villages.) ▶ *L. Huron* ▶ *Lk. Forest, Illinois*

L **1.** el = elevated train. (Initialism. A train that runs aboveground on an elevated track.) ▶ *Peter was mugged under the L tracks.* **2.** 50. (A Roman numeral.) ▶ *MDCCCL = 1850* **3.** Latin. (The language of ancient Rome and the modern Roman Catholic Church. See also *Lat.* Used in dictionaries to show the etymology of a word.) ▶ *dome L domus (house)* **4.** large. (Initialism. A size, usually related to clothing or food. In the series *XS, S, M, L, XL.* See also *lg.*) ▶ *While in New Orleans, Patty bought a T-shirt, size L, that read "Welcome to Cajun Country."* ▶ *french fries S 75¢ M $1.00 L $1.15* **5.** left. (Used in writing directions, including stage directions, or to differentiate between two objects [such as speakers] on a control panel.) ▶ *Juliet crosses L, picks up dagger.* **6.** loss; losses. (Used in sports statistics. Usually appears along with wins. See *W.*) ▶ *Don Drysdale—Inducted into the Baseball Hall of Fame, 1984—209 W/166 L.* **7.** low. (Initialism. Found on control panels that have different speed settings, *low* being the slowest, weakest, or coolest.) ▶ *Matt flicked the AC lever to L after the room chilled down.* **8.** low. (Initialism. A gear setting in a vehicle with an auto-

157

matic transmission.) ▶ *The driver shifted the car into L as it made its ascent up the steep hill.*

l **1.** length. (Algebraic representation of the length of a geometric figure.) ▶ *If the length of one side of a square is l, then the area of the square is 2l.* **2.** AND **L.** lira; lire. (The basic unit of Italian currency.) **3.** liter. (A basic unit of capacity in the metric system, determined by volume of distilled water at 4° Celsius and approximately equal to 1.057 liquid quarts.) ▶ *During the physics experiment, Bill dropped the 2l graduated cylinder filled with hydrochloric acid.*

La. Louisiana. (See also *LA.*) ▶ *Gretna, La.* ▶ *Gov. Bill Rogers (La.)*

LA **1.** Louisiana. (The official two-letter post office abbreviation. See also *La.*) ▶ *New Orleans, LA 70101* **2.** Los Angeles. (Initialism. The second largest city in the United States, located in southern California along the Pacific coast.) ▶ *Jane wanted to be a movie star, so she moved to LA.*

La lanthanum. (The chemical symbol for Element 57.)

Lab. Labrador. (The northern portion of the Canadian province of Newfoundland.)

lab **1.** laboratory. (Clipping. A room for scientific experiments and demonstrations.) ▶ *Harriet and Janie stayed late in the chemistry lab working on their assignment.* **2.** Labrador retriever. (Clipping. A breed of dog.) ▶ *The trusty lab bit the intruder.*

LAN local area network. (Acronym. A computer network consisting of interconnected work stations in an office or a building.) ▶ *Jane's first task in modernizing her department involved researching the LAN systems different computer companies had to offer.*

lang. language. (A system of communication by means of written, spoken, or other expressive representations of conceptual meanings.) ▶ *the English lang.* ▶ *lang. arts* ▶ *body lang.* ▶ *computer lang.*

laser light amplification by stimulated emission of radiation. (Acronym. A device that causes particles of a substance to amplify electromagnetic waves into the visible spectrum. The intense beams so produced are used in medicine and industry for extremely precise procedures.) ▶ *laser beam* ▶ *laser printer* ▶ *Laser surgery corrected Uncle Bob's vision problem.*

Lat. 1. Latin. (The language of ancient Rome and the modern Roman Catholic Church. See also *L.*) ▶ *8:00 Mass (Lat.)* ▶ *equus (Lat. horse)* 2. Latin. (Relating to people from countries where languages derived from Latin are spoken.) ▶ *Lat. America* 3. Latvia. (A nation on the Baltic Sea, a republic of the U.S.S.R. until 1991.) ▶ *Riga, Lat.*

lat. latitude. (The angular distance on a globe north or south of its equator.) ▶ *Tropic of Cancer (23.5° north lat.)*

lb. *libra.* (Latin: pound. A unit of weight equal to 16 ounces avoirdupois or 12 ounces troy. The plural is **lbs.**) ▶ *A 25-lb. asteroid fell to the earth.* ▶ *The newborn weighed 7 lbs., 5 oz.*

LB linebacker. (In football, a player positioned behind the line.) ▶ *Lawrence Taylor—LB*

LBJ Lyndon Baines Johnson. (Initialism. The thirty-sixth president of the United States.) ▶ *LBJ was born in 1908.*

LBO leveraged buyout. (Initialism. A business term. Acquisition of a company by investors using borrowed monies, secured by the assets of the acquired company.) ▶

lbs.

Smithco's LBO of Jones International resulted in the layoff of half of the middle-management staff.

lbs. the plural of *lb.*

L.C. Library of Congress. (Initialism. The United States national library, located in Washington, D.C.) ▸ *L.C. Card Catalog #76-14165 (Remember Me, by Fay Weldon)*

L/C AND **LC** letter of credit. (Initialism. A document issued by a bank to other institutions certifying that its holder is authorized to draw a specified amount from those institutions or from the original bank itself.) ▸ *Part of the mortgage proceeds went to an LC that would be disbursed upon repair of the roof of the collateral.* ▸ *L/C 42-0391-AB1 is hereby extended to August 24, 1977.*

lc lowercase. (Initialism. A proofreader's mark. The opposite of capital letters, also called the minuscule.) ▸ *The designer wrote "Use lc throughout" along the margin of the program layout.*

LCD **1.** AND **lcd** least common denominator. (Initialism. The smallest common multiple of the denominators of at least two fractions.) ▸ *The lcd of 1/2 and 1/3 is 6.* **2.** liquid-crystal display. (Initialism. A device displaying letters and numbers on objects such as digital watches and other control panels. These images are produced when an electrical field causes a capsule of transparent liquid crystal to become opaque.) ▸ *Since LCD watches were first introduced, their price has dropped dramatically.*

LCM AND **lcm** least common multiple. (Initialism. The smallest positive integer evenly divisible by two or more given integers. In the example, 30 is the smallest positive number that can be evenly divided by 2, 5, 6, and 10.) ▸ *The lcm of 2, 5, 6, and 10 is 30.*

LD learning disabled. (Initialism. Relating to students with learning disabilities that place them academically behind other students their age.) ▸ *Terry struggled in math until her teacher placed her in an LD math class, allowing Terry an opportunity to work more closely with an instructor.* ▸ *Ms. Jones demanded that she have no more than eight students in each LD section she taught.*

LDC less developed country. (Initialism. A country that is not as developed as industrialized nations.) ▸ *Sally used the term LDC because she thought underdeveloped was demeaning.* ▸ *Nancy joined the Peace Corps to combat illiteracy in LDCs.*

lea. league. (An association or organization.) ▸ *The candidate was favored by the Lea. of Women Voters.*

Leb. Lebanon. (A country on the eastern shore of the Mediterranean Sea.) ▸ *Beirut, Leb.*

LED light-emitting diode. (Initialism. A diode that emits light when charged. The patterns of the diodes form letters and numbers on a display panel, such as calculators and watches from the early 1970s.) ▸ *After a few hours, Eric's eyes were strained from reading the LED readouts on his father's old calculator.*

leg. 1. legal. (In compliance with the law.) ▸ *leg. holiday* 2. legato. (A musical direction: Smoothly.) 3. AND **legis.** legislation. (Law and the process by which laws are made.) 4. AND **legis.** legislature. (An elected or appointed body that determines the laws within its jurisdiction.) ▸ *state leg.* ▸ *new legis.*

legis. See the previous entry (senses 3 and 4).

legit legitimate. (Clipping. Truthful; lawful; honest.) ▶ *"Of course the scheme is legit. What do you think I am, a crook?" the alderman asked his assistant.*

LEM lunar excursion module. (Acronym. A staffed spacecraft that takes astronauts from the command module to the moon's surface for exploration. See also *LM*.) ▶ *Neil Armstrong made history by leaving the LEM and stepping onto the moon.*

LEO Leo. (The astrological abbreviation for the zodiacal constellation of Leo.) ▶ *LEO (July 23 to August 22)*

Lev. Leviticus. (A book of the Old Testament; the third book of the Pentateuch.) ▶ *Lev. 9:2*

l.f. 1. left field. (In baseball, the outfield position behind third base.) **2.** low frequency. (Initialism. A radio frequency between 30 and 300 kilohertz.) ▶ *l.f. band*

lf lightface. (In typesetting, a type face lighter than the regular text type.) ▶ Hello, there! *(lf)*

lg. large. (A size, usually found on menus or food packaging. See also *L*.) ▶ *Chili sm. $1.50, lg. $2.95*

LG Low German. (The modern German dialect spoken in Northern Germany, also known as *Plattdeutsch*. Linguistically, it is the sub-branch of West Germanic languages from which English, Dutch, and Frisian derived. Compare with High German at *HG*.)

L.I. Long Island. (An island in New York to the east of Manhattan.) ▶ *L.I. Sound* ▶ *Suffolk County, L.I.*

Li lithium. (The chemical symbol for Element 3.)

lib. 1. liberal. (Relating to a progressive political or religious ideology.) **2.** library. (A collection of books and other written materials and the building in which they are kept.) ▶ *New York Public Lib.*

lit.

Lib. Liberia. (A country on the Atlantic Ocean in eastern Africa.) ▶ *Monrovia, Lib.*

LIB Libra. (The astrological abbreviation for the zodiacal constellation of Libra.) ▶ *LIB (September 23 to October 22)*

lib liberation. (Clipping. The freeing from oppression.) ▶ *Gloria Steinem was an early leader of the women's lib movement.*

Liech. Liechtenstein. (A tiny mountain principality between Switzerland and Austria.) ▶ *Vaduz, Liech.*

Lieut. AND **Lt.** lieutenant. (A subordinate in authority during the absence of a superior, as well as a military ranking.) ▶ *Lieut. governor* ▶ *Lt. commander*

LIFO last in, first out. (Acronym. Pronounced "LI-foe." An accounting term. A method of allocating costs between inventory and sales. See also *FIFO*.) ▶ *With LIFO, sold items are valued at the cost of the most recent acquisition.*

ling. linguistics. (The study of language, including its sound systems, word structure, sentence structure, and sentential meaning.) ▶ *historical ling.* ▶ *Alice neatly typed the descriptions of all the courses being taught within the Ling. Dept.*

liq. **1.** liquid. (Fluid; a melted solid and a condensed gas. Used to describe the liquid form of a product, as opposed to a powdered form.) ▶ *liq. latex* **2.** liquor. (Alcoholic spirits.) ▶ *liq. license*

lit. literature. (Sometimes a clipping, especially when used in an academic situation. All writings of prose and verse, as of a culture or of a topic.) ▶ *African Lit.* ▶ *"I wanted to take Early American Lit, but all the sections were closed," Betsy told her advisor.*

Lith. Lithuania. (A nation on the Baltic Sea, a republic of the U.S.S.R. until 1991.) ▸ *Vilnius, Lith.*

Lk. See *L*.

LM lunar module. (Initialism. A manned spacecraft that takes astronauts from the command module to the moon's surface for exploration. See also *LEM*.) ▸ *The LM that took Armstrong and Aldrin to the moon was called the Eagle.*

ln natural logarithm. (Initialism. The mathematical symbol for a logarithm in base *e*.)

loc. cit. *loco citato*. (Clippings. Latin: in the place cited. Used in papers and dissertations to cite a work previously referred to.) ▸ *loc. cit., pg. 32*

long. longitude. (The angular distance on a globe east or west of a particular meridian.) ▸ *The Prime Meridian (0° long.) runs through Greenwich, England.*

LOOM Loyal Order of Moose. (Initialism. A fraternal philanthropic society.) ▸ *LOOM Lodge 4500*

LP 1. long-playing. (Initialism. Full-length albums that play at 33 1/3 rpm.) ▸ *Sue stopped by the record store to buy Neil Diamond's latest LP.* 2. Lower Peninsula. (The lower of the two peninsulas that make up Michigan. Compare with Upper Peninsula. See *UP*.) ▸ *The Marquette native trekked down to the LP to visit the state capital in Lansing.*

LPGA Ladies Professional Golf Association. (Initialism. The organization of professional women golfers.) ▸ *Nancy Lopez won the LPGA Championship in 1989.*

LPM lines per minute. (Initialism. A measure of typing, printing, or reading speed.) ▸ *How many LPM?*

LPN licensed practical nurse. (Initialism. A nurse graduated from a vocational nursing school who has a license to practice nursing.) ▶ *After four years as an LPN, Chris went to college to get a B.S. in nutritional science.*

LR AND **lr** living room. (Found in advertisements.) ▶ *Spacious apartment: 250 sf LR; 2-BR; Eurokitchen*

Lr lawrencium. (The chemical symbol for Element 103.)

LSAT Law School Admission Test. (Partial acronym. Pronounced "EL-sat" A standardized test required for admission to most law schools.) ▶ *After Janet got a B.A. in sociology, she took the LSAT and applied for admission to Harvard Law School.*

LSD lysergic acid diethylamide. (Initialism. An illicit hallucinogenic drug, also known as acid.) ▶ *Kenny and Dexter each dropped a hit of LSD.*

Lt. See *Lieut.*

Ltd. limited. (A partnership or company whose partners are liable only to the degree of their investment in the company.) ▶ *Baker & LaFource, Ltd., invite you to their open house.* ▶ *After receiving her MBA, Jeanette worked for a mortgage broker.*

Lt. Gov. Lieutenant Governor. (In state government, the elected officer ranking just below the governor who takes over the duties of the governor in case of death or illness.) ▶ *Lt. Gov. David Davis (D-Nebraska)*

Lu lutetium. (The chemical symbol for Element 71.)

Luth. Lutheran. (A Protestant denomination.) ▶ *Evangelical Luth. Church in America* ▶ *St. Paul Luth. Church Choir performs the Messiah next Monday at 7:00 pm.*

Lux. Luxembourg. (A small west European country between France, Belgium, and Germany.) ▸ *Troisvierges, Lux.*

LWV League of Women Voters. (Initialism. A nonpartisan women's group organized in 1920 to encourage political education and informed involvement in government.) ▸ *During the confusing primary election, the LWV provided accurate, nonpartisan information on most of the candidates.* ▸ *The LWV representative registered her neighbors to vote.*

M

M. Monsieur. (From French. A title used to address a man, regardless of marital status, equivalent to English *Mister.*) ▸ *M. Hercules Poirot*

M **1.** Mach [number]. (A unit of speed equal to the ratio of the speed of an object to the speed of sound.) ▸ *M1 is the speed of sound; M2 is twice the speed of sound.* ▸ *Shortly after the fighter plane reached M1, it burst into flames.* **2.** male. (Found on forms and other printed material to indicate the sex of the person being described. Compare with female at *F.*) ▸ *Check M or F.* ▸ *Roommate wanted (M only, no pets) 555-2356* **3.** man. (Indicates sex, used to differentiate between man and woman. See also *W.*) ▸ *Pete stood in front of the bathroom doors, staring at two ambiguous symbols, and said, "Wouldn't it be easier if they used an M and a W?"* **4.** March. (Often used in graph columns or rows to chart the month-by-month progress of something. See also *Mar.*) ▸ *Week of M 5-12* **5.** May. (Often used in graph columns or rows to chart the month-by-month progress of something.) **6.** mega- (A prefix meaning 1,000,000, used before certain units of measurement.) ▸ *Mw (megawatt)* ▸ *MHz (megahertz)* **7.** megabyte. (A computer term denoting a million bytes of storage space.) ▸ *Carl quickly filled up his 40M hard drive with essential programs.* **8.** Monday. (A day of the

m

week. In the series *S, M, T, W, T, F, S* or *Su, M, Tu, W, Th, F, Sa.*) ▶ *Dentist appt. M at 9:00!* **9.** money. (Initialism. The term used by the Federal Reserve System to indicate the measure of different money supplies.) ▶ *M1 consists of currency, traveler's checks, demand deposits, and other checkable deposits.* ▶ *M2 consists of M1 plus savings deposits, money market accounts, Eurodollars, and other funds.* **10.** 1,000. (A Roman numeral.) ▶ *The cornerstone of the church built during the Middle Ages was inscribed with an ornate M.* **11.** medium. (Initialism. A size, usually related to clothing or food. In the series *XS, S, M, L, XL*. The same as *med.*) ▶ *Concert T-Shirts (M and L only) $16.00* ▶ *beverages S 75¢ M $1.00 L $1.25*

m **1.** masculine. (A grammatical subclass in languages where nouns are inflected for gender. The biological sex of the object represented by the noun is irrelevant. Found in language textbooks and dictionaries. The same as *masc*. Compare with *f* and *n.*) ▶ *el gato (m)* ▶ *der Kopf (m)* **2.** masculine. (Pertaining to nouns and pronouns that refer to males. Found in language textbooks and dictionaries.) ▶ *his (m)* ▶ *father (m)* **3.** mass (A physics term. The quantity of matter contained in an object.) **4.** meter. (The basic unit of linear measurement in the metric system, approximately equal to 39.37 inches.) ▶ *Height: 1.65m* **5.** mile; miles. (A unit of linear measurement, equal to 5,280 feet.) ▶ *DOWNTOWN (4 M)* **6.** milli- (A prefix meaning 1/1000, used with certain units of measurements.) ▶ *mm (millimeter)* ▶ *mg (milligram)*

M&A mergers and acquisitions. (Initialism. Relating to business strategies regarding two or more firms combining assets [merger] and one firm buying another [acquisition].) ▶ *Sally left the party shortly after her boyfriend got caught up in an argument concerning the M&A practices of his corporation.* ▶ *Chris specialized in business*

mag.

law, working especially with companies involved with M&A.

M.A. Master of Arts; *Magister Artium*. (Initialism. A postgraduate degree ranking above Bachelor and beneath the doctorate. It is awarded to a graduate student who has finished a designated course of study in an area of the humanities.) ▸ *Aunt Blanche returned to school to receive an M.A. in English.*

MA Massachusetts. (The official two-letter post office abbreviation. See also *Mass.*) ▸ *Boston, MA 02134*

mach. machine. (A labor-saving device.) ▸ *For sale: books, beds, sewing mach., kitchen appliances. 555-3021.*

Mad. Madagascar. (An island nation in the Indian Ocean off the coast of Africa.) ▸ *Antananarivo, Mad.*

MAD Mutual Assured Destruction. (Acronym. A group dedicated to stop the proliferation of nuclear weapons and to advance nuclear disarmament.) ▸ *A MAD official sent the presidents of the U.S. and the C.I.S. tens of thousands of petitions urging an end to the threat of a nuclear holocaust.*

MADD Mothers Against Drunk Driving. (Acronym. A group dedicated to preventing drunk-driving deaths by educating people, especially students, about the dangers of driving while intoxicated.) ▸ *Mrs. Davis formed a MADD chapter in her hometown.* ▸ *MADD sponsored a sock hop for local teens as an alternative to wild partying.*

mag. 1. magazine. (Sometimes a clipping. A publication published regularly [e.g., weekly, monthly, quarterly] consisting of news stories and articles relating to a certain topic or audience.) ▸ *Please list mag(s). you subscribe to.* ▸ *I've seen her picture in all the fashion mags.*

maj.

2. magnitude. (The degree of enormity.) ▶ *The Loma Prieta earthquake had a mag. of 7.1 on the Richter scale.* **3.** magnitude. (An astronomy term for the brightness of a celestial object ranging from -26.72 [the brightest object as seen from earth, our sun] to approximately 26.) ▶ *The star Betelgeuse (mag. -9) is part of the constellation of Orion.*

maj. **1.** major. (A field of study leading to a degree.) ▶ *Latin maj.* **2.** major. (A music term for one of the two primary patterns of note intervals that make up the scales most European music is based on. Compare with *minor* at min.) ▶ *D maj. chord* ▶ *C maj. scale* ▶ *Mahler's Symphony No. 2 in C maj.*

Maj. Major. (A military officer of rank.) ▶ *Maj. Thomas died in battle.*

Maj. Gen. AND **M.G.** Major General. (A U.S. military officer of rank, above a brigadier general and beneath a lieutenant general.) ▶ *Maj. Gen. Gordon Johnson.*

Mal. Malaysia. (A nation of Southeast Asia.) ▶ *Kuala Lumpur, Mal.*

Man. Manitoba. (See also *MB*.) ▶ *Portage la Prairie, Man.*

man. manual. (A guidebook explaining the use of a product or the operations of an organization.) ▶ *See owner's man., pg. 2, for equipment list.* ▶ *teacher's man.*

manuf. AND **mfd.** manufactured. (Made; fabricated.) ▶ *Manuf. in Taiwan* ▶ *mfd. in accordance with all gov't regulations*

mar. **1.** maritime. (On or near seas or oceans.) ▶ *Mar. Provinces of Canada include Nova Scotia and New Brunswick.* **2.** married. (Found on forms and in other texts.) ▶ *Mary Walters (mar. Edward Davis) was born in 1915.*

Mar. March. (See also *M.*) ▶ *We will be closed on Mar. 20 for inventory.*

Mart. Martinique. (An island in the Caribbean ruled by the French.) ▶ *Fort-de-France, Mart.*

masc. **1.** masculine. (A grammatical subclass in languages where nouns are inflected for gender. The biological sex [if any] of the object represented by the noun is irrelevant. Found in language textbooks and dictionaries. The same as *m*. Compare with *fem.* and *neut.*) ▶ *el gato (masc.)* ▶ *der Kopf (masc.)* **2.** masculine. (Pertaining to nouns and pronouns that refer to males. Found in language textbooks and dictionaries.) ▶ *his (masc.)* ▶ *uncle (masc.)*

maser microwave amplification by stimulated emission of radiation. (Acronym. A precise energy-emitting device that amplifies electromagnetic waves into the microwave spectrum.) ▶ *The physics professor demonstrated important uses of the maser.*

MASH mobile army surgical hospital. (Acronym. A movable hospital base used to treat soldiers injured in combat during war.) ▶ *The enemy artillery shelled the MASH encampment, leaving no one to treat the wounded.* ▶ *M*A*S*H was a popular motion picture and television program set at a MASH unit.*

Mass. Massachusetts. (See also *MA*.) ▶ *Cambridge, Mass.* ▶ *Gov. William Wolmers (Mass.)*

math mathematics. (Clipping. The science of the relationship of quantities and forms using numbers and symbols.) ▶ *The Math Dept. housed specialists in geometry and calculus.* ▶ *Karen could not watch television until her math homework was completed.*

max. maximum. (Often a clipping. The highest amount possible. The last example is slang.) ▶ *max. weight 800 lbs.* ▶ *max. occupancy 8 persons* ▶ *"Gross me out to the max!" Sue screamed as she stepped on a dead frog.*

MB Manitoba, Canada. (The official two-letter post office abbreviation. See also *Man.*) ▶ *Winnipeg, MB R3B 2E9*

MBA Master of Business Administration. (Initialism. The graduate degree given to a student who has completed a predetermined course of study in business administration and management.) ▶ *Walter found himself in competition with thousands of other MBAs for very few jobs.*

MC **1.** marine corps. (Initialism. See *USMC.*) **2.** master of ceremonies. (Initialism. Someone who presides over a ceremony, narrating the events, filling in gaps, and introducing speakers or guests.) ▶ *The MC apologized for stumbling over the name of the foreign delegate from Nigeria.*

mc micro- (A prefix meaning 1/1,000,000, used with certain units of measurements. μ is the scientific symbol used to express *micro*, but consumer packaging and labeling sometimes uses the prefix *mc.*) ▶ *mcg (microgram)* ▶ *Each tablet contains 400 mcg of Folic Acid, 100% of the United States Recommended Daily Allowance.*

MCAT Medical College Admission Test. (Partial acronym. Pronounced "EM-kat." A standardized test required by most medical schools for admission.) ▶ *After scoring dismally on the MCAT, Aaron decided to work for his father.*

mcg microgram. (1/1,000,000 of a gram. Scientifically expressed as μg. Used on consumer packaging and labeling.) ▶ *Vitamin B-12—6 mcg*

M.D. *Medicinae Doctor.* (Initialism. Latin: Doctor of Medicine. The graduate degree awarded to a student who has successfully completed a predetermined course of study in medicine.) ▸ *Douglas S. Files, M.D.* ▸ *The young M.D. decided to specialize in pediatrics.*

Md. Maryland. (See also *MD.*) ▸ *Annapolis, Md.* ▸ *Gov. William Smith (Md.)*

MD 1. Maryland. (The official two-letter post office abbreviation. See also *Md.*) ▸ *Antietam, MD 21782* 2. muscular dystrophy. (Initialism. A degenerative disorder affecting muscles.) ▸ *Ed used a wheelchair because of his MD.*

Md mendelevium. (The chemical symbol for Element 101.)

MDA 1. methylenedioxy-amphetamine. (Initialism. A synthetic hallucinogenic drug.) 2. Muscular Distrophy Association. (Initialism. An organization devoted to finding a cure for muscular distrophy and to aiding those afflicted by it.) ▸ *Jerry Lewis annually hosts the MDA telethon from Las Vegas.*

MDMA methylenedioxy-methamphetamine. (An antidepressant used in therapy. On the street, it is commonly referred to as Ecstasy. See *E* and *X.*) ▸ *Mark had a prescription for MDMA from his psychiatrist.*

mdse. merchandise. (Consumer goods and commodities.) ▸ *All mdse. 25% off!* ▸ *The marble company had a showroom in the Mdse. Mart.*

MDT Mountain Daylight Time. (Initialism. The adjusted time in the Rocky Mountain region of the United States from early April to late October. It is six hours behind Greenwich Time.) ▸ *Arizona does not go on MDT, so in*

M.E.

the summer its clocks are set the same as those in California.

M.E. **1.** mechanical engineer. (Initialism. A professional title for someone who designs and develops machinery for industrial situations.) ▸ *The elevator system, designed by Wilbur Ross, M.E., efficiently and rapidly transported clients from floor to floor.* **2.** medical examiner. (Initialism. A forensics specialist, coroner, or other official authorized to perform autopsies.) ▸ *Jack Klugman played a forensics specialist on the TV show* Quincy, M.E. ▸ *The M.E. determined that the corpse had been a victim of foul play.* **3.** medical examiner. (Initialism. A health professional hired by corporations or insurance companies to examine applicants.) ▸ *Before Bernard could join the insurance plan, the company M.E. gave him a physical.*

Me. Maine. (See also *ME*.) ▸ *Bangor, Me.* ▸ *Gov. John Thomas (Me.)*

ME **1.** Maine. (The official two-letter post office abbreviation. See also *Me*.) ▸ *Portland, ME 04101* **2.** Middle English. (The written and spoken English language used between approximately AD 1100 and 1500. Used in dictionaries to show the etymology of a word.) ▸ *gutter < ME gotere < OFr gutiere < L gutta*

mech. **1.** mechanical. (Relating to mechanics.) ▸ *mech. eng.* **2.** mechanics. (The science of the relationship between forces and objects. By extension, the technical aspect of any process.) ▸ *physical mech.* ▸ *Home Ec 201: Mech. of Cooking*

med. **1.** medical. (Sometimes a clipping. Relating to the science of preventing and treating disease and relieving pain.) ▸ *med. doctor* ▸ *med. practice* ▸ *After a two-year stint in the Peace Corps, Opal went on to med school, spe-*

mem.

cializing in nutrition. **2.** medicine. (A drug used to treat disease or relieve pain.) ▶ *over-the-counter med.* **3.** medium. (A size, usually related to clothing or food. See also *M.*) ▶ *6 White Tube Socks (med.)* ▶ *coffee sm. 60¢ med. 75¢ lg. 90¢* **4.** medieval. (Referring to the Middle Ages, roughly AD 500 to 1450.) ▶ *Med. Latin* ▶ *Med. Greek* ▶ *Med. European history*

Med. Mediterranean. (Relating to the Mediterranean Sea and nearby land.) ▶ *Med. Sea* ▶ *Med. climate*

medfly Mediterranean fruit fly. (Partial clipping. A pestilent insect that destroys crops.) ▶ *Authorities quarantined portions of the coast to prevent the spread of the medfly.*

Medicaid medical aid. (Blend. A state and federal government public health program for the economically disadvantaged and disabled.) ▶ *The state lagged months behind on its Medicaid payments to the public hospitals, which were in turn put into a financial bind.*

Medicare medical care. (Blend. A government-operated health insurance program primarily for people over sixty-five years of age.) ▶ *Fortunately, Grandma had an excellent health insurance policy and did not have to rely solely on Medicare.* ▶ *For the most part, Medicare is operated with Social Security funds.*

Med. Lat. Medieval Latin. (Latin as it was spoken in Europe from *c.* 600 to *c.* 1500. Used in dictionaries to show the etymology of a word. See also *ModL.*)

mem. **1.** member. (A person who belongs to an organization or community.) ▶ *mem. of Congress* **2.** membership. (The state of belonging to an organization or community.) ▶ *Health Club mem. #4193-2384* **3.** memorial. (Anything that is commemorative.) ▶ *Mem. Day* ▶ *Lincoln Mem.*

mer. meridian. (Longitude; an imaginary circle over the earth's surface passing through both the North and South Poles.) ▶ *45th mer. west of Greenwich* ▶ *120th mer. east*

Messrs. Monsieurs; Sirs; Gentlemen. (From French. A title used to address a group of men, equivalent to the concept that would be expressed in English by a plural of *Mister.*) ▶ *Messrs. Thomas, David, and Daniel Bayer.*

Met The New York Metropolitan Opera House. (Clipping.) ▶ *For her fiftieth birthday, Sandy's children got her tickets to see Luciano Pavarotti at the Met.*

meth methamphetamine. (Clipping. A stimulant, also known as speed.) ▶ *The student was caught shooting meth.*

metro metropolitan. (Clipping. Relating to a large city and its surrounding suburbs or to services offered by or within such a place, such as transportation, police, etc.) ▶ *On a business trip, Rob looked at deals throughout the Detroit metro area.* ▶ *Fred sold encyclopedias throughout the metro Boston area.* ▶ *The metros arrived in the scene with lights flashing.* ▶ *Shall we walk or take the metro?*

Mex. **1.** Mexico. (The North American country to the south of the United States.) ▶ *Mexico City, Mex.* **2.** Mexican. ▶ *Mex. cuisine.*

Mexamerican Mexican-American. (Blend. The mixture of Mexican and American cultures.) ▶ *In San Diego, Jane ate at several Mexamerican restaurants.*

mf **1.** medium frequency. (A radio frequency between 300 and 3,000 kilohertz.) ▶ *All AM radio stations broadcast in the mf range.* **2.** mezzo forte. (A musical direction: Moderately loud.)

M.F.A. Master of Fine Arts. (Initialism. An advanced degree granted upon successful completion of a prescribed course of graduate studies in the fine arts.) ▶ *Claire received an M.F.A. in textile and fabric design.*

mfd. See *manuf.*

mfg. manufacturing. (Fabricating or making products on a large scale.) ▶ *mfg. district*

M.G. See *Maj. Gen.*

Mg magnesium. (The chemical symbol for Element 12.)

mg milligram. (A unit of weight equal to 1/1000 of a gram.) ▶ *Dr. Jones limited the patient to 250 mg of sodium a day.*

MGM Metro-Goldwyn-Mayer. (Initialism. A major motion picture production company.) ▶ *The roaring lion is associated with an MGM movie.*

mgmt. AND **mgt.** management. (The staff in charge of a group of people or the operations of a department.) ▶ *No Smoking in This Section—The Mgmt.* ▶ *Mgmt. Team Mtg. tomorrow at noon*

mgr. AND **mngr.** manager. (A person in charge of a group of people or a department.) ▶ *Joan Davis, Mgr. of Employee Relations* ▶ *stage mngr.*

mgt. See *mgmt.*

MHz megahertz. (A unit of frequency equal to 1,000,000 cycles per second. Associated with FM radio stations.) ▶ *WLUW Chicago, operating at 88.7 MHz*

mi. mile; miles. (A unit of linear measurement equal to 5,280 feet or 1.61 kilometers. See also *MI.*) ▶ *75-mi. trip* ▶ *The Nile River is 4,145 mi. long.* ▶ *A township measures 6 mi. by 6 mi.*

MI   **1.** Michigan. (The official two-letter post office abbreviation. See also *Mich.*) ▶ *Gaines, MI 48436* **2.** middle initial. (Found on forms.) ▶ *Last Name, First Name, MI (Please Print)* **3.** mile. (Found on signs to indicate the distance to the named place. See also *mi.*) ▶ *Detroit (264 MI)* ▶ *Downtown (1.5 MI)* ▶ *Thompson Road, Exit 84 - 1 MI*

MIA   missing in action. (Initialism. Applied to soldiers and other military personnel who become unaccounted for in the line of duty.) ▶ *The senator demanded that the Vietnamese government provide information on all the MIAs remaining on file.*

Mich.   Michigan. (See also *MI.*) ▶ *East Lansing, Mich.* ▶ *Gov. John Jones (Mich.)*

mid.   middle. (In the middle or in between. Sometimes a clipping.) ▶ *Mid-Atlantic States* ▶ *Washington Mid. School*

MIG AND **MiG**   a Soviet jet fighter. (Acronym. Named for its designers, Artem Mikoyan and Mikhail Gurevich.) ▶ *Since Henry was in international airspace, he was surprised when he was informed that he was being followed by 3 MIGs.*

mil.   military. (Relating to soldiers, arms, or war.) ▶ *mil. dictatorship* ▶ *mil. coup*

min.   **1.** minimum. (The smallest possible amount needed to fulfill a requirement.) ▶ *Additional Savings of 25% Off ($100 min. purchase required)* ▶ *$10 cover, 2 drink min.* **2.** minor. (A secondary field of study in conjunction with a primary field of study leading to a degree.) ▶ *maj.: chemistry; min.: computer science* **3.** minor. (A music term for one of the two primary patterns of note intervals that make up the scales most European music is based on. Compare with *major* at *maj.*) ▶ *E min. chord* ▶ *F min. scale* ▶ *Tchaikovsky's Symphony No. 6 in B min.*

4. minute. (A unit of time, equal to 60 seconds.) ▶ *The winner of the 10K race clocked in at 35 min. 24 sec.* **5.** minute. (A unit of angle measurement, equal to 1/60 of a degree. Also shown by the symbol "'.") ▶ *25 deg. 14 min. 07 sec. (25° 14' 07")* ▶ *The latitude of Green Bay, Wisconsin, is 44 deg. 31 min. North, and the longitude is 88 deg. 00 min. West.*

Minn. Minnesota. (See also *MN*.) ▶ *Edina, Minn.* ▶ *Gov. Sam Carlson (Minn.)*

MIPS million instructions per second. (Acronym. A unit of processing speed.) ▶ *The 25 MIPS computer broke down in the middle of the day, so everyone went home.*

MIRV multiple independently targeted reentry vehicle. (Acronym, pronounced "MERV." A missile equipped with several warheads that can each be aimed at a different target.) ▶ *The military uses MIRVs to foil the enemy's antiballistic shields.*

misc. miscellaneous. (Used to label files, boxes, column headings, and other items that do not belong to any other listed category.) ▶ *Yuri's bills were arranged in files marked Credit Cards, Utilities, Fines and Tickets, Subscriptions, and Misc.*

Miss. Mississippi. (See also *MS*.) ▶ *Biloxi, Miss.* ▶ *Gov. Ray Thomas (Miss.)*

MIT Massachusetts Institute of Technology. (Initialism.) ▶ *Dr. Chomsky held the interview from his MIT office.*

mks meter/kilogram/second. (Initialism. One of two international measurement systems used to measure force, work, energy, and power. The mks system is for large measurements. Compare with *cgs*.) ▶ *The mks unit for the measurement of force is the newton.*

mkt. market. (A place, region, store, or street where goods are sold, bought, and traded; trade in specific goods or commodities.) ▸ *Metzger's Meat Mkt.* ▸ *the stock mkt.* ▸ *the precious metals mkt.* ▸ *950 West Fulton Mkt.*

mktg. marketing. (The science and business of moving consumer goods from production to consumption, including selling, advertising, and packaging.) ▸ *Mktg. Dept.*

ML Medieval Latin; Middle Latin. (The Latin language used in Europe from approximately the seventh through sixteenth centuries AD. Used in dictionaries to show the etymology of a word.) ▸ *mediation < ME mediacioun < ML mediatio*

ml milliliter. (1/1000 of a liter.) ▸ *Add 4 ml of solution for every liter of water.*

MLF multilateral force. (Initialism. The military forces of more than one nation joined together to fight a common enemy.) ▸ *The United Nations authorized the MLF occupying the capital city to destroy all plants capable of generating nuclear power.*

Mlle. Mademoiselle. (From French. A title used to address an unmarried woman, equivalent to English *Miss*.) ▸ *Mlle. Agnes Renoir*

Mlles. Mesdemoiselles. (From French. A title used to address unmarried women, equivalent to English *Misses*.) ▸ *Mlles. Babette Croix and Elsa duBois.*

m.m. *mutatis mutandis.* (Initialism. Latin: with the necessary changes having been made. Marked on materials such as plans or manuscripts to indicate that requested editorial changes have been incorporated.) ▸ *Manuscript returned 4/1/81, m.m.*

MM. Messieurs. (From French. A title used to address men, regardless of marital status, equivalent to English *Misters.*)

mm millimeter. (1/1000 of a meter.) ▶ *1 in. = 254 mm* ▶ *Measure to the nearest mm.*

Mme. Madame. (From French. A title used to address a married woman, equivalent to English *Mrs.*) ▶ *Mme. Margaret Trudeau*

Mmes. Mesdames; Ladies. (From French. A title used to address married women. There is no equivalent in English, but the concept would be expressed by a plural of *Mrs.*) ▶ *Mmes. Nancy Reagan and Raisa Gorbachev*

Mn manganese. (The chemical symbol for Element 25.)

MN Minnesota. (The official two-letter post office abbreviation. See also *Minn.*) ▶ *Duluth, MN 55801*

mngr. See *mgr.*

M.O. **1.** *modus operandi.* (Initialism. Latin: mode of operation. A term used in criminal investigations to describe the typical methods used by a particular criminal. Extended metaphorically into noncriminal circumstances.) ▶ *Max used the same M.O. in all his thefts.* ▶ *This boor's typical M.O. of ruining a party is to talk incessantly of nothing but insignificant trivia.* **2.** money order. (Initialism. An order for payment of a specific amount of money, issued at a bank, post office, or appointed agency, and redeemable at similar institutions.) ▶ *People without checking accounts use M.O.'s to pay bills.* ▶ *M.O. #2401-2941221* **3.** medical officer. (Initialism. A doctor who is an elected official or a member of the military.) ▶ *The private's appendix was removed by the M.O. on duty.* ▶ *We had to get a form from the M.O.'s office before we could transport the body.*

Mo. Missouri. (Sometimes a clipping. See also *MO.*) ▸ *Jefferson City, Mo.* ▸ *Gov. John Stevens (Mo.)*

mo. month. (A unit of time and a division of a year equal to 28, 29, 30, or 31 days. The plural is **mos.**) ▸ *6-mo. money market certificate*

MO Missouri. (The official two-letter post office abbreviation. See also *Mo.*) ▸ *Kansas City, MO 64101*

Mo molybdenum. (The chemical symbol for Element 42.)

mod. 1. modern. (Contemporary, up to date.) ▸ *Mod. American furniture* ▸ *Mod. English.* 2. moderato. (A musical direction: medium speed.)

mod modern. (Clipping. A slang word reflecting the stylish and fashionable fads of that particular time.) ▸ *"Those bell-bottom pants Marcia is wearing are so mod!" Jan thought to herself.*

ModGr Modern Greek. (Written and spoken Greek since the 1500s. Used in etymologies in dictionaries to compare with Old Greek.)

ModL Modern Latin. (Written and spoken Latin since the 1500s primarily in the scientific community for biological classifications. See also *NL.*)

mol. 1. molecule. (The smallest physical unit of an element or compound. One molecule of an element is made up of one or more similar atoms, and one molecule of a compound is made up of two or more different atoms.) ▸ *Water mol. = two hydrogen atoms and one oxygen atom* 2. molecular. ▸ *mol. weight* ▸ *mol. structure*

MOMA Museum of Modern Art. (Acronym. Pronounced "MOE-ma" A museum of contemporary art in New York.) ▸ *Bob attended the opening of each new MOMA exhibit.*

mon. monastery. (The building and grounds that house a religious order, particularly monks.)

Mon. Monday. (See also *M.*) ▶ *Mon., April 10.*

Mong. Mongolia. (A landlocked Asian country between Russia and China.) ▶ *Ulan Bator, Mong.*

Mont. Montana. (See also *MT.*) ▶ *Butte, Mont.* ▶ *Gov. Fred Stephens (Mont.)*

Mor. Morocco. (An African country on the Atlantic coast.) ▶ *Casablanca, Mor.*

MOR middle of the road. (Initialism. A radio format that plays soft pop music, no hard rock, and no "elevator" music.) ▶ *After months of declining ratings, the radio station switched to an MOR format and put its acid rock collection into storage.*

mos. the plural of *mo.*

Moz. Mozambique. (An African country on the Indian Ocean.) ▶ *Maputo, Moz.*

mp 1. melting point. (A physics term. The temperature at which a solid becomes liquid.) ▶ *Jane's science paper included a chart of the mp of every element.* 2. mezzo piano. (A musical direction: Moderately soft.)

MP 1. military police. (Initialism. The police branch of the armed forces.) ▶ *The MP picked up the soldiers who had gone into town without permission.* 2. mounted police. (Initialism. A police force that patrols on horse. In Canada, the mounted police are called Mounties. See *RCMP.*) ▶ *The protestors could not read the badge numbers of the MPs for fear of being trampled by a horse.* 3. member of parliament. (Initialism. In the United Kingdom, a representative who has been elected to serve in the House of

Commons.) ▶ *The newly-elected MPs wrote thank-you letters to their constituents.*

mpg miles per gallon. (Initialism. The distance in miles that something travels using one gallon of fuel.) ▶ *Ed's 1967 Chrysler gas hog gets only 12 mpg.*

mph miles per hour. (Initialism. A measure of velocity or speed determined by the distance covered in one hour.) ▶ *The taxi driver sped at 85 mph in an attempt to get the woman passenger to the hospital before she delivered her baby.*

Mr. Mister. (A title used to address a man, regardless of his marital status.) ▶ *Mr. Jones and Mr. Phelps played gin every afternoon at 3:00.*

MRE meal ready to eat. (Initialism. Prepackaged food supplied to the coalition forces in the Persian Gulf War.) ▶ *After weeks of eating MREs, the soldiers who liberated Kuwait City looked forward to real food.*

MRI magnetic resonance imagery. (Initialism. A sophisticated imaging technique performed instead of exploratory surgery by using a magnetic field and radio waves. The end result is a highly-detailed 3-D image of internal organs.) ▶ *The MRI performed on the aging patient showed the brain to be free of tumors.*

mRNA messenger RNA. (Initialism. A form of RNA that carries chemical information necessary to make protein.) ▶ *Dr. Wolcott researched amino acids and their relationship with mRNA.*

Mrs. Mistress. (Pronounced "MISS-iz." A title used to address a married woman.) ▶ *Mrs. Richard M. Nixon* ▶ *Mr. and Mrs. John Wilson*

M.S. *Magister Scientae*. (Initialism. Latin: Master of Science. A postgraduate degree ranking above Bachelor and beneath Doctor. It is awarded to a graduate student who has finished a designated course of study in an area of science.) ▶ *Jerry received an M.S. in chemistry from Indiana University.* ▶ *M.S. program*

ms AND **msec** millisecond. (1/1000 of a second.) ▶ *The isotope had a half-life of 21 ms.*

Ms. a title used to address a woman, regardless of marital status. (An abbreviation of both *Mrs.* and *Miss.* When spoken, usually pronounced "MIZ.") ▶ *Ms. Romano kept her maiden name because Zbignew's last name was unpronounceable.* ▶ *Ms. Molly Yard*

ms. manuscript. (Initialism. Usually found in written form only, but pronounced as an initialism in the publishing business. A copy of an author's work submitted to a publisher or printer. The plural is **mss.**) ▶ *ms. received Oct. 12* ▶ *ms. due Oct. 30* ▶ *Mr. Edwards shouted to his secretary across the office, "Where did I put those mss. that Weston sent last week?"*

MS 1. Mississippi. (The official two-letter post office abbreviation. See also *Miss.*) ▶ *Yazoo City, MS 39194* **2.** multiple sclerosis. (Initialism. A chronic disease that affects the central nervous system.) ▶ *The local fire department raised $2,500 for the MS telethon.*

msec See *ms.*

msg. message. (Used in memos and note taking.) ▶ *You have a msg. from Mom on the machine.*

MSG monosodium glutamate. (Initialism. A seasoning that looks like salt, is made from vegetable protein, and is used as a flavor enhancer.) ▶ *Helen requested that no MSG be put in her shrimp fried rice because it usually gave her a headache.*

Msgr. Monsignor. (A title given to certain Roman Catholic officials.) ▶ *8:00 Mass—Msgr. Belliotti*

M. Sgt. Master Sergeant. (A level of rank of noncommissioned officers in the U.S. armed forces.) ▶ *M. Sgt. William Simpson, U.S.A.F.*

mss. the plural of *ms.*

MST Mountain Standard Time. (Initialism. The time in the Rocky Mountain region of the United States from late October to early April. It is seven hours behind Greenwich Time.) ▶ *4:50 MST* ▶ *Arizona remains on MST year-round.*

MSU Michigan State University. (Initialism.) ▶ *MSU Spartans*

M.S.W. Master of Social Work. (Initialism. A postgraduate degree awarded to a student who has completed a predetermined course of study in the area of social work.) ▶ *After Jane got her M.S.W. at Columbia, she got a job in the Bronx assisting the poor.*

m.t. metric ton. (A unit of weight equal to 1,000 kilograms or approximately 2,205 pounds.) ▶ *Weight Limit on Bridge: 6 m.t.*

Mt. 1. mount. (The term used in naming a mountain.) ▶ *Mt. Shasta* ▶ *Mt. Ranier* **2.** AND **Mtn.** mountain. (A part of the earth's surface that has an elevation significantly higher than the areas around it. Used in place names after the proper name. Found on maps and signs and in addresses.) ▶ *Iron Mt., Michigan*

MT 1. Montana. (The official two-letter post office abbreviation. See also *Mont.*) ▶ *Helena, MT 59601* **2.** Mountain Time. (Initialism. The standard time in the Rocky Mountain area of the United States.) ▶ *Denver (MT)* ▶ *The tele-*

cast will be broadcast live from Salt Lake City (8 MT/7 PT).

mtg. 1. meeting. (A gathering of people for discussion and decision making.) ▶ *Dept. mtg.—5:00 p.m. today* 2. AND **mtge.** mortgage. (A loan whose payment is secured by property.) ▶ *2nd mtg.* ▶ *low-cost mtge.*

mtge. See the previous entry.

Mtn. See *Mt.*

MTV Music Television. (Initialism. A cable television network that plays videos of songs and shows related to the rock music industry.) ▶ *It is almost impossible for a musical group to be financially successful without exposure on MTV.*

mun. 1. municipal. (Relating to a local community government.) ▶ *Mun. workers struck yesterday at noon.* ▶ *Violation of Mun. Code* 2. municipality. (An incorporated city, town, or village.) ▶ *large mun.*

muni municiple [bond]. (Clipping. A unit of bonded indebtedness issued by a city, state, or local governmental body. The income is not subject to federal taxes.) ▶ *Fred bought a number of muni bonds to shelter part of his investment income from federal taxes.*

mus. 1. museum. (A place where objects relating to a particular topic are placed on display.) ▶ *Mus. of Science and Industry* 2. music. (The art and science of the arrangement and production of vocal and instrumental tones. Also used in dictionaries and associated with other word lists to denote that a term is related to music.) ▶ *School of Mus.* ▶ *arpeggio (mus.)*

MV megavolt. (1,000,000 volts.) ▶ *2.4 MV*

MVP most valuable player. (Initialism. A sports designation awarded to the most valuable player of a game or a season.) ▸ *The Baseball Writers Association of America annually selects one MVP for each league.* ▸ *Yogi Berra won the MVP award in 1954 and 1955.*

MW megawatt. (One million watts.) ▸ *1 MW = 1,340 horsepower*

MYOB mind your own business. (Initialism. Used as a response to rude or intrusive questions. Often found in advice columns.) ▸ *Ann Landers advised, "Tell the neighborhood busybody to MYOB."*

N

n. **1.** *natus.* (Latin: born. Used in legal, medical, and scholarly texts.) ▶ *Charlemagne, n. AD 742.* **2.** noun. (A person, place, thing, or idea. Found in language textbooks and dictionaries. See also *N.*) ▶ *cat (n.)* ▶ *fish (sing. n. and pl. n.)*

N **1.** Avogadro's number. (Initialism. The chemistry symbol for the number of molecules in one mole of a substance.) ▶ $N = 6.022 \times 10^{23}$ *particles per mole* **2.** knight. (A game piece in chess.) **3.** neutral. (Initialism. Found on gearshifts, indicates that the motor of a vehicle is running but not in gear.) **4.** newton. (A physics term. A unit of force. One newton is the force needed to accelerate a one-kilogram mass one meter per second each second.) **5.** nickel. (1/20 of a dollar or 5¢. Used as a column heading to keep track of loose change, as in a cash register, for instance.) **6.** nitrogen. (The chemical symbol for Element 7.) **7.** noon (12:00 PM; midday.) ▶ *Open 8 to 11, N to 5.* **8.** AND **N., no., nor.** north. (A compass direction. Found on maps and signs and in addresses. See also *S, E, W.*) ▶ *N. Dakota* ▶ *Turn left at the library and walk two blocks N.* ▶ *1999 N. Sheridan Road* **9.** noun. (Initialism. A grammar symbol for *noun*, used in describing the structure of the syntax of a sentence. See also *n.*) ▶ *NP (noun phrase)* ▶ *det. + adj. + N* **10.** November. (Often used in graph columns or rows to chart the month-by-month progress of something. See also *Nov.*) ▶ *Thanksgiving Break: N 24-28*

n neutron. (A subatomic particle with a neutral charge located in the nucleus of the atom.)

N.A. North America. (Initialism. The northern continent of the Western Hemisphere. The United States is a part of North America.)

NA 1. not applicable. (Initialism. Used to fill in the blank of a question that is not pertinent.) ▶ *Name of spouse: NA* 2. not available. (Initialism. Used in tables and charts to indicate that the information is not available.) ▶ *1965 Effective Gross Income: NA*

Na sodium. (The chemical symbol for Element 11. The symbol is derived from Latin *natrium*.)

NAACP National Association for the Advancement of Colored People. (Initialism. Usually pronounced the "EN double A SEE PEE." A national organization established in 1909 to integrate Americans of African descent fully by ending racial prejudice and intolerance and by providing equal opportunities in all aspects of life.) ▶ *The NAACP campaign to end educational segregation was brought to the Supreme Court in the* Brown v. Topeka Board of Education *decision.*

NARAL National Abortion Rights Action League. (Acronym. A political action organization that combats attempts to restrict abortions.) ▶ *Members of NARAL escorted patrons into the health clinic held under siege by antiabortion demonstrators.*

NASA National Aeronautics and Space Administration. (Acronym. The government agency responsible for exploration of outer space.) ▶ *The explosion of the* Challenger *shuttle dealt NASA a severe blow.*

NASDAQ National Association of Securities Dealers Automated Quotations. (Acronym. The second largest stock market in the United States, established in 1971. Millions of securities for heavily traded over-the-counter stocks are exchanged each day.) ▶ *Complex telecommunication systems monitor securities traded through NASDAQ.*

nat. 1. AND **natl., nat'l.** national. (Relating to a country.) ▶ *Nat. League* ▶ *Nat'l. Assoc. for the Advancement of Colored People* 2. native. (A life form, including humans, indigenous to a region.) ▶ *Nat. American Indian* 3. natural. (Occurring in nature; organic.) ▶ *nat. gas exploration* ▶ *nat. disaster*

natl. AND **nat'l.** See the previous entry.

NATO North Atlantic Treaty Association. (Acronym. An international defense organization established in 1949. During the Cold War, its power was balanced by the Warsaw Pact countries.) ▶ *NATO's membership as of 1991 included Belgium, Canada, Denmark, France, Germany, Greece, Iceland, Italy, Luxembourg, the Netherlands, Norway, Portugal, Spain, Turkey, the United Kingdom, and the United States.)*

naut. nautical. (Relating to water navigation.) ▶ *naut. mile*

Nazi a member of the *Nationalsozialistische Deutsche Arbeiterpartei.* (Clipping. German: National Socialist German Workers' Party, the political party seized by Adolf Hitler. The term now connotes the facist, racist, and prejudiced aspects of Hitler's regime.) ▶ *Nazi war criminal* ▶ *The neo-Nazis and skinheads attacked the Turkish immigrants.*

N.B. **1.** *nota bene.* (Initialism. Latin: mark well. Used in writing to highlight something important.) ▸ *N.B.: No weapons were found at the scene of the crime.* **2.** New Brunswick, Canada. (See also *NB.*) ▸ *Moncton, N.B.*

NB New Brunswick, Canada. (The official two-letter post office abbreviation. See also *N.B.*) ▸ *Fredericton, NB E38 5A3*

Nb niobium. (The chemical symbol for Element 41.)

NBA National Basketball Association. (Initialism. The professional basketball league of the U.S.) ▸ *NBA Commissioner David Stern autographed a basketball for charity.*

NBC National Broadcasting Company. (Initialism. A radio and television network in the U.S. See also *ABC, CBS.*) ▸ *In Detroit, Channel 4 is the local NBC television station.*

NBS National Bureau of Standards. (Initialism. From 1901 to 1988, a government research agency designed to improve and enhance the United States position in the scientific community throughout the world. In 1988, the mission of the NBS became a part of the National Institute of Standards and Technology.) ▸ *The NBS provided the military defense contractor with the precise measurements of the physical properties of the new compound.*

N.C. See *N. Car.*

NC **1.** no charge. (Initialism. Marked on bills, receipts, and other similar items to indicate a product or service was free of charge.) ▸ *extra pickles (NC)* **2.** North Carolina. (The official two-letter post office abbreviation. See also *N. Car.*) ▸ *Raleigh, NC 27601*

NC-17 no children 17 and under. (Initialism. A movie rating in the series *G, PG, PG-13, R, NC-17, X.* It indicates that no one aged 17 or younger is allowed to view the film.) ▶ *The NC-17 rating was developed for films whose producers did not want an X rating, which indicates pornography.*

NCAA National Collegiate Athletic Association. (Initialism. Pronounced "EN SEE double A." The governing organization of college and university athletic departments.) ▶ *The NCAA determines guidelines for the players' eligibility.* ▶ *Michigan State was the 1979 NCAA Division I Men's Basketball champion.*

N. Cal. New Caledonia. (An island chain in the South Pacific under French rule.) ▶ *Nouméa, N. Cal.*

N. Car. AND **N.C.** North Carolina. (See also *NC*.) ▶ *Cape Hatteras, N.C.* ▶ *Sen. Terry Thomas (N. Car.)*

NCC National Council of Churches. (Initialism. An organization of ecumenical and cooperative church groups to promote religious justice and coordinate evangelistic, ecumenical, educational, and social welfare programs.) ▶ *Over thirty different denominations are represented by the NCC.*

NCO noncommissioned officer. (Initialism. An enlisted member of the military with lesser rank than a commissioned officer.) ▶ *The NCOs all stayed ashore as long as possible.*

N.D. See *N. Dak.*

ND 1. North Dakota. (The official two-letter post office abbreviation. See also *N. Dak.*) ▶ *Fargo, ND 58102* 2. Notre Dame. (Initialism. A Roman Catholic university in South Bend, Indiana.) ▶ *ND Fighting Irish*

Nd neodymium. (The chemical symbol for Element 60.)

N. Dak. AND **N.D.** North Dakota. (See also *ND*.) ▸ *Bismarck, N. Dak.* ▸ *Sen. Tom Smith (N.D.)*

N.E. New England. (The area of the United States comprised of Maine, Vermont, New Hampshire, Massachusetts, Rhode Island, and Connecticut.) ▸ *The N.E. Coastline*

NE **1.** Nebraska. (The official two-letter post office abbreviation. See also *Neb.*) ▸ *Omaha, NE 68112* **2.** northeast. (A compass direction halfway between due east and due north. In addresses and signs, it refers to a location in the northeast quadrant of a city.) ▸ *Zimbabwe is NE of Botswana.* ▸ *Tomorrow's forecast: Winds 15 to 20 mph from the NE* ▸ *Chicago is in NE Illinois.* ▸ *Amtrak, 60 Massachusetts Ave., NE, Washington, DC.*

Ne neon. (The chemical symbol for Element 10.)

NEA **1.** National Education Association. (Initialism. A professional education organization dedicated to the improvement of public education.) ▸ *The NEA struggles to improve classroom conditions, including reducing class size.* **2.** National Endowment for the Arts. (Initialism. An independent government agency supporting progress in the arts by offering grants to artists and subsidizing programs.) ▸ *The quilt-maker from West Virginia applied for an NEA grant so she could teach her craft throughout the Appalachians.*

Neb. AND **Nebr.** Nebraska. (See also *NE*.) ▸ *Lincoln, Neb.* ▸ *Gov. Ben Thomas (Nebr.)*

Nebr. See the previous entry.

neg. **1.** negative. (A mathematical term for a quantity less than zero.) ▸ *neg. integer* **2.** negative. (Pertaining to words and phrases that mean "no" or "none.") ▸ *neg. pronoun* ▸ *neg. sentence* **3.** negative. (In photography, exposed and developed film on which light and dark are opposite what they normally are.) ▶ *Reprint neg. #14.* **4.** negative. (A physics term for an electric charge with a surplus of electrons.) ▶ *The neg. end of a battery is marked with a "–."*

NEH National Endowment for the Humanities. (Initialism. An independent government agency that offers grants to people pursuing research and education in the humanities.) ▶ *Professor Xie received an NEH grant to bring Asian-American literature to public schoolchildren on the Pacific Coast.*

Nep. Nepal. (A mountainous country in the Himalayas between Tibet and India.) ▶ *Kathmandu, Nep.*

NET National Educational Television. (Acronym. An agency that facilitates educational television programming in the United States.) ▶ *NET has been responsible for much of the useful classroom programing done in the past few years.*

Neth. Netherlands. (A country in western Europe on the North Sea.) ▶ *Amsterdam, Neth.*

neut. **1.** neuter. (In biology, belonging to neither sex. In grammar, a gender denoting something neither masculine nor feminine. In English, *it* is a neuter pronoun. The nouns of highly inflected languages may be masculine, feminine, or neuter. The same as *n*. See also *masc.* and *fem.* Found in language textbooks and dictionaries.) ▶ *das Boot (neut.)* **2.** neutral. (To abstain from taking sides.) ▶ *Switzerland (neut.)* **3.** neutral. (In chemistry, 7 on the pH scale; that is, a substance that is neither alkaline nor acidic.)

Nev. Nevada. (See also *NV.*) ▶ *Lake Tahoe, Nev.* ▶ *Gov. Alice Miller (Nev.)*

Newf. AND **Nfld.** Newfoundland. (See also *NF.*) ▶ *Gander, Newf.*

New Hebr. See *N. Heb.*

New Test. AND **N.T.** New Testament. (Clipping AND initialism. The second half of the Christian Bible, beginning with the four gospels chronicling the birth of Jesus Christ and ending with Revelations or the Apocalypse.) ▶ *New Test. books include Matthew, Mark, Luke, and John.* ▶ *Todd studied N.T. Greek.*

NF Newfoundland, Canada. (The official two-letter post office abbreviation. The same as *Newf.*) ▶ *St. John's, NF A1C 5S7*

NFC National Football Conference. (Initialism. One of two divisions of the National Football League. See *AFC, NFL.*) ▶ *NFC teams include the New York Giants, the Chicago Bears, and the Los Angeles Rams.*

NFL National Football League. (Initialism. The professional football league of the United States.) ▶ *1990 NFL Draft* ▶ *The First NFL Championship playoff pitted the New York Giants against the Chicago Bears.*

Nfld. See *Newf.*

NG National Guard. (The militia force recruited by the individual states of the United States. It can be called into service by the state or the federal army.) ▶ *NG Recruitment Office*

N.H. New Hampshire (See also *NH.*) ▶ *Concord, N.H.* ▶ *Gov. Greg Smith (N.H.)*

NH New Hampshire. (The official two-letter post office abbreviation. See also *N.H.*) ▶ *Exeter, NH 03833*

N. Heb. AND **New Hebr.** New Hebrides. (An island chain in the South Pacific once governed by France and Great

Britain, known as the Republic of Vanuatu since July 30, 1980.) ▶ *They never reached the New Hebr., and were lost at sea.*

NHI National Health Insurance. (Initialism. A government-run medical insurance system which, if implemented, would provide basic care and treatment for all citizens.) ▶ *NHI was a major component of Democratic platforms in the 1992 election.* ▶ *The professor believed that NHI would succeed if a strong emphasis were placed on prevention and nutrition.*

NHL National Hockey League. (Initialism. The major professional hockey league of the United States and Canada.) ▶ *The NHL is comprised of the Campbell Conference and the Wales Conference.* ▶ *The NHL team that wins the postseason playoffs is awarded the Stanley Cup.*

Ni nickel. (The chemical symbol for Element 28.)

Nic. Nicaragua. (A Central American country.) ▶ *Managua, Nic.*

Nig. 1. Niger. (A sub-Saharan African country.) ▶ *Niamey, Nig.* **2.** Nigeria. (A populous African nation on the Gulf of Guinea.) ▶ *Lagos, Nig.*

NIH National Institutes of Health. (Initialism. A government agency within the Department of Health and Human Services that conducts research for better health care and disease control.)

NIMBY Not in my backyard. (Acronym. Describes the phenomenon of neighborhood groups organizing to keep jails, waste dumps, halfway houses, or other things perceived as undesirable from being established or built in their vicinity.) ▶ *If everyone adopted a NIMBY attitude, no more landfills would be built.*

NIMH National Institute of Mental Health. (Initialism. A government agency within the Department of Health and Human Services that conducts research concerning mental health.) ▶ *NIMH released a report on stress-related anxiety.*

N. Ire. Northern Ireland. (The northern part of the island of Ireland and a division of the United Kingdom.) ▶ *Belfast, N. Ire.*

N.J. New Jersey. (See also *NJ.*) ▶ *Hoboken, N.J.* ▶ *Gov. James Smith (N.J.)*

NJ New Jersey. (The official two-letter post office abbreviation. See also *N.J.*) ▶ *Paterson, NJ 07501*

NL 1. National League. (Initialism. Often abbreviated when spoken. One of the two professional baseball leagues of the United States and Canada. See also *AL.*) ▶ *Orlando Cepeda was the 1958 NL Rookie of the Year.* ▶ *The 1977 and 1978 World Series pitted the New York Yankees (AL) against the Los Angeles Dodgers (NL).* **2.** New Latin. (Latin used since the 1500s, particularly in science and classification. See also *ModL.*)

NLRB National Labor Relations Board. (Initialism. An independent government agency that oversees the implementation of federal labor laws.) ▶ *The right to form unions is protected by the NLRB.* ▶ *The long strike against the factory had to be mediated by the NLRB.* ▶ NLRB v. Jones & Laughlin Steel Corporation *(1937) was an important Supreme Court decision.*

N.M. *See N. Mex.*

NM New Mexico. (The official two-letter post office abbreviation. See also *N. Mex.*) ▶ *Truth or Consequences, NM 87901*

N. Mex. AND **N.M.** New Mexico. (See also *NM*.) ▸ *Santa Fe, N. Mex.* ▸ *Sen. Pete Davis (N.M.)*

nmi no middle initial. (Initialism. Used on forms in the blank provided for a person's middle initial to indicate the lack of a middle name.) ▸ *Doe, John nmi*

NNE north-northeast. (A compass direction halfway between northeast and due north.) ▸ *After touching down on a farm, the tornado moved NNE toward the shopping mall.* ▸ *Syracuse is about 50 miles NNE of Ithaca, New York.*

NNW north-northwest. (A compass direction halfway between northwest and due north.) ▸ *Niagara Falls is about 25 miles NNW of Buffalo.*

no. 1. north. (A compass direction. The same as *N.* and *nor.*) ▸ *900 No. Michigan Avenue* ▸ *No. Dakota* **2.** northern. ▸ *No. California* **3.** AND **num.** number. (One of a numerical sequence of things. The abbreviation is from the Latin word *numero*. The plural of *no.* is **nos.**) ▸ *Amy lives in apartment no. 2.* ▸ *Main Street Bank Account No. 45612.*

No nobelium. (The chemical symbol for Element 102.)

nom. nominative. (A grammar term for the case that marks the subject of a sentence. In English, this case is marked only on personal pronouns. *I, you, he, she, it, we,* and *they* are all in the nominative case. Found in textbooks.) ▸ *she (nom.)* ▸ *der Kopf (nom.) [German]*

Nor. 1. Norman. (The tenth-century Scandinavian people of Normandy. The French and English occupants of England after 1066.) ▸ *Nor. Conquest (1066).* **2.** Norway. (A country of northern Europe.) ▸ *Oslo, Nor.*

nor. 1. north. (A compass direction. Also *N* and *no.*) ▸ *Nor. Korea* 2. northern ▸ *Nor. Europe (Norway, Sweden, Finland)* ▸ *Aurora Borealis (nor. lights)*

NORAD North American Air Defense Command. (Acronym. A command established in 1957 to detect attacks from incoming missiles and satellites.) ▸ *Information collected by NORAD is relayed to the president of the United States and the prime minister of Canada.*

norm. normal. (Typical.) ▸ *norm. temp.* ▸ *norm. for this time of year.*

nos. the plural of *no.* (sense 3).

Nov. November. (See also *N*.) ▸ *Theresa's birthday is on Nov. 16.*

NOW National Organization for Women. (Acronym. An organization that supports causes related to women.) ▸ *The new president of NOW was elected by a landslide vote.*

N.P. notary public. (A public officer who certifies and authenticates documents and is authorized to take depositions and affidavits.) ▸ *Signed: Ulla Johannsen, N.P.* ▸ *The N.P. affixed his seal beneath his signature.*

Np neptunium. (The chemical symbol for Element 93.)

NPR National Public Radio. (Initialism. A nonprofit, federally funded radio network.) ▸ *NPR's lack of commercials appealed to Jim.* ▸ *During the Gulf War, Elizabeth listened to NPR for news coverage that was not discussed on the major networks.*

NRA National Rifle Association. (Initialism. The primary organization for people who own and collect guns and other firearms.) ▸ *The NRA lobbies against legislation that would restrict the use or purchase of firearms.*

NRC Nuclear Regulatory Commission. (Initialism. The government agency that licenses and regulates nuclear energy in order to prevent damage to the environment and public health.) ▶ *The NRC inspected the new nuclear reactor in all stages of construction.*

ns AND **nsec** nanosecond. (1/1,000,000,000 [one billionth] of a second.) ▶ *The scientist discovered a rare compound whose half-life was a mere 23 ns.*

NS Nova Scotia, Canada. (The official two-letter post office abbreviation.) ▶ *Halifax, NS B3J 3J6*

NSC National Security Council. (Initialism. An agency of the executive office that keeps the president informed of domestic and foreign policies in conjunction with national security.) ▶ *The president met with the NSC to discuss the recent activities in the Middle East.*

nsec See *ns.*

n.s.f. not sufficient funds. (Initialism. Marked on a check returned by a bank because there is not enough money in the account to be drawn upon.) ▶ *Enclosed please find check #412 returned n.s.f.*

NSF National Science Foundation. (Initialism. A government agency supporting research and education programs to encourage interest in science.) ▶ *Rodney decided to become a mechanical engineer after attending a program sponsored by the NSF at his high school.*

N.S.W. New South Wales. (An Australian state.) ▶ *Sydney, N.S.W.*

N.T. See *New Test.*

NT Northwest Territories, Canada. (The official two-letter post office abbreviation. See also *N.W.T.*) ▶ *Yellowknife, NT*

nt. wt. net weight. (Used on packaging and labeling to show the weight of the product itself, not including the weight of the packaging the product is stored in.) ▶ *nt. wt. 24 oz.*

Num. Numbers. (A Old Testament book; the fourth book of the Pentateuch.) ▶ *Num. 5:10*

num. See *no.*

NV Nevada. (The official two-letter post office abbreviation. See also *Nev.*) ▶ *Henderson, NV 89015*

NW northwest. (A compass direction halfway between due north and due west. In addresses and signs, it refers to a location in the northwest quadrant of a city.) ▶ *The aldermen from the NW side of the city sided with the mayor.* ▶ *Albania is NW of Greece.* ▶ *Department of the Treasury, 1500 Pennsylvania Ave., NW, Washington, DC*

N.W.T. Northwest Territories. (A Canadian territory. See also *NT.*) ▶ *District of Keewatin, N.W.T.* ▶ *Paulatuk, N.W.T.*

N.Y. New York. (See also *NY.*) ▶ *Ithaca, N.Y.* ▶ *New York, N.Y.* ▶ *Gov. Perry Smith (N.Y.)*

NY New York. (The official two-letter post office abbreviation. See also *N.Y.*) ▶ *New York, NY 10025*

NYC New York City. (Initialism. The largest city in the United States.) ▶ *Sandra moved to NYC to be an actress.* ▶ *NYC, NY.*

NYNEX New York New England Exchange. (Acronym. A regional Bell telephone company formed after the divestiture of AT&T in 1984, serving the states of Maine, Vermont, New Hampshire, Massachusetts, Connecticut, Rhode Island, and New York.) ▶ *After receiving a Masters Degree in Communications, NYNEX offered Aaron* *an attractive job in programming.* ▸ *Erika's five years of experience at Central Bell enabled her to work for NYNEX when she moved east.*

NYSE New York Stock Exchange. (Initialism. The major American stock exchange headquartered in the financial district of Manhattan.) ▸ *Almost forty billion shares were traded in 1990 on the NYSE.* ▸ *NYSE Composite Prices*

NYU New York University. (Initialism.) ▸ *Freddie had never been to Manhattan until he attended NYU.*

N.Z. New Zealand. (A country in the southern Pacific Ocean east of Australia.) ▸ *Auckland, N.Z.*

O

O. **1.** AND **Oc.** ocean. (A body of salt water. Found on maps.) ▶ *Pacific. O.* ▶ *Pac. O.* **2.** Ohio. (See also *OH.*) ▶ *Xenia, O.* ▶ *Gov. George Smith (O.)*

O **1.** a blood type. ▶ *People with Type O blood can receive only Type O.* ▶ *Type O blood can be used by everyone.* **2.** October. (Often used in graph columns or rows to chart the month-by-month progress of something. See also *Oct.*) **3.** out. (A baseball term. Used on scoreboards to denote the number of times one team's batters have struck out or have not safely reached a base in the current inning. The example is interpreted to mean that there are two outs and the current batter has one strike and three balls.) ▶ *O 2 S 1 B 3* **4.** oxygen. (The chemical symbol for Element 8.)

o/a on or about. (Used in memos and note taking.) ▶ *The defendant left Idaho o/a August 4, 1986.* ▶ *The property was inspected o/a Oct. 3, 1991.*

OAS Organization of American States. (Initialism. An international organization established in 1948 by several Western Hemisphere nations as an anticommunist security pact.) ▶ *In 1962, although Cuba's membership in OAS was not revoked, it was prohibited from participating in OAS activities.*

OASDI old age, survivors, and disability insurance. (Initialism. Commonly known as Social Security, a government program that provides benefits for the elderly and disabled. It is funded by a compulsory Social Security tax.) ▶ *In 1990 there were almost 40 million OASDI beneficiaries.*

OAU Organization of African Unity. (Initialism. An international organization consisting of most independent African countries, formed in 1963 to expel colonialism from the African continent and promote independence.) ▶ *Goals of the OAU in 1991 included integration of regional economies.*

ob. 1. *obiit.* (Latin: he, she, or it died.) ▶ *Frank Capra (ob. 9/3/91) directed the film* It's a Wonderful Life. 2. obstetrics. (Initialism. The area of medicine specializing in the treatment of women during pregnancy, birth, and the postnatal period.)

ob-gyn obstetrics/gynecology. (Acronym. A medical department or doctor who specializes in the female reproductive system.) ▶ *Harriet visited her ob-gyn to verify her pregnancy.*

obj. object. (A noun or noun phrase that is affected by or receives the action of a verb or that follows a preposition. Found in language textbooks.) ▶ *prepositional obj.* ▶ *direct obj.* ▶ *indirect obj.*

obl. 1. oblique. (The cases other than the nominative and the vocative in languages that exhibit a grammatical case system. Oblique cases usually have inflectional endings. The most common oblique cases are the accusative, dative, genitive, ablative, and instrumental. Found in language textbooks and dictionaries.) 2. oblique. (A geometry term for a geometrical solid whose axis does not form a 90° angle with the base.) ▶ *obl. cylinder* 3.

o.b.o.

oblong. (Ovoid or rectangular.) ▶ *I want an obl. throw rug for the hallway.*

o.b.o. AND **obo** or best offer. (Found in classified advertisements and for sale signs.) ▶ *Two tickets round-trip to Seattle, $200 each, o.b.o.* ▶ *Oak bookshelf, $100 obo*

obs. **1.** obscene. (By legal definition, something that involves printed or visual representations that appeal to a prurient interest in sex or excrement.) ▶ *The adult bookstore violated several passages of the city's Obs. Works Act.* **2.** observation. (Watching and keeping record of events, for instance, in science or medicine.) ▶ *Visitors for patients under med. obs. may not smoke.* **3.** observatory. (An institution or building, usually with a very powerful telescope, for scientific research and astronomical observation.) ▶ *Owens Valley Radio Obs. at Cal. Tech.* **4.** observed. (Found on calendars to mark the date a holiday is legally observed even though the actual holiday may be earlier or later in the month.) ▶ *January 20, 1992, Martin Luther King, Jr.'s Birthday (obs.)* **5.** obsolete. (Something no longer used; out of date. Found in dictionaries to indicate words or definitions of words once but no longer used.) ▶ *fain (obs.)*

o.c. AND **op. cit.** *opere citato.* (Pronounced as a clipping. Latin: in the work cited. Used in dissertations and research papers to refer to a work previously cited.)

Oc. See *O*.

occ. **1.** occidental. (To the west; Western. Used in contrast to oriental.) ▶ *She was confused by occ. culture.* **2.** occupation. (Relating to one's job. Found on forms to indicate a job title.) ▶ *occ.: fire fighter*

occas. occasionally. (From time to time. Used in notes.) ▶ *Patient occas. has blurred vision.*

OCS Old Church Slavonic. (Initialism. The medieval language that developed into modern Slovenian, Serbo-Croatian, Macedonian, and Bulgarian. Old Church Slavonic is also the liturgical language of Slavic Orthodox churches.) ▶ *Saint Cyril, the inventor of the Cyrillic script used in Eastern Europe, and Saint Methodius translated the Bible into OCS in the ninth century A.D.*

Oct. October. (See also *O*.) ▶ *The stock market crashed on Oct. 29, 1929.*

O.D. Doctor of Optometry. (Initialism. The medical degree awarded to optometrists.) ▶ *Eye exams by Anthony Warner, O.D.*

o.d. outer diameter. (Initialism. The distance from the center of the opening of a tube to the outside edge of the material the tube is made from.) ▶ *The copper tubing didn't fit properly, so Emily bought a pipe with a half-inch o.d.*

OD **1.** overdose. (Initialism. The ingestion of a fatal amount of a drug. The meaning has been broadened to include the intake of too much of anything.) ▶ *The paramedics took the addict who OD'd on heroin to the morgue.* ▶ *The fourth-graders bounced around the classroom, OD'ing on sugar from the Halloween candy they ate at lunch.* **2.** overdrawn. (Initialism. A checking account whose outstanding checks total more than the amount in the account.) ▶ *Jane's bank sent her three OD slips in one month and finally closed her account.*

OE Old English. (Initialism. A West Germanic language spoken by Anglo-Saxons in England from the fifth to twelfth century A.D. Old English evolved into Middle English, which in turn evolved into Modern English. Used in dictionaries to show the etymology of a word.) ▶ *heaven < ME heven < OE heofon*

OECD Organization for Economic Cooperation and Development. (Initialism. An international organization encouraging and promoting economic growth and social welfare among member countries and aiding the global economy by helping the developing nations.) ▸ *Members of the OECD include most of Western Europe, Canada, the United States, Australia, and New Zealand.*

OED Oxford English Dictionary. (Initialism. A comprehensive, unabridged compilation of the vocabulary of the English language.) ▸ *Stan cleared an entire shelf of books to make way for all of the volumes of his newly purchased OED.* ▸ *While researching currency, April checked the OED for the earliest use of the word* dollar.

off. **1.** office. (A division of a department or organization, especially used in government.) ▸ *Off. of Mgmt. & Budget* **2.** office. (The room or building a particular department or person of authority is housed in.) ▸ *Personnel Off.* ▸ *principal's off.* **3.** officer. (A person in a position of authority.) ▸ *Susan Jones, Human Relations Off.* **4.** officer. (The title used to address a police officer.) ▸ *Off. O'Neill arrested the felon who attempting to burglarize the donut shop.*

OFr Old French. (The French language between the ninth and fourteenth centuries. Used in dictionaries to show the etymology of a word.) ▸ *mutation < ME mutacioun, OFr mutacion < L mutatio*

OH Ohio. (The official two-letter post office abbreviation. See also *O.*) ▸ *Springboro, OH 45066*

OJ orange juice. (Initialism.) ▸ *Stella offered Stanley some soda, OJ, or whatever he could find in the fridge.*

OK **1.** Oklahoma. (The official two-letter post office abbreviation. See also *Okla.*) ▸ *Oklahoma City, OK 73101* **2.** all right. (Origin unknown. One theory links *OK* to *oll* *korrect,* a misspelling of *all correct,* or to an abbreviation for *Old Kinderhook.* The term has spread globally to indicate everything is all right.) ▸ *If you study every night, you should do OK in this class.* **3.** a degree of intensity, below "very good," but above "poor." ▸ *I like chocolate OK, but I really like vanilla.* **4.** a confirmation of comprehension. ▸ *OK, I understand.* **5.** a request for approval or permission. ▸ *I'm going to the mall with Janie, OK?* **6.** a conversation filler. ▸ *OK, so are you like ready to go?*

Okla. Oklahoma. (See also *OK* .) ▸ *Tulsa, Okla.* ▸ *Gov. Joan Waters (Okla.)*

Om. Oman. (A country on the Arabian peninsula in the Middle East.) ▸ *Muscat, Om.*

OMB Office of Management and Budget. (Initialism. Established in 1970 to help the president of the United States assess the efficiency of the management of the executive branch and prepare the government's budget.) ▸ *The OMB keeps the president informed of work and programs planned and executed by different government agencies.*

ON **1.** Old Norse. (A North Germanic language spoken in Scandinavia before the fourteenth century. The modern languages of Icelandic, Faeroese, Norwegian, Swedish, and Danish have developed from Old Norse. Used in dictionaries to show the etymology of a word.) ▸ *skirt < ON skyrt* **2.** Ontario, Canada. (The official two-letter post office abbreviation.) ▸ *Toronto, ON M4W 1B8*

Ont. Ontario. (See also *ON.*) ▸ *Windsor, Ont.*

op. **1.** operation. (A military or other organized action.) ▸ *Op. Desert Storm.* **2.** opus. (A musical composition. The plural is **opp.**) ▸ *Chopin's Sonata in G, op. 65, was written in 1847.*

op. cit. See *o.c.*

OPEC Organization of Petroleum Exporting Countries. (Acronym. Organization established in 1970 to set global oil prices by coordinating oil production. The thirteen member countries—Algeria, Ecuador, Gabon, Indonesia, Iran, Iraq, Kuwait, Libya, Nigeria, Qatar, Saudi Arabia, United Arab Emirates, and Venezuela—possess about two-thirds of oil reserves and about one-third of natural gas reserves.) ▶ *The Texas economy throughout the 1980s was directly affected by OPEC policies.*

opp. the plural of *op.*

opt. 1. optical. (Relating to vision.) ▶ *opt. illusion* ▶ *opt. department* 2. optional. (Not mandatory; an available choice.) ▶ *Math 212 req. for physics majors; opt. for bio. majors.* ▶ *Equipped with power steering, power brakes (A/C and AM/FM radio opt.)*

Or. AND **Ore.** Oregon. (See also *OR.*) ▶ *Salem, Or.* ▶ *Gov. Barbara Smith (Or.)*

OR 1. Oregon. (The official two-letter post office abbreviation. See also *Or.*) ▶ *Eugene, OR 97401* 2. operating room. (Initialism. A room in a hospital or clinic where surgery and other operations are performed.) ▶ *The nurse wheeled the bleeding patient into the OR.*

orch. 1. orchestra. (A group of musicians led by a conductor, usually performing classical music.) ▶ *Detroit Symphony Orch.* 2. orchestra. (The main floor of a theater. Found on tickets.) ▶ *Orch. Row E, Seat 4*

ord. 1. ordinal. (A dictionary term denoting something in a series, usually numbers. *Two* is a cardinal number. *Second* is an ordinal number.) ▶ *third (ord.)* 2. ordinance. ▶ *City ord. prohibits smoking in public places.* ▶ *City Ord. 3-14159(p) prohibits smoking in public places.*

ordn. ordnance. (Military weaponry and related supplies, equipment, and vehicles.) ▶ *mil. ordn.*

Ore. See *Or.*

org. 1. organic. (Occurring in nature. Used frequently in advertising, labeling, and packaging to stress the natural attributes of a product.) ▶ *org. compound* ▶ *org. produce* ▶ *Org. Hair Shampoo with Vitamin E* 2. organization. (A systematically unified group of people working together for a common cause.) ▶ *World Health Org.* ▶ *Org. of American States* 3. organized. (Established; systematically unified. Frequently used to indicate the date an organization was established.) ▶ *org. May 1, 1891*

orig. 1. originally. (Referring to the origin of something; how something was when it was first begun.) ▶ *Stuffed Animals $19.95 (orig. priced at $29.95)* 2. origin. (The place where something or someone began or came from.) ▶ *of foreign orig.* ▶ *On the Orig. of Species by Means of Natural Selection.*

ornith. ornithology. (The study of birds.) ▶ *Room 205, Avis Hall—Dept. of Ornith.*

orth. orthopedic. (Relating to the medical science of treating injured bones and muscles.) ▶ *orth. surgeon* ▶ *orth. shoes*

OS Old Saxon. (A West Germanic language of the ninth and tenth centuries, spoken in what is now northern Germany.)

Os osmium. (The chemical symbol for Element 76.)

OSHA Occupational Safety and Health Administration. (Acronym. Established in 1970 under the jurisdiction of the Department of Labor to maintain safety and health standards in work environments, investigate violations of safety and health regulations, and to set penalties.)

OSU

▸ *The factory superintendent was able to keep the OSHA investigator from discovering the mysterious sludge leaking from one of the assembly lines.*

OSU Ohio State University. (Initialism.) ▸ *OSU Buckeyes*

OT **1.** occupational therapy. (Initialism. The use of arts and crafts within therapy to remedy a physical or mental defect or to provide job skills to the disabled.) ▸ *Despite difficult hours and occasional setbacks, Nancy found her work in OT to be very rewarding.* **2.** Old Testament. (Initialism. The first of two parts of the Christian Bible; the Christian term for the Judaic Scriptures.) ▸ *Reverend Klemm was an OT authority and spoke at many churches throughout the South.* **3.** offensive tackle. (A football term for one of the two players on either side of the offensive end.) **4.** overtime. (Initialism. An extra amount of playing time to settle a sporting event that ended in a tie. Used in reporting sporting events scores that went into overtime.) ▸ *Pistons 112 - Bulls 110 (OT)* **5.** overtime. (Initialism. Work done after the regular quitting time, usually more than eight hours a day or forty hours a week. Used on time sheets and pay checks to denote the extra hours worked.) ▸ *OT wages are one and one-half times regular wages.* ▸ *Taxable Hours: 40 (reg.) 5 (OT)*

OTB offtrack betting. (Initialism. Legal places of betting, not at the site of the actual race.) ▸ *After work, Larry went to the OTB parlor near his office to relax.*

OTC over-the-counter. (Initialism. Relating to medicine and drugs that are available without a prescription.) ▸ *Aspirin and other OTC medicines are readily available at most grocery stores.*

OTEC ocean thermal energy conversion. (Acronym. A method of producing energy by solar power, using hot and cold ocean water.) ▶ *Dr. Walters moved to Hawaii after he was transferred to the OTEC research department.*

Oxbridge Oxford and Cambridge Universities. (Blend. Characteristic of Oxford and Cambridge.) ▶ *"Neville has this phony Oxbridge intellectual attitude that I cannot stand," Anne confided to her best friend.*

Oxfam Oxford Committee for Famine Relief. (Acronym. An international organization established in 1942 providing aid and training for developing countries and disaster-stricken areas.) ▶ *After joining Oxfam, Raymond moved to Senegal and worked with farmers whose land had been stricken by drought.*

oz. **1.** ounce; ounces. (A unit of dry weight equal to 1/16 of a pound or 1/12 of a pound in troy and apothecaries' measure. Found on packaging and labeling.) ▶ *5 lb. 6 oz.* **2.** ounce; ounces. (A unit of liquid measure equal to 1/16 of a pint. Found on packaging and labeling.) ▶ *fl. oz.* ▶ *Free—Extra 6 oz.!*

oz. advp. avoirdupois ounce(s). (1/16 of an avoirdupois pound—the standard American pound.) ▶ *12 oz. advp.*

oz. ap. apothecaries' ounce. (1/12 of a pound, used in pharmacy.) ▶ *1 oz. ap. = 480 grains*

oz. t. troy ounce. (1/12 of a pound, used in the measurement of precious stones.) ▶ *1 oz. t. = 20 pennyweight*

P

p. **1.** AND **pg.** page. (One of the sides of a leaf of printed material. The plural is **pp.**) ► *See p. 925 for further explanation.* ► *Ron read 23 pp. in one hr.* **2.** participle. (An adjective derived from the present participle or past participle form of a verb. In the following sentence, *cooked* is a participle: Poorly cooked rice can be very sticky. Found in language textbooks and dictionaries.) ► *flown (p.)* **3.** past. (Pertaining to a tense describing an action completed or in progress at a former time. Compare with *pres., fut.* Found in language textbooks and dictionaries.) ► *had (p.), have (pres.)* **4.** AND **pt.** pint. (A dry or liquid measure equal to 1/2 quart.) ► *4 pt. heavy cream* **5.** parts. (In *ppb.* and *ppm.*)

p **1.** momentum. (A mechanical physics symbol for the mass of an object multiplied by its velocity.) ► $p = M \times v$ **2.** penny. (A unit of money equal to 1/100 of an English pound since 1971. The ¢ symbol is used in the United States for 1/100 of a dollar. See also *P.*) ► *20 p* **3.** peso. (A unit of currency in Chile, Colombia, Cuba, Dominican Republic, Guinea-Bissau, Mexico, Republic of the Philippines, and Uruguay. In the U.S., if a country is not specified, it usually refers to Mexican currency.) ► *Dr. Frauer bought the ceramic pig for 25 p.* **4.** piano. (A musical direction: Soft.) **5.** proton. (A particle with a positive charge found in the nucleus of an atom.)

P **1.** penny. (1/100 of a dollar or 1¢. Used as a column heading to keep track of loose change, as in a cash register, for instance. See also *p.*) **2.** phosphorus. (The chemical symbol for Element 15.) **3.** pitcher. (A baseball abbreviation for the player who throws the ball to the batter.) ▸ *Mark Fidrych (P) was the American League's Rookie of the Year in 1976.* **4.** pawn. (A game piece in chess.) **5.** park. (Initialism. Found on gearshift levers.) ▸ *Is the lever in D or P?*

p.a. *per annum.* (Initialism. Latin: each year. Annually.) ▸ *Effective interest rate: 19.8% p.a.*

PA **1.** Pennsylvania. (The official two-letter post office abbreviation. The same as *Pa., Penn.,* and *Penna.*) ▸ *Reading, PA 19601* **2.** public address system. (Initialism. A method of amplifying and broadcasting sound throughout a building or within a room.) ▸ *When the principal's voice boomed through the PA, the unruly students quickly found their seats.* **3.** power of attorney. (Initialism. A written legal statement authorizing an individual to act on behalf of another.) ▸ *David Warner, PA for Herbert Rothschild, gave testimony to Judge Shriver.* **4.** press agent. (Initialism. Someone who promotes a person or organization to news media.) ▸ *The starlet paid her PA over $100,000 to ensure that favorable articles concerning her career would appear in national magazines every month.* **5.** production assistant. (Initialism. A member of a movie crew who assists the director by being responsible for organizing many tasks behind the scenes.) *During the filming of a crucial scene, three PAs were needed to keep the gawking crowds away from the actors.* **6.** prosecuting attorney. (Initialism. A public official who conducts criminal prosecutions for

Pa

the state or the people.) ▸ *The PA assigned to the case was a withered old lawyer who had grown tired of the system.*

Pa protactinium. (The chemical symbol for Element 91.)

Pa. AND **Penn., Penna.** Pennsylvania. (See also *PA*.) ▸ *Altoona, Pa.* ▸ *Gov. Robert Thomas (Penn.)* ▸ *Reg. Penna. Dept. Agr.*

PABA para-aminobenzoic acid. (Acronym. An organic acid found in yeast. It absorbs ultraviolet light and is used in suntan lotions. Found on labeling and packaging.)

Pac. AND **Pacif.** Pacific. ▸ *Pac. Ocean.* ▸ *Pacif. Islander*

PAC Political Action Committee. (Acronym. An organization that receives contributions and expends money to elect or influence legislators.) ▸ *The senator received several thousand dollars from PAC groups organized by labor unions.*

Pacif. See *Pac.*

Pak. Pakistan. (An Asian country between Iran and India on the Arabian Sea.) ▸ *Karachi, Pak.*

Pal. Palestine. (A parcel of land on the east coast of the Mediterranean Sea comprised of parts of modern Israel, Jordan, and Egypt. It was a British territory from 1923 to 1948, until the formation of Israel by the United Nations.)

Pan. Panama. (The southernmost country of Central America.) ▸ *Panama City, Pan.*

par. **1.** paragraph. (A section of a document. Also denoted by the ¶ symbol.) ▸ *The words "are to endeavor to" shall be deleted from par. 20.* **2.** parish. (A subdivision of a diocese; the residential area occupied by the congregation of a church.) ▸ *Par. of St. Rita.* **3.** parish. (A political division in Louisiana, equivalent to counties in other states.) ▶ *Lafourche Par.*

Par. Paraguay. (A landlocked country of South America.) ▶ *Asunción, Par.*

paren. parenthesis. (A mark of punctuation that sets off information. Sometimes a clipping. This definition is enclosed by an open parenthesis and a closed parenthesis.) ▶ *open paren.* ▶ *closed paren.*

parl. parliament. (A body of government similar to Congress. In England, Parliament is comprised of the House of Commons and the House of Lords.)

parsec AND **pc** parallax second. (Acronym. A unit used to measure astronomical distances, equal to 3.26 light-years.) ▶ *The spacecraft zoomed toward Quasar 2B13, 5 parsecs past the galaxy they were from.*

part. participle. (One of the forms of an English verb. An example of a present participle is *flying*. An example of a past participle is *flown*. When such words are used as adjectives, they are called participles. Found in language textbooks and dictionaries.) ▶ *past part.* ▶ *pres. part.*

pass. 1. passive. (Pertaining to the "voice" of a sentence whose object is being acted on by someone or something. "Mary was hugged by John" is the passive construction of the active sentence "John hugged Mary." Found in language textbooks and dictionaries.) ▶ *pass. voice* **2.** passenger. ▶ *twelve pass. in first class and 200 pass. in coach.*

pat. patent. (A document granting the exclusive right to produce and profit from an invention or process.) ▶ *pat. applied for*

patd. patented. (Describing an object or process for which a patent has been obtained.) ▶ *patd. ingredients*

path. pathology. (The study of disease and the biological changes caused by disease.) ▶ *path. lab*

pat. pend. patent pending. (Describing a product or process for which a patent has been applied but not yet granted.) ▶ *manuf. USA, pat. pend.*

PAYE pay as you enter. (Describing an event for which tickets are not available in advance, and where admission must be paid upon entry.) ▶ *Tickets $15 PAYE*

payt. AND **pmt.** payment. (Money remitted toward an account, bill, or other financial obligation.) ▶ *payt. rec'd. 6/12/81*

Pb lead. (The chemical symbol for Element 82. The symbol is derived from Latin *plumbum*.)

PBB polybrominated biphenyl. (Initialism. A carcinogenic fire retardant.) ▶ *Cattle feed was inadvertently mixed with PBB in Missouri, exposing thousands to the dangerous toxin.*

PBJ peanut butter and jelly [sandwich]. (Initialism.) ▶ *Every day after school, Alvin ate a PBJ and drank a glass of milk.*

PBS Public Broadcasting System. (Initialism. A network whose operating income comes from federal funds and private donations instead of the revenue from commercials. PBS broadcasts many educational and cultural programs.) ▶ *During a PBS fund-raiser, a mysterious tycoon donated $100,000.* ▶ *Sesame Street and Masterpiece Theatre are two of the best-known series broadcast by PBS stations.*

PBX private branch exchange. (Initialism. A telephone system for private use.) ▶ *The condominium association disbanded the PBX system and put a private line into* *each unit instead.* ▸ *Mr. Potter was fined for making personal long distance calls on the company's PBX system.*

p.c. *post cibum.* (Initialism. Latin: after a meal. Found on prescriptions, indicating that the medication is to be taken following a meal.) ▸ *1 tablet orally, p.c.*

PC **1.** politically correct. (Initialism. The actions and beliefs of the progressive left. *PC* is often used in ridicule of extreme, trendy behavior and social attitudes.) ▸ *The PC students demanded that European Civilization studies be replaced with Asian and African culture.* ▸ *Some people join every radical group on campus just to be PC.* **2.** personal computer. (Initialism. A home computer for private use.) ▸ *Tad wrote his English paper on the PC his parents bought for his birthday.* **3.** petty cash. (Loose collection of change and small denominations not specifically accounted for in a budget, used for small purchases as needed.) ▸ *The amount is too small to write a check for. Take it out of petty cash.* **4.** peace corps. (Initialism. The United States overseas volunteer program, established in 1961, to aid developing nations and foster world peace.) ▸ *Nancy, a PC volunteer in Honduras, coordinated a number of learning programs.* ▸ *Paul and Jeff learned Amharic when they worked for the PC in Ethiopia.*

pc **1.** AND **pct.** percent. (Initialism. The number of parts per 100. Often expressed with the % symbol.) ▸ *25 pc muratic acid, by volume* **2.** See *parsec.* **3.** piece. (A part of a whole.) ▸ *9-pc. chicken dinner* ▸ *24-pc. Tupperware set*

PCB polychlorinated biphenyl. (Initialism. A toxic carcinogenic liquid used as insulation in electrical transformers.) ▸ *Before the mortgage was issued, the lender demanded that the transformers on the property be checked for PCBs.*

PCP   **1.** phencyclidine. (Initialism. A veterinary tranquilizer and a psychedelic drug that can cause severe hallucinations and death.) ▸ *While tripping on PCP, Pamela thought she could fly, and leaped out the fifth-floor window to her death.* **2.** Pneumocystis Carinii pneumonia. (Initialism. A parasitic lung infection; an opportunistic infection frequently striking people with AIDS.) ▸ *Four months after being diagnosed with AIDS, Tanya contracted PCP and died shortly thereafter.*

pct.   See *pc.*

p.d.   *per diem.* (Initialism. Latin: by the day. A legal and medical term to denote something occurring on a daily basis.) ▸ *p.d. interest charges of $145.34 are applicable.*

P.D.   police department. (Initialism. The branch of municipal government whose duty is to uphold and enforce the laws of that community.) ▸ *L.A.P.D. (Los Angeles Police Department)*

pd.   paid. (Marked on receipts and bills to indicate payment.) ▸ *$100—pd. 12/24*

Pd   palladium. (The chemical symbol for Element 46.)

PDA   public display of affection. (Initialism. A display of kissing or even hand-holding in public.) ▸ *The high school handbook strictly forbids any form of PDA on the school grounds.*

PDQ   pretty darn quick; pretty damn quick. (Initialism. Slang expression. Caution with *damn*.) ▸ *If you don't clean your room PDQ, I am not taking you to soccer practice tonight.*

PDT   Pacific Daylight Time. (Initialism. The adjusted time in the westernmost contiguous United States from early April to late October. See also *PST*.) ▸ *Please remit your* *payment today to the Bank of Oxnard by 2:00 PM PDT or incur an additional day's interest charges.*

P.E. physical education. (Initialism. A physical education class.) ▶ *Annie hated her first-period P.E. class because her hair was frizzed for the rest of the day.*

PE Prince Edward Island, Canada. (The official two-letter post office abbreviation. See also the following entry.) ▶ *Charlottetown, PE C1A 4P3*

P.E.I. Prince Edward Island. (Initialism. A Canadian island province in the Gulf of St. Lawrence. See also the previous entry.) ▶ *Montague, P.E.I.*

pen. peninsula. (Land surrounded on three sides by water. Found on maps and in texts.) ▶ *Kamchatka Pen.*

PEN International Association of Poets, Playwrights, Editors, Essayists, and Novelists. (Acronym. A literary organization.) ▶ *The recipient of the Nobel Prize for Literature was invited to speak at an upcoming PEN convention.*

Penn. See *Pa.*

Penna. See *Pa.*

per. period. (A division of time.) ▶ *1st per.—English Lit—Room 203* ▶ *3rd per. earnings: $125,000,000*

P/E ratio price earnings ratio. (Initialism. The ratio of the current market price of a company's stock to the earnings per share. The higher the P/E ratio, the more likely a company's earnings will rise faster than others.) ▶ *A P/E ratio of 10 means that stock has a value ten times greater than the earnings per share.* ▶ *Investors tend to have a negative view of low P/E ratios.*

perm.

perm. permanent. (Not temporary. Found in classified advertising, especially in relation to jobs.) ▶ *Intl. House of Clay hiring sales clerks, perm. and seasonal.*

perm permanent. (Clipping. A type of hairstyle.) ▶ *Jeanne's new perm flatters her facial features.*

perp. perpendicular. (Describing two lines whose intersection form a right angle.) ▶ *12° from perp.*

Pers. Persian. (Having to do with Persia, the former name of *Iran*.) ▶ *Pers. cat* ▶ *Pers. Gulf War*

PERT program evaluation and review technique. (Acronym. A system of analyzing events, usually by using a computer, in order to execute a project in the quickest and most efficient way possible.) ▶ *On the basis of the PERT analysis, Veronica outlined a number of recommendations to her superiors in an effort to improve productivity.*

PET positron emission tomography. (Acronym. An imaging technique used to study blood circulation and distribution.) ▶ *PET scan*

PETA People for the Ethical Treatment of Animals. (Acronym. A radical animal rights group.) ▶ *The women wearing fur coats were hassled by members of PETA on the street.* ▶ *PETA protested against the cosmetics company that tested products on animals.*

Pfc Private first class. (Initialism. A military rank.) ▶ *Pfc John A. Doe*

pg. See *p.*

PG 1. pregnant. (Initialism. A slang term for pregnancy.) ▶ *Did you hear that Mary is PG again?* 2. parental guidance. (Initialism. A movie rating in the series *G, PG, PG-13, R, NC-17, X*. It indicates that some scenes may be

pH

inappropriate for young children; therefore, parental guidance is suggested.) ▶ Little Man Tate *(PG) is Jodie Foster's directorial debut.*

PG-13 parental guidance [for children under age] 13. (Initialism. A movie rating in the series *G, PG, PG-13, R, NC-17, X*. It indicates that some scenes may not be suitable for children under 13.) ▶ *Red Dawn (PG-13)*

PGA Professional Golfers' Association. (Initialism. The men's league of professional golfers.) ▶ *Jack Nicklaus has won the PGA golf tournament five times.*

Pg Dn page down. (A key on a computer keyboard that moves a document down one page.) ▶ *Press Ctrl—Pg Dn to delete a document to the end of the page.*

Pg Up page up. (A key on a computer keyboard that moves a document up one page.) ▶ *Mr. Carsons couldn't figure out why his screen was blank, but Bill merely tapped the Pg Up key and the end of the speech appeared on the monitor.*

p&h postage and handling. (The additional cost levied when purchased items are shipped to cover postage and handling expenses. See also *s&h*.) ▶ *Order Your Slice-O-Matic Now (Only $29.95 plus $4.95 p&h)* ▶ *As promised, Rita's money was refunded, less the p&h charge.*

P.H. purple heart. (A military award given to members of the armed forces killed or wounded in action.) ▶ *The soldier was awarded the P.H. for his act of heroism.*

pH *pouvoir hydrogene.* (Initialism. French: hydrogen power. The measurement of the acidity or alkalinity of a substance on a scale from 0 [very acidic] to 14 [very alkaline].) ▶ *The pH of distilled water is 7, or neutral.*

phar. AND **pharm.** 1. pharmacy. (A drugstore.) ▸ *Stop at pharm. and get the Rx I phoned in.* 2. pharmaceutical. (A medical product or drug.) ▸ *pharm. co.*

pharm. See the previous entry.

Ph.D. *Philosophiae Doctor.* (Initialism. Latin: Doctor of Philosophy. The highest graduate degree awarded for research in a particular study.) ▸ *Sam Smith, Ph.D.* ▸ *Susan received her Ph.D. in sociology from Northeastern University.*

Phil. Philippines. (A nation of several islands between the South China Sea and the Pacific Ocean.) ▸ *Luzon City, Phil.*

phil. philosophy. (The study of the sciences and liberal arts exclusive of medicine, law, and theology.) ▸ *Dr. Lewis taught Phil. 401—Introduction to Hegelian Thought.*

phon. 1. phonetic(s). (The study and description of different sounds in a language.) ▸ *phon. pronunciation* 2. phonology. (The study of the sound systems of languages. For some people, the study of phonology also embraces the study of phonetics.) ▸ *I took two phon. courses in college.*

photo photograph. (Clipping. A reproduction on film.) ▸ *photo album* ▸ *Grandma took a photo of all her grandchildren at Christmastime.*

photog. photography. (The process of using film to reproduce images.) ▸ *Photog. Dept.*

phr. phrase. (A string of words functioning as a part of speech. Found in language textbooks.) ▸ *participial phr.* ▸ *adjective phr.*

PHS Public Health Service. (Initialism. An administration within the Department of Health and Human Services that regulates and coordinates federal health policies.) ▶ *The Food & Drug Administration and the Centers for Disease Control are a part of the PHS.*

phys. 1. physical. (Relating to the body.) ▶ *phys. fitness* ▶ *phys. ed.* ▶ *phys. disability* 2. physician. (A doctor of medicine.) 3. physics. (The science of the properties of matter and energy.) ▶ *quantum phys.* ▶ *nuclear phys.* 4. physicist. (A person trained in one or more areas of physics.) ▶ *molecular phys.*

p & i principal and interest. (Initialism. A banking term. A payment on a loan comprised of the principal and interest, as opposed to interest only.) ▶ *Brad's monthly p & i payment on his business loan was $3,500.*

PID pelvic inflammatory disease. (Initialism. The inflammation of the pelvic cavity in females, often a symptom of other diseases or disorders.) ▶ *Mary was stricken with PID.*

PIN personal identification number. (Acronym. A secret number associated with a credit card or ATM card that provides access to do business with that card. See also *ATM*.) ▶ *Sam forgot his PIN number, so he had to wait until the bank opened to withdraw cash from his account.*

pix picture; pictures. ▶ *I had my pix taken for the yearbook.* ▶ *Are your pix back from the lab yet?*

pixel picture element. (Acronym. A unit that is part of an image on a video screen. *Pix* is usually assumed to be in the plural, but that is irrelevant in this acronym. See also *pix*.) ▶ *The greater the number of pixels on a monitor, the higher the resolution of the image will be.*

PJ's

PJ's pajamas. (Initialism.) ▸ *Sally put on her PJ's at 8:00 and brushed her teeth.*

Pk. **1.** park. (Found on maps and signs and in addresses.) ▸ *Forest Pk., Illinois* ▸ *Central Pk.* ▸ *Gorky Pk.* **2.** peak. (The summit of a mountain. Found on maps and signs.) ▸ *PIKE'S PK. NEXT EXIT* ▸ *Lenin Pk.*

PK psychokinesis. (Initialism. The paranormal ability to move physical objects with the power of the mind.) ▸ *When toys flew around the nursery, Sally's parents brought her to a paranormal institute specializing in PK.*

pkg. package. (An enclosed box or container.) ▸ *Get one pkg. free with $5 purchase with coupon!* ▸ *Pick up pkg. at post office.*

pkt. packet. (A small package.) ▸ *5 pkts. per crate*

PKU phenylketonuria. (Initialism. A metabolic disorder that can cause mental retardation in infants if not treated. Found in medical texts and on packaging of products that contain certain artificial sweeteners.) ▸ *Some diet soft drinks can be dangerous for people with PKU.*

Pkwy. parkway. (Found on maps and signs and in addresses.) ▸ *935 Diversey Pkwy.*

P&L profit and loss. (Initialism. A financial statement that details an individual's or company's profits and losses over a given time period.) ▸ *Smithco's P&L statement sent many investors into a panic.*

pl. AND **plur.** plural. (Denoting more than one; the opposite of singular. Found in language textbooks and dictionaries.) ▸ *fox—sing.; foxes—pl.* ▸ *1st pers. pl.*

Pl. place. (Found on maps and signs and in addresses.) ▶ *9351 Park Pl.* ▶ *St. James Pl.*

Plat. plateau. (A geological term for a elevated flat stretch of land. Found on maps and in addresses and geography texts.) ▶ *Tavaputs Plat., Utah*

plat. platoon. (A military term for a group of squads and a subsection of a troop.) ▶ *4th plat.*

PLO Palestine Liberation Organization. (Initialism. A political organization whose main objective is to establish the secular nation of Palestine as it existed before 1948.) ▶ *The PLO and Israelis met in Madrid to discuss peace in their wartorn homeland.*

plur. See *pl.*

P.M. post mortem. (Initialism. Latin: after death. Usually refers to a post mortem examination or an autopsy.) ▶ *The coroner's P.M. examination revealed that the poet had been bludgeoned with a brick.*

PM **1.** postmaster. (Initialism. The head of a post office.) ▶ *PM General.* ▶ *Arthur Williams, PM Chase Park Branch* **2.** *post meridiem.* (Initialism. Latin: after noon. Used to designate the time from noon to midnight. Not used with the phrases *in the afternoon* or *in the evening*, which mean the same thing as *PM*. Commonly seen abbreviated with periods, [P.M.], in lower-case letters, [pm, p.m.], or in small caps [PM, P.M.]. Compare with *ante meridiem* at *AM.*) ▶ *The news is broadcast at 10:00 PM.* ▶ *Taylor was born at 4:32 pm.* **3.** prime minister. (Initialism. The chief executive of a parliamentary government.) ▶ *PM Thatcher greeted President and Mrs. Reagan as they left Air Force One.*

Pm promethium. (The chemical symbol for Element 61.)

PMG postmaster general. (The head of the United States postal system.) ▶ *Until the creation of an independent postal service in 1970, the PMG was a member of the president's cabinet.* ▶ *The first PMG was Samuel Osgood, who served under George Washington from 1789 to 1791.*

PMS premenstrual syndrome. (Initialism. Physical and emotional afflictions, such as bloating and irritability, that precede a menstrual period.) ▶ *Pauline remarked that PMS never gave her cramps, only slight headaches.* ▶ *"Don't irritate me today, I've got PMS," Lily warned everyone.*

pmt. See *payt.*

p/n AND **p.n.** promissory note. (Initialism. A written pledge to pay a specified amount of money to a specific person or institution on demand or a predetermined date.) ▶ *p/n #3404821, due January 31, 1956*

p.n.g. *persona non grata.* (Initialism. Latin: an unwelcome person.) ▶ *What famous financier was seen hiding behind the Clark-Smith's piano, a true p.n.g.?*

P.O. post office. (Initialism. An office where mail is routed, stamps can be purchased, and mailboxes can be rented.) ▶ *P.O. Box 350*

PO **1.** Petty Officer. (A position of rank in the U.S. Navy.) ▶ *He hoped to make PO in a year.* **2.** purchase order. (Initialism. A document authorizing and detailing the purchase of specific items.) ▶ *PO #43-321023* ▶ *The Art Department's PO for acrylic paint was returned because it had been filled out incorrectly.*

Po polonium. (The chemical symbol for Element 84.)

P.O.E. port of entry. (Initialism. A port with a customs office that admits aliens and foreign goods into a country. Found on forms.) ▶ *P.O.E.: New York City*

PO'ed pissed off. (Initialism. Annoyed. Vulgar slang. Caution with *piss.*) ▶ *"Don't get me PO'ed, or I'm liable to slug you," Keith told his roommate.*

Pol. 1. Poland. (A country of eastern Europe.) ▶ *Warsaw, Pol.* 2. Polish. ▶ *Pol. sausage*

pol. polite. (A form of the word *you* used in languages that distinguish between a polite "you" and a familiar "you." The polite form is usually used in addressing superiors and strangers. Found in language textbooks and dictionaries. See *fam.*) ▶ *German: du (fam. sing.), Sie (pol. sing.), ihr (fam. plur.), Sie (pol. plur.)*

pol politician. (Clipping.) ▶ *A month before the election, all the pols up for reelection began making contact with their constituents.* ▶ *The gossip columnist made note of the pols that were obnoxious at the awards banquet.*

poli sci political science. (Acronym. Pronounced "PAHL-ee SY" The study of the principles and organization of governments.) ▶ *Sally dated a poli sci major her junior year and endured political arguments throughout the presidential campaign.*

pop. population. (The number of people living in a certain area. Found on signs and maps and in texts, charts, and atlases.) ▶ *El Paso (1990 pop. 515,342)* ▶ *Welcome to Mud River—Pop. 253*

Port. Portugal. (A western European country between Spain and the Atlantic Ocean.) ▶ *Lisbon, Port.*

pos. 1. positive. (A mathematical term for a quantity greater than zero.) ▶ *pos. integer* 2. positive. (Pertaining to an uninflected adjective or an adverb, as opposed to the comparative and the superlative. Found in language texts and dictionaries.) ▶ *hot (pos.), hotter (comp.), hottest (sup.)* 3. positive. (A medical term for the presence of a

poss.

condition.) ▶ *pos. antibody* **4.** positive. (A photography term for a print where light and shadow correspond to the light and shadow of the subject.) **5.** positive (A physics term for an electric charge with a deficiency of electrons.) ▶ *The pos. end of a battery is marked with a "+."*

poss. **1.** possession. (Ownership.) ▶ *Jane Roe, charged w/ poss. of marijuana, Cell 34.* **2.** possessive. (Pertaining to the relationship between an owner and the object owned. Found in language textbooks and dictionaries.) ▶ *poss. adjective* ▶ *poss. case* ▶ *my (poss. pronoun.)* **3.** possible. (Something that could happen or could be truthful.) ▶ *If poss., pick up Liz at 5.*

POSSLQ person of opposite sex sharing living quarters. (Acronym. Pronounced "POSS-il-KYU." A United States Census term.) ▶ *"Are you seeing each other or just POSSLQing?" Sandra asked her sister.*

pot. potential. (Something that could be, but is not yet; latent.) ▶ *pot. energy*

POW Prisoner of War. (Initialism. A member of the military held captive by the enemy.) ▶ *Hank was captured by the Viet Cong and placed in a POW camp.*

pp. the plural of *p.*

pp **1.** past participle. (A form of a verb used with an auxiliary verb to indicate completion of an action. The past participle in the following sentence is italicized: "The Eagle has *landed*." Found in grammar textbooks.) ▶ *eaten (pp)* ▶ *run (pp)* **2.** pianissimo. (A musical direction: Very soft.)

PP prepositional phrase. (A linguistic symbol used in analyzing sentence structure to indicate prepositional phrases.) ▶ *prep. + NP = PP* ▶ *"in the huge purple box" (PP)*

ppb parts per billion. (Initialism.) ▶ *Gold makes up 2 ppb of the earth's crust.*

ppd. 1. postpaid. (Indicating that postage has been prepaid.) ▶ *It was shipped ppd.* 2. prepaid. (Indicating that something has been paid for in advance. Found on bills, invoices, and the like.) ▶ *$30.00 ppd. 6/1/90*

ppm parts per million. ▶ *Zinc makes up 76 ppm of the earth's crust.*

P.P.S. post postscript. (Initialism. A second additional thought added to the bottom of the letter, used after the postscript. See also *P.S.*) ▶ *P.P.S.: Call me immediately!!!*

PQ 1. *Parti Québécois.* (A political party in Quebec favoring separation from Canada.) 2. Province of Quebec, Canada. (The official two-letter post office abbreviation. See also *Que.*) ▶ *Montreal, PQ H3C 3J7*

pr. AND **pres.** present. (A verb tense denoting a current action or condition, as opposed to the future or the past. Found in language textbooks and dictionaries.) ▶ *pr. indicative* ▶ *go (pr.), went (past), will go (fut.)*

pr. pair. (A set of two objects.) ▶ *6 pr. sunglasses* ▶ *12 pr. contact lenses*

Pr. Prince. (The son of a king or queen; the head of a principality.) ▶ *Pr. Andrew* ▶ *Pr. Charles is next in line to the British throne.*

PR 1. public relations. (Initialism. Relating to the use of media publicity to develop a positive image.) ▶ *The chemical company's PR team wrote a series of commercials emphasizing its beneficial products in order to downplay the recent toxic spill.* ▶ *The last-place candidate hired a top-notch PR firm to enhance his name recognition among the electorate.* ▶ *All the PR in the world couldn't salvage the mayor's position in the community* *after he was caught smoking cocaine with his children.* **2.** Puerto Rico. (The official two-letter post office abbreviation.) ▸ *San Juan, PR 00904* **3.** Puerto Rican. (Initialism. A slang term; usually derogatory.) ▸ *Protesters demonstrated at City Hall the day after the mayor referred to the Puerto Rican community as "a bunch of PRs."*

Pr praseodymium. (The chemical symbol for Element 59.)

PRC People's Republic of China. (Initialism. The official name of China.) ▸ *Beijing, PRC* ▸ *The PRC is the most populous nation on the planet.*

pred. predicate. (The part of the sentence consisting of the verb and its auxiliaries, modifiers, and complements; the opposite of the subject. The predicate of the following sentence is in italics: "The poodle with short white hair *bit the old dog that limped across the sidewalk.*" Found in language textbooks and dictionaries.) ▸ *pred. nom.* ▸ *pred. adj.*

pref. **1.** preface. (An introduction to a book.) ▸ *Pref.—p. 3* **2.** preference. (A choice. Used as a clipping in the phrase "no pref," referring to college students who have not chosen a course of study.) ▸ *After declaring "no pref" for two years, Kelly was forced to think about what she wanted to major in.* **3.** prefix. (A particle added to the front of the word to create a new word with a new meaning.) ▸ *un- (pref. meaning "not")* ▸ *re- (pref. meaning "again")*

prem. **1.** premium. (A periodic payment for insurance.) ▸ *ins. prem. $45/month* **2.** premium. (A grade of gasoline that has a higher octane rating than regular.) ▸ *prem. $1.35/gal.*

prep. preposition. (Pertaining to a word that indicates a grammatical or spatial relationship. Found in grammar

prob.

textbooks and dictionaries.) ▸ *prep. phrase* ▸ *above (prep.)*

prep preparatory (Clipping. A class or school that prepares students for college.) ▸ *Bill's parents sent him to an exclusive prep school.* ▸ *Theresa's schedule was jammed with college prep classes, including calculus, physics, and advanced placement English.* ▸ *"Did you know Bob prepped at Choate?"*

pres. 1. See *pr.* 2. president. (Sometimes pronounced as a clipping, "prez." The leader of a political entity or organization.) ▸ *Pres. Bush addressed the electorate of New Hampshire.* ▸ *Pres. Smith spoke to the shareholders of the company.* ▸ *Elect Monica Jones for Student Council Pres!*

Presb. Presbyterian. (A Protestant denomination.) ▸ *First Presb. Church of Boston*

prev. previous. (Prior.) ▸ *prev. experience required* ▸ *see prev. entry*

prim. primary. (The first; the original; the most basic.) ▸ *prim. colors (red, blue, yellow)* ▸ *St. Stephen Prim. School*

prin. principal. (The head of a school, college, or organization.) ▸ *Prin. Kathy Jones will speak at the May 15 board meeting.*

priv. AND **pvt.** private. (Belonging to a person or a group and not the public.) ▸ *priv. property* ▸ *pvt. office*

pro professional. (Clipping. An expert in a field or sport.) ▸ *pro sports* ▸ *Brad played pro ball for the Giants.* ▸ *Sally's a pro when it comes to poker.*

prob. 1. probable. ▸ *prob. cause of death* 2. probably. ▸ *"Jim, I can't go today. Tomorrow is prob. OK," wrote*

prod.

Anne. **3.** problem. (A question of some degree of difficulty. Used as a clipping in the phrase *no prob*, meaning "it wasn't difficult" and sometimes "you're welcome.") ▸ *Homework: even-numbered probs. on page 42.* ▸ *Prob. 2: Find the cube root of 329,321.* ▸ *"How was the physics test?" Mark's parents asked him. "No prob," he replied.* ▸ *"Thanks for running to the store for me," Aunt Martha said. "No prob," replied Stephanie.*

prod. **1.** produce. (Fresh food, as in a supermarket.) ▸ *prod. section* **2.** product. (An item available for consumer consumption.) ▸ *Consumer Prod. Safety Comm.* **3.** production. (The process of making items available for consumer consumption.) ▸ *prod. line* ▸ *prod. plant* ▸ *U.S. STEEL PROD. (1979, by month)*

prof. **1.** professional. (Not amateur. See also *pro*.) ▸ *prof. wrestling* ▸ *prof. actor* **2.** professor. (Sometimes a clipping. A tenured instructor in a university.) ▸ *The prof didn't show after twenty minutes, so we all left.* ▸ *Prof. Williams kept a supply of hard candy on her desk to give to students who stopped by to visit her.*

pron. **1.** pronoun. (A word that takes the place of a noun or noun phrase. Found in language textbooks and dictionaries.) ▸ *she (pron.)* ▸ *il (French pron.)* ▸ *indef. pron.* **2.** pronounced. (The way that something is spoken.) ▸ *P. G. Wodehouse (pron. "wood-house") 1881-1975*

prop. **1.** proper. (Pertaining to a noun that names a person, a specific place [city, state, community], or a specific group of people. In English, proper nouns are capitalized and rarely follow an article. Contrast with common nouns.) ▸ *dog (com.); Fido (prop.)* ▸ *month (com.); April (prop.)* **2.** property. (Something that is owned.) ▸ *Keep out: Private Prop.* **3.** property. (A piece of land or real estate.) ▸ *For sale: 20-acre prop. next to river* **4.** property. (An attribute or quality of something.)

▸ *List 3 prop. common to mammals* **5.** proposition. (In logic and mathematics, a statement that is to be proven or analyzed.) ▸ *Prop.: If sheep are white and clouds are white, then sheep are clouds.* **6.** proprietor. (The owner of a store or property.) ▸ *Marshalltown General Store, Jake Wilson, prop.*

prop property. (Clipping. A theater, film, and television term for an object used on the set, except for costumes and the set itself.) ▸ *prop manager* ▸ *The actor playing King Richard placed his dagger and his hump on the prop table.* ▸ *"Prop check! The house will open in five!" announced the stage manager to all the actors.*

pros. atty. prosecuting attorney. (A public official who prosecutes suspected lawbreakers on behalf of the people or the government.) ▸ *I want to see the pros. atty. in my chambers immediately.*

Prot. Protestant. (The non-Catholic, non-Orthodox Christian denominations, such as Methodist, Baptist, and Lutheran, among many others.) ▸ *member of a Prot. demonination.*

prov. **1.** province. (A political division of a larger government entity.) ▸ *Prov. of Manitoba* **2.** provost. (The administrative head of a college or university.) ▸ *Prov. Clark officiated at commencement.*

Prov. Proverbs. (An Old Testament book of the Bible. See *O.T.*) ▸ *Prov. 15:2—The tongue of the wise adorneth knowledge: but the mouth of fools bubbleth out folly.*

PRT personal rapid transit. (Initialism. An automated light rail transportation system consisting of cars for four to six passengers that travel along a track to a specific destination.) ▸ *Four congested suburbs vied to be the testing site of the newly developed PRT system.*

P.S.

P.S. 1. postscript. (Initialism. An additional thought added to the bottom of a letter.) ▸ *P.S.: Jean just walked in, and she says "Hi!"* **2.** public school. (Initialism. A school that is funded by public taxes.) ▸ *John attended P.S. 54 until his dad was transferred, and they moved to another district.* ▸ *The mayor visited P.S. 91 today to speak with fourth graders about their view of the future.*

Ps. Psalms. (An Old Testament book of the Bible. See *O.T.*) ▸ *Ps. 129:1 Out of the depths I have cried to thee, O Lord.*

PSA public service announcement. (Initialism. A free television or radio announcement of a public event, health tip, and other information broadcast for the benefit of the listening audience.) ▸ *In between sets, Cindy played PSAs that detailed the warning signs of diabetes, the dangers of drunk driving, and the upcoming local high school football games.* ▸ *Instead of commercials, the college radio station played a specific amount of PSAs each hour.*

p's and q's (Found in the phrase *Mind your p's and q's*, meaning to behave oneself. Alternate theories of the origin include (a) "pints and quarts," meaning to keep track of the pints and quarts of alcohol consumed, and (b) p's and q's are easily mistaken for each other and one needs to keep aware of them.) ▸ *"Mind your p's and q's," the baby-sitter warned the children.*

PSAT/NMSQT Preliminary Scholastic Aptitude Test/National Merit Scholarship Qualifying Test. (Initialism. A standardized test taken in high school to determine National Merit Scholars.) ▸ *"All students taking the PSAT/NMSQT, please report to the library with two sharpened #2 pencils."*

PSC Pisces. (The astrological abbreviation for the zodiacal constellation of Pisces.) ▸ *PSC (February 20 to March 20)*

Pt

psi pounds per square inch. (Initialism. A unit of pressure.) ▶ *Air pressure at sea level is equal to 14.7 psi.*

PST Pacific Standard Time. (Initialism. The standard time in the western United States from late October to early April. It is seven hours behind Greenwich Time.) ▶ *12:30 P.M. PST* ▶ *When traveling to Los Angeles, Irwin forgot to change his watch to PST and missed his first five appointments.*

psych. psychology. (Sometimes a clipping. Pronounced "SIKE." The study of the mind and mental processes.) ▶ *We'll need two volunteers for a psych experiment.* ▶ *I fell asleep in psych class this morning.* ▶ *Psych. Dept.*

pt. **1.** part. (A division of a larger entity or group.) ▶ *I need pt. 2 of the manuscript.* ▶ *A Nightmare on Elm Street—Pt. 4* **2.** See *p*.

Pt. **1.** Point. (A piece of land that sticks out into a body of water.) ▶ *Cedar Pt., Ohio* **2.** Port. (A harbor where cargo ships can load and unload. Also used as a place name in cities with harbors. Found on maps and signs and in addresses.) ▶ *Pt. Authority* ▶ *Pt. Elizabeth, New Jersey* ▶ *Pt. Huron, Michigan*

PT **1.** Pacific Time. (Initialism. The standard time in the western United States.) ▶ *Seattle (PT)* ▶ *The State of the Union Address will be broadcast live (9 ET/6 PT)* **2.** part-time. (Initialism. Employment less than a full work week. Used in classified advertisements and in employment descriptions. Compare with full-time at *FT*.) ▶ *PT help wanted, AM only, donut counter. 555-2022* **3.** physical therapy. (Initialism. The treatment of injury or disease using exercise, massage, and other techniques instead of drugs.) ▶ *She was in PT for three months after the accident.*

Pt platinum. (The chemical symbol for Element 78.)

PTA Parent-Teacher Association. (Initialism. An organization of parents and teachers within a school district who meet to address issues facing the school.) ▸ *The PTA urged the school board to ban the books they found offensive.*

pty. proprietary. (An owner or a group of owners, or relating to them.)

Pu plutonium. (The chemical symbol for Element 94.)

pub. **1.** public. (Relating to the people or the community.) ▸ *pub. utilities* ▸ *New York Pub. Library* ▸ *pub. service announcement* **2.** published. (Refers to the issuance of a written work.) ▸ *The 1976 Old Farmers Almanac (pub. 1975)* ▸ *City Government Finances (pub. by the U.S. Bureau of the Census)* **3.** publisher. (The company or person who publishes written materials.) ▸ *Pub.: Random House*

PUD planned unit development. (Acronym. A thoroughly designed commercial and/or residential project in which all aspects, including the buildings, the streets, the infrastructure, and the environmental impact are controlled.) ▸ *The legislature rezoned 160 acres of farmland to allow the construction of a PUD along the tollway.*

Pvt. Private. (A military title for the lowest rank of the Army and the Marine Corps.) ▸ *Pvt. MacDonald and Pvt. Hendricks reported to the mess hall for KP.*

pvt. See *priv.*

Q

q. **1.** AND **qt.** quart. (A unit of liquid volume, equal to 2 pints or 32 ounces; a unit of dry volume equal to 2 pints.) ▶ *one q. milk.* ▶ *It needs three qts. of oil.* **2.** quarter. (1/4 of the total. See also *Q* and *quar.*) **3.** AND **qto.** quarto. (A book made up of quarto pages, which are sheets folded twice to make up four leaves [eight pages] about 9″ × 12″.)

Q **1.** quarter. (One-fourth of a dollar or 25¢. Used as a column heading to keep track of loose change, as in a cash register.) **2.** question. (Often used in conjunction with A—Answer.) ▶ *Q: Have you ever voted for the communist party?* **3.** queen. (Used on playing cards. In the series *J, Q, K, A.*) *With a poker face, Arthur bluffed, holding only 2♥, 3♣, 8♦, 10♠, and Q♥ in his hand.* **4.** queen. (A game piece in chess.)

Q&A question and answer. (Initialism. Relating to speeches and lectures, the time when people in the audience can ask specific questions of the speaker or panel.) ▶ *After Mrs. Smith lectured about day-care centers, she fielded a Q&A session.*

QB quarterback. (A football term for the offensive player who calls the signals and controls the plays.) ▶ *The QB*

QC

for the New York Giants was traded to the Minnesota Vikings.

QC 1. quality control. (Initialism. A business concept involving the production of defect-free products through rigorous inspection and maintenance of materials and machinery so that defective parts never reach the consumer.) ▸ *The QC department analyzed the broken spring in order to correct the situation.* 2. [to] quality control [something]. (Initialism. To act aggressively to assure the quality of one's products or services.) ▸ *We have two full-time people QC-ing our systems at all times.*

q.d. *quaque die.* (Initialism. Latin: daily. A medical term used on prescriptions indicating a drug or medicine should be taken once a day.) ▸ *4 tbsp. q.d.*

Q.E.D. *quod erat demonstrandum.* (Initialism. Latin: that which was to be demonstrated. Used in geometry and other branches of mathematics at the end of formal proofs to indicate that the initial hypothesis was proven.)

q.i.d. *quater in die.* (Initialism. Latin: four times a day. A medical term used on prescriptions indicating a drug or medicine should be taken four times a day.) ▸ *2 tablets q.i.d.*

QM 1. quartermaster. (Initialism. A petty officer who attends to the ship's helm and its navigational equipment.) ▸ *The QM on duty when the frigate hit the iceberg went down with the ship.* 2. quartermaster. (Initialism. A military officer who provides troops with quarters, clothing, supplies, and equipment.) ▸ *Private Smith tore his pants and obtained a new pair from the QM.*

QSO quasi-stellar object. (Initialism. A celestial object that produces a vast amount of energy. The same as *qua-*

sar.) ▶ *QSO's might be the centers of very distant galaxies.*

qt. See *q*.

qto. See *q*.

qty. quantity. (An amount. Found on forms and labels to indicate the number of objects being referred to.) ▶ *qty. 350*

quad. 1. quadrangle. (Sometimes a clipping. A four-sided figure.) ▶ *The students hung out on the quad between classes.* 2. quadrant. (One of four parts; in geometry, one of the four sections determined by the horizontal and vertical axes.) ▶ *(-3,-2) is a point in quad. III.*

quar. 1. quarter. (A division into four, often refers to the division of a school or fiscal year. See also *q, Q*.) ▶ *Advanced Lighting Design—Fall Quar.—Room 205/10:20 am.* ▶ *4th Quar. earnings were better than expected.* 2. quarterly. (Occurring four times a year. Often in reference to a publication.) ▶ *Ethan's story was printed in the university's Quar. Review.*

quasar quasi-stellar object. (Blend. A celestial object that produces a vast amount of energy. The same as *QSO*.) ▶ *Quasars might be the centers of very distant galaxies, but the scientific community has not yet proven this.*

Que. Quebec. (See also *PQ*.) ▶ *Ottawa, Que.*

quint quintuplet. (Clipping. One of five children born at one birth.) ▶ *My grandmother's attic had a lot of memorabilia concerning the Dionne Quints.*

q.v. *quod vide.* (Initialism. Latin: which see.) ▶ *frog (q.v.)*

R

® registered trademark. (Appears on packaging and written information about a brand-name product.) ▶ *Sue cleaned her windows with Glass Plus®, a cleaning product manufactured by Dow.*

R. **1.** Rabbi. (The spiritual leader of a Jewish congregation.) ▶ *R. Wallenstein organized a Hebrew school trip to Israel.* **2.** AND **Riv.** river. (Found on maps and in texts. A natural stream of water that empties into a lake, ocean, or another river.) ▶ *Missouri R.* ▶ *Amazon R.*

r AND **rad.** radius. (The line segment from the center of a circle to its circumference.) ▶ *The diameter of a circle is equal to 2r.* ▶ *The area of a circle is equal to πr^2*

R **1.** receiver. (A football player whose duty is to catch a forward pass.) **2.** restricted. (Initialism. A movie rating in the series *G, PG, PG-13, R, NC-17, X*. It indicates that children under the age of 17 cannot be admitted unless accompanied by a parent or guardian.) ▶ *Friday the 13th (R)* ▶ *A concerned group of parents protested the lax management of the theater complex that had been allowing 12- and 13-year olds to see R-rated movies.* **3.** repeat. (Initialism. Used in television listings to denote a program that has already been broadcast.) ▶ *Laverne & Shirley (R)* **4.** AND **Rep.** Republican. (One of the two national political parties in the United States.) ▶ *Sen. Robert Davis (R)* **5.** reverse. (Initialism. Found on gearshifts. It indicates that a vehicle is in reverse.) **6.** AND **rew.** rewind. (Found on tape recorders, VCRs, and other devices. It indicates the button that will reverse the tape.) ▶ *Press R and then play it again.* **7.** AND **rt.** right. (Used in writing directions, including stage directions, or to differentiate between two objects, such as speakers, on a control panel.) ▶ *Turn R at the stoplight past the bowling alley.* **8.** Roentgen. (A unit of radiation measurement, named for Wilhelm Roentgen, the discoverer of X rays.) **9.** rook. (A game piece in chess.) **10.** run(s). (A baseball term. A point scored by a player rounding the bases and touching home plate. Used in charts following the progress of a baseball game. The example is to be interpreted to mean 5 runs, 7 hits, 2 errors.) ▶ *5 R 7 H 2 E*

R.A. Rear Admiral. (Initialism. A ranking position in the U.S. Navy.) ▶ *Walter Stoker, R.A.*

Ra radium. (The chemical symbol for Element 88.)

RA resident assistant. (Initialism. A student living in a wing or floor of a college dormitory who is employed by the university to provide counsel and watch over the students living there.) ▶ *Eileen calmly explained to her RA that her pet snake had escaped.*

rad. **1.** See *r.* **2.** radian. (A unit used to measure angles, equal to approximately 57.296°, or the angle formed at the center of the circle with the length of the arc between the points of intersection of the angle and the circle equal to the radius.) ▶ *30° = π/6 rad.*

radar radio detecting and ranging. (Acronym. A device using radio waves to detect an object, usually aircraft, and to pinpoint its location, distance, altitude, and speed.) ▶ *Radar enables pilots to fly planes when visibility is zero.*

RAF Royal Air Force. (Initialism. The air force of the United Kingdom.) ▶ *The Queen awarded a posthumous medal of honor to the brave RAF pilot shot down by enemy aircraft.*

RAM random-access memory. (Acronym. The temporary storage space for a computer program in use and the document on the screen, which is erased when the computer is turned off.)

R&B rhythm and blues. (Initialism. A style of blues music with a strong rhythm.) ▶ *While visiting Chicago, Randy went to see a few R&B combos in his old neighborhood.*

Rb rubidium. (The chemical symbol for Element 37.)

RB running back. (A football position.) ▶ *Bo Jackson (RB) was the number one NFL draft pick in 1986.*

RBC red blood cell. (Initialism. Also known as an erythrocyte. A cell without a nucleus that circulates in the bloodstream, carrying oxygen from the lungs to body tissues and carbon dioxide from body tissues to the lungs.) ▶ *A low RBC count indicates anemia.*

RBI run(s) batted in. (Initialism. A baseball term found in statistic charts and other texts. A batter whose action allows a teammate to score a run receives an RBI.) ▶ *Hank Aaron holds the record for the most RBIs with 2297.*

RC **1.** Red Cross. (An international organization that administers health programs and provides relief to victims of war and natural disasters. See also the American Red Cross at *ARC*.) ▶ *A team of RC workers flew to northern Iraq to assess the plight of the Kurds.* ▶ *The RC was formed as a result of the Geneva Convention in 1864.* **2.** Roman Catholic. (Initialism. A Christian denomination, headquartered in the Vatican, in Italy, under the authority of the Pope.) ▶ *John F. Kennedy (RC)* ▶ *Within the city limits are five secondary schools (3 public, 1 Bapt., 1 RC).*

RCA Record Corporation of America. (Initialism. An American record company.) ▶ *RCA was bought out by General Electric in 1986.*

RCAF Royal Canadian Air Force. (Initialism. The air force of Canada.) ▶ *Sam saw no future in his tiny village in Manitoba, so he joined the RCAF.*

RCMP Royal Canadian Mounted Police. (Initialism. The Canadian police force that patrols by horse. Members are known as *Mounties*.) ▶ *Davis Johnson, RCMP.*

rcpt. receipt. (The written acknowledgement of a bill payment.) ▶ *This bill was paid on 5/15 (see copy of rcpt. #4302), so it would be appreciated if you would stop sending past-due notices.*

rct. recruit. (A new member of an organization, particularly of the armed forces.)

R&D research and development. (Initialism. The division of a company dedicated to researching and developing new products or services or improving upon old products and services.) ▶ *A healthy business firm requires a strong R&D department to prevent stagnation.*

Rd. road. (Found on maps and signs and in addresses.) ▶ *Irving Park Rd.* ▶ *Elizabeth lives on Grand Blanc Rd. east of Nichols Rd.*

RD rural delivery. (Postal delivery to rural, outlying areas. See also *RFD*.)

RDA recommended daily allowance. (Initialism. Found primarily on food labeling and in nutritional charts. The

R.E.

amount of vitamins, minerals, and other substances that the Food and Drug Administration recommends should be taken every day.) ▸ *Sugar Overdrive Cereal provides 10% of the RDA of six essential nutrients and can be a part of your balanced breakfast!*

R.E. real estate. (Initialism. The acquisition and ownership of land and buildings on it.) ▸ *Alan worked for an R.E. investment office.*

Re rhenium. (The chemical symbol for Element 75.)

rec. 1. record. (The label for the record button on a video or audio tape recorder.) ▸ *To record, press rec. and play simultaneously.* 2. record. (A document or file of an account of events, information, or political papers.) ▸ *Rec. #420-10293-C* 3. recorder. (A government official whose duty is to keep records of official documents.) ▸ *Rec. of Deeds* 4. recreation. (Often a clipping. Activities pursued in one's free time.) ▸ *Director of Parks and Rec.* ▸ *The rec room had a pool table, a pinball machine, and a wide-screen TV.*

rec'd. AND **recd.** received. (Marked on a document to indicated that money or a product has been received.) ▸ *Rec'd. 4/12/90* ▸ *$50 recd. Jan. 15, 1973*

red. reduced. (A lesser amount, usually in reference to sale prices or caloric intake.) ▸ *Entire inventory red. 30% to 50%! Buy now and save!* ▸ *Red. Calorie Formula!*

ref. 1. refer. (An indication to reference a source.) ▸ *Ref. to page 45 for further discussion.* 2. reference. (Dictionaries, encyclopedias, almanacs, and other books of information used for research.) ▸ *Materials from the ref. section cannot be checked out and must be used here at the library.* 3. reformed. (Protestant denominations descended from Calvinism, including the Presbyterian Church and the United Church of Christ.) ▸ *Christian*

Ref. Church. **4.** refrain. (A verse repeated as marked after the stanza of a song or poem. Found in hymnals and other songbooks.) ▸ *Verses 1-3 and Ref. by J.S. Bach.*

ref **1.** referee. (Clipping. The arbiter of a sporting event.) ▸ *"Come on, ref, that was a foul!" the irate fan yelled from the stands.* ▸ *On the first day of the job, the ref stood in front of the mirror, admiring his black-and-white striped shirt.* **2.** reference. (A person who can provide a recommendation. Used in hiring situations, usually in the plural.) ▸ *Working parents seek live-in nanny. Refs required.* ▸ *We followed up on your refs, and they all liked you.*

reg. **1.** regent. (A board member of certain state universities.) ▸ *Reg. Knowles motioned to adjourn the budget meeting.* **2.** regent. (The person running a government in a monarchy when the monarch is not old enough or healthy enough to do so.) **3.** AND **regt.** regiment. (A military division comprised of two or more battalions.) ▸ *4th reg.* **4.** region. (An extensive, homogeneous area of earth.) ▸ *the sub-Saharan reg.* ▸ *the midwest reg.* **5.** register. (The range of a musical instrument or human voice.) ▸ *upper reg.* **6.** registrar. (An official whose duty is to keep records, primarily a school official who registers students, issues report cards, and maintains student records.) ▸ *Ofc. of the Reg., Room 345.* **7.** regular. (A size in between small and large, often found on menus. See also *med.*) ▸ *Buy two burgers and get a reg. fries free.* ▸ *Hot Coffee (small $1, reg. $1.25, large $1.50)* **8.** regular. (A grade of gasoline. Originally used to refer to leaded gasoline. Toward the late 1980s it came to mean the cheapest grade of unleaded gasoline.) ▸ *reg. unleaded $1.21/gal.* **9.** regular. (A geometrical shape whose angles and sides are equal.) ▸ *reg. polygon* ▸ *reg. octagon* **10.** regulation. (A directive issued by the government or other authority.) ▸ *Fire Code Reg. 1432.23* **11.** registered. (Something offi-

regt.

cially recorded or authenticated. The second example means "Registered with the United States Patent Office.") ▶ *Send Grandma's present by reg. mail today.* ▶ *Reg. U.S. Pat. Ofc.*

regt. See *reg.*

REIT real estate investment trust. (Initialism and acronym. A firm that invests its shareholders' capital in real estate acquisition and financing.) ▶ *When the recession undermined a weak real estate portfolio, the president of the largest REIT in the city declared bankruptcy.*

rel. 1. relative. (A member of the family.) ▶ *Name of closest rel. to contact in emergency.* 2. relative. (Pertaining to a dependent clause that refers to an antecedent.) ▶ *rel. pronoun* ▶ *rel. clause* 3. AND **relig.** religion. (A denomination of worship. Found on forms.) ▶ *rel. orientation* ▶ *relig. preference*

relig. See the previous entry.

REM rapid eye movement. (Initialism. The stage of sleep during which dreaming occurs, accompanied by quick, jerky movements of the eyeballs under closed eyelids.) ▶ *The scientist studied the effects of rousing people during the REM stage of sleep.*

rep. 1. republic. (A government with the supreme power vested in an electorate who elects representatives responsible to them.) ▶ *Rep. of Finland* ▶ *Rep. of Peru* 2. republic. (A political unit of the former Soviet Union and Yugoslavia.) ▶ *Ukranian Soviet Socialist Rep.* ▶ *The Rep. of Croatia declared independence from Yugoslavia on June 25, 1991.* 3. republic. (A government whose head of state is not a monarch but usually a president.) ▶ *People's Rep. of China*

Rep. See *R.*

rep 1. repertory. (Clipping. Referring to a theater company presenting more than one play on alternating nights or weekends.) ▶ *"I'm playing Ariel in* The Tempest *and Tybalt in* Romeo & Juliet *at the Shakespeare Rep."* ▶ *After three months of doing four Edward Albee plays in rep, Janet was exhausted.* 2. representative. (Clipping. A member at a meeting or an assembly acting on behalf of a larger group of people.) ▶ *"Our congressional rep voted against the president's veto," the farmer told the patrons at the diner.* ▶ *The Pakistani and the Afghani reps conferred in the corner of the assembly hall.*

req. requirement. (A necessary or mandatory thing.) ▶ *Econ. 401 (req. for finance majors)*

res. 1. reservation. (An arrangement that sets aside a restaurant table, tickets, and other things in advance.) ▶ *Res. Desk* ▶ *res. for 4 at 6:00* 2. reserved. (Something that has been set aside.) ▶ *This section res. for nonsmokers.* 3. resident. (A person who lives in a place; not a visitor.) ▶ *The Plaintiff is a res. of New Smyrna Beach, Florida.* 4. residence. (The place where a person lives.) ▶ *place of res.: 500 Main Street* ▶ *250 Main St. (res.)/10 W. Broad St. (work)*

Res. 1. Reservation. (Public land granted to Native Americans. Used on maps and signs and in addresses.) ▶ *Navajo Indian Res.* ▶ *Ute Mountain Indian Res.* 2. reservoir. (A place where water is collected and stored in large amounts to serve nearby communities.) ▶ *Lake Mead Res.*

ret. retired. (Referring to someone who has withdrawn from working, often due to having reached a certain age. Frequently seen in reference to people who have retired from the military.) ▶ *Cpl. William A. Smith (ret.)*

rev. 1. revenue. (A source of income.) ▶ *Internal Rev. Serv.* ▶ *Dept. of Rev.* 2. revised. (Used to describe publica-

Rev.

tions and statutes that have been corrected and/or updated.) ▶ *Tourists' Guide to Attractions in Ohio (rev.)* ▶ *pursuant to Rev. Stat. 34-1022* ▶ *Statistics from the Commerce Dept., rev. to March* **3.** revolution. (An uprising resulting in radical change.) ▶ *Bolshevik Rev.* ▶ *American Rev.* **4.** revolution. (One full orbit of an object around another object. Used in tables charting the periods of revolution of satellites to planets, planets to stars, stars to centers of galaxies, etc.)

Rev. **1.** Reverend. (A title for the clergy. The term can be used in conjunction with other titles.) ▶ *The Rev. Jesse Jackson presented a speech to the high school class.* ▶ *the Rev. Dr. Pat McCarter* **2.** Revelations. (The final book of the New Testament of the Bible; the Apocalypse.) ▶ *The Rev. of St. John the Divine* ▶ *Rev. 6:8*

rew. See *R*.

r.f. right field. (The baseball outfield position behind first base.) ▶ *Sam Ryan (r.f.)*

rf radio frequency. (Initialism. Any frequency between audible sound and infrared light, approximately .01 to 1,000,000 megahertz.) ▶ *rf transmitter*

Rf rutherfordium. (The chemical symbol for Element 104.)

RFD rural free delivery. (Initialism. Postal delivery to rural, outlying areas, now called rural delivery. See *RD*.)

Rh **1.** rhodium. (The chemical symbol for Element 45.) **2.** a property of red blood cells. (Initialism. The abbreviation is from Rhesus monkeys, the animal in which the substance was first studied. When Rh comes in contact with anti-Rh antibodies, the blood clots.) ▶ *The nurse immediately checked the newborn's Rh factor.*

RH relative humidity. (Initialism. A meteorological term. The ratio of moisture in the air to the maximum amount of moisture possible at that temperature. Used in weather reports and statistical tables.) ▸ *RH 80%*

rhet. rhetoric. (The practice of using words eloquently and effectively.)

R.I. Rhode Island. (See also *RI*.) ▸ *Pawtucket, R.I.* ▸ *Gov. Bruce Smith (R.I.)*

RI Rhode Island. (The official two-letter post office abbreviation. See also *R.I.*) ▸ *Newport, RI 02840*

RICO Racketeer Influenced and Corrupt Organizations. (Acronym. A federal statute providing legislation to curb the influence of organized crime.) ▸ *The bank had to fight off RICO charges when it was rumored that it had secret dealings with the mob.*

R.I.P. *requiescat in pace.* (Initialism. Latin: rest in peace. Inscribed on tombstones, printed on prayer cards, and used in relation to other aspects of death.)

Riv. See *R*.

rm. room. ▸ *Rm. 222* ▸ *detention rm.* ▸ *Returning students, please report to Rm. 100.*

Rn radon. (The chemical symbol for Element 86.)

RN Registered Nurse. (Initialism. Someone who has a degree in nursing, has passed a state board examination, and is licensed to practice nursing. Compare with licensed practical nurse at *LPN*.) ▸ *Chris Werner, RN* ▸ *With the help of two RNs and an intern, Dr. Whitcomb managed to sedate the hysterical patient.*

RNA ribonucleic acid. (Initialism. A nucleic acid and an essential part of every living cell.) ▸ *For her science pro-*

Rom.

ject, Sally made a model of a strand of RNA. ▶ *mRNA* ▶ *tRNA*

Rom. 1. Roman. ▶ *Rom. Catholic* ▶ *Rom. numerals* 2. Romance. (A linguistic term. A branch of the Indo-European language family, from which the modern languages of Italian, French, Spanish, Portuguese, Romanian, Catalan, and Provençal were derived.) ▶ *Rom. languages* 3. Romania. (A country in eastern Europe.) ▶ *Bucharest, Rom.*

ROM read-only memory. (Acronym. A computer term for the permanent information a computer uses to run the system. It is not erased when the power is turned off.) ▶ *All of the basic instructions for starting the computer are in ROM.*

ROTC Reserve Officers' Training Corps. (Usually an initialism. Sometimes an acronym, pronounced "ROT-see.") ▶ *Tom's in ROTC.*

rpm revolutions per minute. (Initialism. The number of times an object goes around each minute, especially used to denote record speed.) ▶ *33-1/3 rpm* ▶ *Most singles are played at 45 rpm.* ▶ *In her grandmother's attic, Inez found some old 78 rpm jazz records.*

RPN reverse Polish notation. (Initialism. A method of entering calculations on certain sophisticated computers and calculators.) ▶ *I had to teach Uncle Earl RPN when he bought a new Hewlett Packard calculator.*

R&R rest and recreation; rest and relaxation. (Initialism. A vacation period spent away from everyday hectic activities.) ▶ *Sam left work at noon on Friday and drove to the club for some well-deserved R&R.*

R.R. 1. Right Reverend. (A religious title for high-ranking church officials.) ▶ *Next Sunday's guest lector will be the*

R.R. E. Vincent Cooley, who will speak on the wages of sin. **2.** rural route. (Initialism. Part of a rural address for mail delivery where there is no street numbering system.) ▶ *Mr. Frank Racek, R.R. #1, Chesaning, Mich.*

RR railroad. (The tracks trains travel on; a railroad company.) ▶ *RR crossing* ▶ *Chicago & Northwestern RR*

RSFSR Russian Soviet Federated Socialist Republic. (Initialism. One of the former fifteen Soviet Republics within the Union of Soviet Socialist Republics that comprised three-fourths of the Soviet Union. See also *USSR*.) ▶ *Boris Yeltsin, president of the RSFSR, guided the breakup of the Soviet Union.*

RSVP *répondez s'il vous plaît.* (Initialism. French: respond if you please. Appears at the bottom of invitations to indicate that the invited guest is to inform the host if he or she will attend.) ▶ *Dinner—7:30 p.m. RSVP.* ▶ *Molly's mother was rather upset because half of the invited guests had not bothered to RSVP.*

Rt. AND **Rte.** Route. (A federal, state, or county, highway. Found on maps and signs.) ▶ *U.S. Rt. 66.* ▶ *RTE. 23 NEXT EXIT*

rt. See *R*.

RTC Resolution Trust Company. (Initialism. The company formed to sell the assets of failed savings and loan institutions following the collapse of the Federal Savings & Loan Insurance Corporation.) ▶ *The developer contacted the RTC about buying a few office buildings.*

Rte. See *Rt*.

Ru ruthenium. (The chemical symbol for Element 44.)

Rus. Russian. (The adjective form of Russia.) ▶ *Rus. literature* ▶ *Rus. president Boris Yeltsin.*

RV recreational vehicle. (Initialism. A trailer, motor home, or other vehicle that can be lived in during travel and camping.) ▸ *Uncle Bob bought an RV and took Aunt Ellen and the kids on a three-week trip to the Grand Canyon.*

Rx prescription. (The pharmacy symbol for prescription, derives from the Latin *recipe*. It is pronounced either "prescription" or "AR-EX." The meaning has been extended to mean an antidote for a problem.) ▸ *All Rx filled here, pharmacist on staff 24 hours a day.* ▸ *The country is suffering a recession; the president's Rx is lowering interest rates and encouraging people to spend money they don't have.*

S

s. AND **sing.** singular. (Denoting or referring to a single item. Compare with *pl.* Found in language textbooks and dictionaries.) ▸ *cat (sing.) cats (pl.)* ▸ *1st person s. (I am)* ▸ *2nd person s. (you are)* ▸ *3rd person s. (it is)*

S. Sea. (A large body of salt water, surrounded entirely or partly by land. Found on maps and in texts.) ▸ *Caribbean S.* ▸ *S. of Okhotsk*

s AND **sec.** second. (A unit of time equal to 1/60 of a minute.) ▸ *The race was completed in 4h 12m 32s.*

S 1. Saturday; Sunday. (A day of the week. In the series *S, M, T, W, T, F, S*. If context will not distinguish Saturday from Sunday, *Sa* should be used. See also *Sa, Sat.*) **2.** September. (Often used in graph columns or rows to chart the month-by-month progress of something. See also *Sep.*) ▸ *S 28 1966* **3.** AND **sm.** small. (Initialism. A size, usually related to clothing and food. In the series *XS, S, M, L, XL.*) ▸ *"I have this blouse in S or M. Which would you prefer?" the clerk asked.* ▸ *Cotton Candy S $1.50 L $2.50* **4.** soprano. (In most choral music arrangements, the highest range of a female voice. In the series *S, A, T, B*. See also *sop.*) **5.** AND **S.** south. (A compass direction. Found on maps and signs and in addresses. See also *N, E, W.*) ▸ *#9 S to 95th Street* ▸ *S. America* ▸ *400 S. State*

Street ▸ *S. Bend, Indiana* ▸ *Turn S at the stoplight.* **6.** sulfur. (The chemical symbol for Element 16.)

s.a. *sine ano.* (Initialism. Latin: without date. Refers to undated correspondence and materials.) ▸ *Mr. Smith's letter to me (s.a., copy enclosed) made several accusations that I would like to address.*

S.A. 1. South Africa. (A country in southern Africa.) ▸ *Soweto, S.A.* **2.** South America. (The southern continent of the Western Hemisphere.) ▸ *Banco de Buenos Aires, S.A.*

Sa Saturday. (A day of the week. In the series *Su, M, Tu, W, Th, F, Sa*. See also *S, Sat*.) ▸ *Sa Aug 15*

Sab. Sabbath. (The day of rest and worship: Jewish people observe Saturday as the Sabbath; most Christians observe Sunday as the Sabbath.)

SAC Strategic Air Command. (Acronym. The United States Air Force's long-range bomber and missile force, headquartered at Offut Air Force Base in Nebraska.) ▸ *Warren dreaded living in Omaha, knowing a large portion of the Soviet arsenal was aimed at SAC headquarters.*

SADD Students Against Drunk Driving. (Acronym. A student organization whose goal is to reduce alcohol-related driving accidents and deaths.) ▸ *Sally started up a SADD chapter in her high school.*

SAG 1. Sagittarius. (The astrological abbreviation for the zodiacal constellation of Sagittarius.) ▸ *SAG (November 23 to December 21)* **2.** Screen Actors Guild. (Acronym. The professional labor union of motion picture, television, video, and commercial actors.) ▸ *Becky moved to Chicago, earned her SAG card, and then moved to Hollywood to audition for television.*

SALT Strategic Arms Limitation Talks. (Acronym. A series of meetings beginning in 1969 between the United States and the Soviet Union in an attempt to limit nuclear weapon production.) ▶ *SALT I (1969-1972)* ▶ *SALT II (1979)*

SASE self-addressed stamped envelope. (Initialism or acronym, pronounced "SAY-zee." An envelope, with the sender's address and proper postage, included in a request for information or materials so that the person returning the SASE does not have to pay for postage or take the time to address an envelope.) ▶ *For more information, send $5 and a SASE to this station.*

Sask. Saskatchewan. (A Canadian province. See also *SK*.) ▶ *Saskatoon, Sask.*

Sat. Saturday. (See also *S, Sa.*) ▶ *Open House—Sat., May 25, at 4:00 PM.*

SAT Scholastic Aptitude Test. (Initialism. A standardized exam required by many colleges for admission. It tests verbal and mathematical ability.) ▶ *Jane's excellent SAT score enabled her to select whichever university she preferred.* ▶ *Hal went to a wild party the night before the SAT but managed to stay awake for the duration of the test.*

Sax. Saxon. (Referring to one of the German tribes that entered what is now England in the fifth century. Used in dictionaries.)

sax saxophone. (Clipping. A woodwind [musical] instrument.) ▶ *The newly formed jazz band advertised in the local newspaper for another sax player.*

Sb antimony. (The chemical symbol for element 51. The symbol is derived from Latin *stibium*.)

SBA Small Business Administration. (Initialism. Created in 1953, a United States government agency that protects the interests of small businesses by providing loans, offering management information, and ensuring that a proportionate amount of government contracts are awarded to them.) ▸ *Colette opened her bakery as soon as her SBA loan was approved.*

sc small capitals. (Initialism. In typesetting, a font of capital letters smaller than the regular text font.) ▸ HELLO, THERE *(uc);* HELLO, THERE *(sc)*

S.C. **1.** See *S. Car.* **2.** Supreme Court. (The highest federal tribunal, a nine-member court that interprets the United States Constitution. Also, the highest court in most states.) ▸ *Arkansas S.C.* ▸ *United States S.C.*

sc. **1.** scene. (A division of play, usually a division of an act.) ▸ *"Life's but a walking shadow, a poor player that struts and frets his hour upon the stage and then is heard no more."*—Macbeth *Act V, sc. v.* **2.** science. (An area of knowledge or study.) ▸ *soc. sc.*

SC **1.** Security Council. (Initialism. The branch of the United Nations that works to maintain peace by arbitrating or preventing disputes before they escalate into international conflict.) ▸ *Members of the UN must adhere to decisions made by the SC.* ▸ *The five permanent members of the SC are China, France, Russia, the United Kingdom, and the United States.* **2.** South Carolina. (The official two-letter post office abbreviation. See also *S. Car.*) ▸ *Aiken, SC 29801*

Sc scandium. (The chemical symbol for Element 21.)

S. Car. AND **S.C.** South Carolina. (See also *SC.*) ▸ *Georgetown, S. Car.* ▸ *Sen. Sam Harris (S. Car.)*

sch. school. (An institution of education or one of its divisions.) ▸ *Sch. of the Performing Arts.* ▸ *Sch. of Music at State Univ.*

sci-fi science fiction. (Acronym. A genre of film and literature involving real, imagined, or anticipated scientific advances. The same as *SF.*) ▸ *Kevin read Asimov's* The Foundation Trilogy *and immediately got hooked on sci-fi novels.*

SCO Scorpio. (The astrological abbreviation for the zodiacal constellation of Scorpio.) ▸ *SCO (October 23 to November 22)*

scuba self-contained underwater breathing apparatus. (Acronym. A device that allows divers to breathe under water.) ▸ *Marty and Ginnie went scuba diving off the Bahamas on their honeymoon.*

S.D. AND **S. Dak.** South Dakota. (See also *SD*.) ▸ *Pierre, S.D.* ▸ *Gov. George Thomas (S.D.)*

SD South Dakota. (The official two-letter post office abbreviation. See also *S.D.*) ▸ *Aberdeen, SD 57401*

S. Dak. See *S.D.*

SDI Strategic Defense Initiative. (Initialism. A highly technical United States defense program that, if built, would destroy incoming missiles and other objects in flight.) ▸ *As the Cold War came to a close, critics suggested that money allocated to SDI might be better spent on social services, such as housing for the poor.*

SDS Students for a Democratic Society. (Initialism. A radical political organization created in 1962 that used student strikes and demonstrations to oppose social injustice and the Vietnam Conflict.) ▸ *The university police broke up the SDS march through the center of campus.*

SE **1.** southeast. (A compass direction halfway between due south and due east. In addresses and signs, it refers to a location in the southeast quadrant of a city.) ▶ *The path of the total eclipse passed over SE Asia.* ▶ *Detroit is located in the SE part of Michigan.* ▶ *Library of Congress, 100 Independence Ave., SE, Washington, DC* **2.** Standard English. (The variation of English used in formal writing and speaking.) ▶ *The bidialectical students conversed in SE at school and used the local variant on the streets.*

Se selenium. (The chemical symbol for Element 34.)

SEATO Southeast Asia Treaty Organization. (Acronym. From 1954 to 1976, an alliance of nations located or having interest in Southeast Asia to combat Communist aggression.) ▶ *Australia, Britain, France, New Zealand, Pakistan, the Philippines, Thailand, and the United States were members of SEATO.* ▶ *Pakistan discontinued membership in SEATO in 1973.*

sec. AND **secy., sec'y.** **1.** secretary. (Someone who takes care of correspondence and record keeping for an individual, a company, or a club.) ▶ *Now hiring: Office sec. w/ 5 yrs. exp.* ▶ *Student Council Secy.* **2.** secretary. (The chief of a government department.) ▶ *Sally Rand, Sec. of State* ▶ *Max Fox, Sec'y. of the Treasury* **3.** See *s*.

sec secant. (In trigonometry, the reciprocal of the cosine, or, in a right triangle, the ratio of the hypotenuse to the adjacent side of a given acute angle.) ▶ $sec x = 1/cos x$

SEC Securities and Exchange Commission. (Initialism. A federal agency established in 1934 that enforces federal laws concerning buying and selling stocks and bonds. Also investigates complaints and regulates national stock exchanges.)

secy. AND **sec'y.** See *sec*.

sem. **1.** seminary. (A school where people are trained to become members of a religious order or to pursue a vocation in religion.) ▸ *St. John's Theological Sem.* **2.** semester. (A division of a school year.) ▸ *fall sem.* ▸ *Spring Sem., 1988*

Sem. Semitic. (Relating to the language and culture of the Semites, including the languages of Aramaic, Arabic, and Hebrew.)

sen. **1.** senate. (A legislative body of politicians; in the United States and most of the states, the upper house of the legislature.) ▸ *a member of the Colorado Sen.* ▸ *the U.S. Sen.* **2.** senator. (An appointed or elected representative who serves in a senate.) ▸ *Sen. Tom Harris (D-Iowa)* ▸ *Sen. Todd Davis (R-New Hampshire)* **3.** AND **sr.** senior. (The fourth year of high school or college.) ▸ *English 401—sen. level* **4.** AND **sr.** senior. (Of a higher status or level.) ▸ *sen. member* ▸ *sr. vice president*

Sep. AND **Sept.** September. (See also *S.*) *Sep. 14, 1941*

Sept. See the previous entry.

seq. *sequentes; sequentia.* (Latin: the following [singular; plural]. Used in texts to reference a series.) ▸ *Pp. 45-60, seq.*

SF science fiction. (Initialism. A genre of film and literature involving unique life forms or real or imaginary science. The same as *sci-fi.*) ▸ *Greg was caught reading SF comic books in class.*

sf **1.** square feet. (A measure of area equal to 144 square inches.) ▸ *200 sf.* **2.** See the following entry.

sfz AND **sf** sforzando. (A musical direction: Sharply accented.)

SG AND **surg. gen.** surgeon general. (The head medical officer of the United States Public Health Service.) ▸ *Former SG Koop issued a statement about the dangers of cigarettes.*

Sgt. Sergeant. (A noncommissioned military officer or police officer.) ▸ *Sgt. Wilson was released by the enemy after being held hostage for forty-five days.* ▸ *Sgt. Edwards filed the missing persons report.*

s&h shipping and handling. (The additional cost levied when purchased items are mailed to cover shipping and handling expenses. See also *p&h*.) ▸ *Order Your Crush-O-Matic Now (Only $39.95 plus $4.95 p&h)* ▸ *As promised, Rita's money was refunded, less the s&h charge.*

SI *Systeme Internationale d' Unités.* (Initialism. French: International System of Units. The internationally accepted system of weights and measures, using the metric system along with additional scientific units of measure.) ▸ *The basic SI unit of weight is the gram.*

Si silicon. (The chemical symbol for Element 14.)

SIDS sudden infant death syndrome. (Acronym. Applied to babies who die unexpectedly and of undetermined cause, usually during sleep. Also called crib death.) ▸ *The coroner stated that the many cases of SIDS in the previous month were coincidental.*

sin sine. (In trigonometry, the ratio of the opposite side of a given acute angle in a right triangle to the hypotenuse.)

sing. See *s*.

sitcom situation comedy. (Acronym. A television program comedy format involving a set of characters in a succession of episodes.) ▸ *The critic felt that few of the season's new sitcoms were even remotely funny.* ▸ The Cosby Show *(sitcom)*

S.J. Society of Jesus. (Initialism. A Roman Catholic religious order founded by Ignatius Loyola in 1534. Its members are called Jesuits.) ▶ *Fr. Peter Flanagan, S.J.*

SK Saskatchewan, Canada. (The official two-letter post office abbreviation. See also *Sask.*) ▶ *Moose Jaw, SK S6H 4R4*

Slav. Slavic. (A branch of the Indo-European language family.) ▶ *Slav. Studies majors meet at 3:00 for orientation.* ▶ *Czech is a W. Slav. language.*

S&M sadism and masochism. (Initialism. Relating to the derivation of sexual pleasure from the infliction of pain.) ▶ *There were many ads in the personal section placed by people interested in S&M.*

sm. See *S*.

Sm samarium. (The chemical symbol for Element 62.)

SMU Southern Methodist University. (Initialism.) ▶ *SMU Mustangs*

s.n. *sine nomine*. (Initialism. Latin: without name; anonymous or unknown.) ▶ *A copy of the June 15 letter (s.n.) addressed to my father is enclosed.*

Sn tin. (The chemical symbol for Element 50. The symbol is derived from Latin *stannum*.)

SNAFU AND **snafu** situation normal all fouled up. (Acronym. A term of military origin that describes events that have not gone as planned; a glitch. See the note at *FUBAR*.) ▶ *A snafu in the software caused all the phone lines on the East Coast to go dead.*

s.o. strike out. (Initialism. A baseball term for an out made by a batter after getting three strikes.)

so. 1. See *S*. 2. southern. (Relating to the south.) ▶ *so. accent* ▶ *So. California*

SOB son of a bitch. (Initialism. A derisive term directed at someone held in contempt. Use caution with *bitch*.) ▶ *"That stupid SOB in the red car cut me off!" Harry yelled to the police officer at the scene of the accident.*

soc. 1. social. (Relating to the people of a community or society.) ▶ *soc. worker* ▶ *soc. Darwinism* 2. socialism. (A system by which all members of a society share the work and the production; private ownership is eliminated.) 3. socialist. (Relating to or adhering to the Socialist Party.) ▶ *Union of Soviet Soc. Rep.* ▶ *Eugene V. Debs (Soc.)* 4. society. (A distinct group of people who form a community; an organization of people based on a common element.) ▶ *Soc. of Friends.*

SoHo south of Houston Street. (Acronym. An artsy neighborhood on Manhattan's lower west side.) ▶ *On Saturdays, Terry often browsed through the galleries in SoHo but never bought anything.*

sol. 1. solution. (The answer to a problem.) ▶ *sol. on next page* 2. soliloquy. (A theater term for a monologue that reveals the thoughts of a character to the audience but not to other characters in the play.) ▶ *During sol., Anne crosses L to corpse.*

SOL shit out of luck. (Initialism. An offensive expression meaning totally without success or luck. Sometimes euphemized as "short out of luck." Use caution with *shit*.) ▶ *Having just missed the last bus back to the city, John turned to his friend and muttered, "Well, I guess we're SOL."*

Sol. Is. Solomon Islands. (A chain of islands in the southwest Pacific near New Guinea. About three-fourths of the land area is part of the nation of the Solomon Islands.

The remainder is part of Papua New Guinea.) ▶ *Honiara, Sol. Is.*

Som. Somalia. (A country in eastern Africa along the Indian Ocean and Gulf of Aden.) ▶ *Mogadishu, Som.*

sonar sound navigation and ranging. (Acronym. A device that sends sound waves through water. The vibrations reflect off objects, enabling the detection of submarines or other objects, and the depth of the water.)

sop. See *S*.

SOP standard operating procedure. (Initialism. The rules and regulations underlying the way a job is done or an office is run. The term has bureaucratic overtones and suggests there is no flexibility to bend from the rules.) ▶ *The clerk let the water overflow from the basin because SOP mandated that only a union janitor could unclog the sink.*

soph. sophomore. (Also a clipping. A student in the second year of high school or college.) ▶ *soph. class* ▶ *You look sort of old for a soph.*

Sov. Soviet. (Relating to the former Soviet Union.) ▶ *Armenian Sov. Soc. Rep.*

Soweto Southwest Townships. (Acronym. A segregated district southwest of Johannesburg, South Africa.) ▶ *The news correspondent traveled to Soweto and Johannesburg to show the disparity of living conditions under apartheid.*

s.p. *sine prole*. (Initialism. Latin: without issue. A legal abbreviation to denote that someone is childless. See also *d.s.p.* and *s.p.s.*) ▶ *Mr. and Mrs. Henry P. Smith (s.p.)*

Sp. 1. Spain. (A country in western Europe on the Atlantic Ocean and Mediterranean Sea.) ▸ *Toledo, Sp.* 2. AND **Span.** Spanish. ▸ *Sp. cuisine.* ▸ *Span. Riviera*

sp. 1. species. (A biology term, referring to a grouping of similar organisms that can produce fertile offspring.) ▸ *gen. Homo; sp. sapiens* 2. AND **sp** spelling. (Indicates a spelling error or spelling uncertainty.) ▸ *Meet with Mr. Szczepanski (sp?) at 3:00.*

Sp Spanish. (The Spanish language. Used in dictionaries to show the etymology of a word.) ▸ *mesquite < Sp mezquite*

Span. See *Sp.*

SPCA Society for the Prevention of Cruelty to Animals. (Initialism. An organization found in many countries to protect the welfare of animals. See also *ASPCA*.) ▸ *Henry took the abandoned puppy to the local SPCA.*

spec. special. ▸ *spec. education* ▸ *spec. edition*

specs specifications. (Clipping. Exact, detailed characteristics.) ▸ *plans and specs* ▸ *The architect spilled coffee all over the specs and had to start from scratch.*

SPF sun protection factor. (Initialism. Used on suntan lotion and sun-block products to indicate the level of protection from sunburn; the higher the number, the more protection provided.) ▸ *Joan's skin was so fair that she used SPF 24 whenever she went outside.*

s.p.s. *sine prole superstite.* (Initialism. Latin: without surviving issue. A legal term describing someone whose offspring are all dead. See also *d.s.p.* and *s.p.*) *The tycoon died s.p.s., so the estate was split among cousins and second cousins.*

Sq. Square. (An abbreviation used in addresses.) ▶ *Buckingham Sq.* ▶ *Fashion Sq. Mall*

sq. square. (Of two dimensions. Compare with *cu.*, an indication of three dimensions.) ▶ *sq. ft.* ▶ *sq. root*

Sr. **1.** Senior. (A man who has a son with the same name.) ▶ *Desi Arnaz, Sr.* **2.** Señor. (Spanish title, equivalent to the English *Mister.*) ▶ *Sr. Octavio Paz.* **3.** Sister. (A religious title for a nun.) ▶ *Sr. Mary Elizabeth*

sr. See *sen.*

Sr strontium. (The chemical symbol for Element 38.)

SRO **1.** standing room only. (Initialism. Used in theaters, stadiums, and auditoriums to indicate that all of the seats are sold out.) ▶ *The enthusiastic SRO crowd at the Ella Fitzgerald concert persuaded her to do a third encore.* **2.** single room occupancy. (Initialism. A welfare housing unit similar to a studio or kitchenette.) ▶ *The alderman prohibited the developer from transforming badly needed SROs into condominiums.*

SS. Saints. (The plural of *St.*) ▶ *SS. Peter & Paul Parish is sponsoring a clothing drive next weekend. Donations are most welcome.*

SS **1.** *Schutzstaffel.* (Initialism. German: protective rank, an elite military unit. The special police of the Nazi Party.) ▶ *The sight of the SS in the streets frightened the Dutch townsfolk.* **2.** Social Security. (Initialism. The United States life insurance and old age pension system.) ▶ *SS #* ▶ *SS benefits* **3.** steamship. (A large naval vessel, usually, but not necessarily, powered by steam.) ▶ *The SS Minnow crashed onto an uncharted desert isle.*

SSA Social Security Administration. (Initialism. An agency within the United States Department of Health and Human Services that administers Social Security benefits to the retired, disabled, the families of wage earners who have died, etc.) ▶ *I had to write the SSA six times before they even looked at my problem.*

SSE south-southeast. (A compass direction halfway between due south and southeast.) ▶ *Winds from the SSE at 10 mph.*

SSI Supplemental Security Income. (Initialism. A government cash assistance program that provides money to the economically disadvantaged, the elderly, and the disabled.) ▶ *State governments may supplement federal SSI payments with state-supported programs.* ▶ *The SSI program is administered by the Department of Health and Human Services.*

SSR Soviet Socialist Republic. (Initialism. One of the fifteen divisions of the former Union of Soviet Socialist Republics.) ▶ *Estonian SSR* ▶ *Kirghizian SSR*

SSS Selective Service System. (Initialism. The United States military draft program.) ▶ *The SSS requires that every American male must register for the draft by his eighteenth birthday.*

SST supersonic transport. (Initialism. An aircraft that operates faster than the speed of sound.) ▶ *The Concorde is an example of an SST.*

SSW south-southwest. (Initialism. A compass direction halfway between southwest and due south.) ▶ *The aircraft flew SSW toward the airport.*

St. **1.** Saint. (A holy person officially recognized by a church.) ▶ *St. Peter* ▶ *St. Anne* ▶ *St. Valentine's Day* **2.** street. (Found on maps and signs and in addresses.) ▶ *Take the 87th St. bus to the end of the line.* ▶ *400 South State St.*

st. 1. state. (A major political or governmental unit; pertaining to such a unit. Capitalized when referring to a particular state.) ▸ *St. of Illinois.* ▸ *Jane attended Oklahoma St. for two years.* ▸ *st. capitol* 2. AND **stat.** statute. (An official regulation.) ▸ *The city officials bickered about St. 24A-89 regarding smoking in public places.*

ST standard time. (Initialism. Universalized time, expressed in terms of the time at Greenwich, England. Contrast with Daylight Time at *DT* in which clocks are set an hour behind to allow more daylight in the evening. Used in combination with the names of the time zones. See *EST*, *CST*, *MST*, and *PST*.) ▸ *Arizona and portions of Indiana always remain on ST.*

sta. station. (A building used as a regular stopping place in a transportation system.) ▸ *Penn. Sta.*

START Strategic Arms Reduction Treaty. (Acronym. A treaty signed on July 31, 1991, by the presidents of the USSR and the United States to reduce strategic offensive arms by almost a third during the 1990s.) ▸ *START, negotiated since 1982, was signed by Bush and Gorbachev in Moscow in 1991.*

stat. See *st.*

stats statistics. (Clipping. Numeric data providing information about a specific topic.) ▸ *The coach posted the players' stats on the board for last week's game.*

STD sexually transmitted disease. (Initialism. A disease such as gonorrhea, syphilis, genital herpes, chlamydia, and AIDS spread through sexual contact. See also *VD*.) ▸ *The university's STD clinic provided testing and counseling at no cost.*

Ste. saint. (French: saint [fem.]. Used in place names settled by the French and named for female saints.) ▶ *Sault Ste. Marie*

STOL short takeoff and landing. (Partial acronym. Pronounced "STALL." Aircraft that can take off and land on a shorter runway than conventional aircraft.) ▶ *STOL runway*

STP 1. standard temperature and pressure. (Initialism. A constant used in science to compare phenomena that vary depending on temperature and pressure.) 2. Scientifically Treated Petroleum. (Initialism. A brand name of a popular motor oil.) ▶ *Joe filled his gas tank and bought a couple of cans of STP.*

Str. Strait. (A narrow passage of water connecting two larger bodies of water. Found on maps.) ▶ *The Str. of Hormuz connects the Persian Gulf and the Gulf of Oman.* ▶ *Bering Str.*

stud. student. (Someone enrolled at a school, college, or university.) ▶ *Stud. Council meeting today during 5th period.*

Su Sunday. (In the series *Su, M, Tu, W, Th, F, Sa.* See also *S* and *Sun.*) ▶ *Su Feb 2*

sub. 1. suburb. (An incorporated city or town outside of a major metropolis.) ▶ *Balwin (St. Louis sub.), Missouri* 2. suburban. (Relating to the suburbs.) ▶ *Sub. Transportation Authority*

sub 1. submarine. (Clipping. A ship that can operate under water.) ▶ *The sub torpedoed the enemy aircraft carrier.* 2. submarine. (A large sandwich with several ingredients.) ▶ *David ordered five ham and cheese subs to go.* 3. substitute. (Clipping. A replacement; a stand-in for the regular thing.) ▶ *The detention room monitor* *subbed for the calculus teacher, so the class ordered pizza.* ▶ *The physics class had a sub for the day, so they goofed off.*

subj. 1. subject. (A topic, as of a lecture or article.) ▶ *Tonight's subj.: Toxic waste* 2. subject. (A noun or noun phrase that performs the action carried out by the verb. In the following sentence, the subject is italicized: "*The old man with a cane ate an apple.*" Found in language textbooks.) ▶ *simple subj.* 3. subjunctive. (The semantic state of a sentence with a verb expressing a condition contrary to fact, such as doubt or supposition. In English, the subjunctive is limited to the use of *were* instead of *was* in contrary-to-fact clauses beginning with *if*. Found in language books and dictionaries.) ▶ *"If I were..."/subj.*

Sud. Sudan. (A northeast African nation.) ▶ *Khartoum, Sud.*

suff. suffix. (A particle or morpheme placed at the end of a word. Found in language textbooks and dictionaries.) ▶ *-ite (suff.)* ▶ *-al (suff.)*

Sun. Sunday. (See also *S* and *Su.*) ▶ *Sun. Special— 2 eggs, 2 pieces of bacon for $2.22*

SUNY State University of New York. (Initialism. The state university system of New York state.) ▶ *SUNY-Binghamton* ▶ *SUNY at Oswego*

sup. 1. superlative. (A form of an adjective or an adverb indicating the greatest amount of the sense of the adjective or adverb, as compared to the positive degree and the comparative degree. Most superlative constructions use the suffix *-est* or are preceded by the word *most*. Found in language textbooks and dictionaries.) ▶ *wet (pos.); wetter (comp.); wettest (sup.)* ▶ *tedious (pos.); more tedious (comp.); most tedious (sup.)* 2. supine. (Denotes the infinitive construction, consisting of the word *to* and an uninflected verb. Found in language textbooks.) ▶ *to exacerbate—(sup.)*

super superintendent. (Clipping. The manager of a building or an institution. The written abbreviation is usually *supt.*) ▶ *Julie, call the super, the kitchen sink is leaking again!*

supt. **1.** superintendent. (Someone in charge of an institution, such as the head of a school district.) ▶ *Central School District Supt. Eilene Anderson did not comment on the strike.* **2.** a super. ▶ *Timothy Sanders, Building Supt.*

sur. surplus. (An excess quantity remaining at the end of a specific period.) ▶ *Grain Sur. by State—1988*

surg. gen. See *SG*.

Sw. Swedish. ▶ *Sw. meatballs*

SW **1.** shortwave. (Referring to shortwave radio, which receives or transmits radio waves shorter than those used by commercial broadcasters. Found on the panels of radios that can be tuned into shortwave stations.) ▶ *AM/FM/SW Brand Name Radios—25% NOW!* **2.** southwest. (A compass direction halfway between due south and due west. In addresses and signs, it refers to a location in the southwest quadrant of a city.) ▶ *The weather bureau reported tornado funnels SW of the city.* ▶ *Federal Emergency Management Agency, 500 "C" St., SW, Washington, DC 20472*

SWAT special weapons attack team; special weapons and tactics. (Acronym. A paramilitary police squad.) ▶ *The authorities called in the SWAT team to rescue the people being held hostage by the crazed bank robber.* ▶ *The*

SWAT team burst into the warehouse and made the largest drug bust in the state's history.

Swaz. Swaziland. (A south African country between South Africa and Mozambique.) ▶ *Mbabane, Swaz.*

Switz. Switzerland. (A landlocked central European country.) ▶ *Zurich, Switz.*

sym. **1.** symphony. (A musical composition for a full orchestra.) ▶ *Beethoven's Sym. #5 in C minor* **2.** symphony [orchestra]. (Describing orchestras that perform symphonies.) ▶ *Detroit Sym. Orch.*

syn. synonym. (A word that has a similar meaning to another word. Found in language textbooks and dictionaries.) ▶ *mad (syn. angry; upset)*

Syr. Syria. (A Middle East country on the east shore of the Mediterranean Sea.) ▶ *Damascus, Syr.*

T

T. AND **tbsp.** tablespoon. (Initialism. A unit of measurement equal to three teaspoons or 1/2 fluid ounce, used primarily in recipes. Sometimes called a "big T" to distinguish it from *t.*) ▸ *Add 1 T. vanilla.*

t. 1. AND **tsp.** teaspoon. (Initialism. A unit of measurement equal to 1/3 of a tablespoon or 1/6 fluid ounce, used primarily in recipes. Sometimes called a "small T" to distinguish it from *T.*) ▸ *Mix in 2 t. salt.* **2.** tense. (The quality of the verb expressing the time of the action. Found in language textbooks and dictionaries.) ▸ *future t. (future tense)* **3.** time. (In physics, chemistry, and other sciences, the variable used to represent time in algebraic formulas.) **4.** transitive. (Pertaining to a verb that has a direct object. More commonly abbreviated as *vt.*) ▸ *run (t.)*

T 1. tenor. (In most choral music arrangements, the highest range of a male voice. In the series *S, A, T, B.*) **2.** Tuesday; Thursday. (A day of the week in the series *S, M, T, W, T, F, S*. If context does not distinguish Tuesday from Thursday, *Th* should be used for Thursday. See also *Thur., Thurs.*) ▸ *Thanksgiving—T Nov. 25* ▸ *Election Day —T Nov. 4* **3.** treasury. (Initialism. Relating to the United States Treasury Department.) ▸ *At the birth of each grandchild Frank bought a T bond that would mature* *after the child had gone to college.* ▸ *All T bills mature within one year.* ▸ *$1000 T Note* **4.** true. (Initialism. Used in logic and in true and false tests. See also *F.*) ▸ *Robert blanked out during the history test and marked every answer T.*

T&A tits and ass. (Initialism. Visible or notable breasts and buttocks, especially in a stage, film, or television production. Use caution with this expression.) ▸ *The musical production was filled with T&A.*

TA **1.** teaching assistant. (Initialism. Someone, usually a graduate student, teaches college classes or assists a professor in doing so.) ▸ *The TA's accent was so thick that Brian couldn't understand his lecture.* **2.** to be a teaching assistant. (Initialism.) ▸ *As part of her stipend, Jane had to TA two classes a term.*

Ta tantalum. (The chemical symbol for Element 73.)

Tan. Tanzania. (A country in eastern Africa on the Indian Ocean.) ▸ *Dar es Salaam, Tan.*

tan tangent. (Clipping. A trigonometric function. In a right triangle, it is the ratio of the opposite side of an acute angle to its adjacent side.) ▸ $tan x = sin x / cos x$

taser tele-active shock electronic repulsion. (Acronym. The trademarked name of a stun gun that shoots electrified projectiles.) ▸ *The woman fired her taser at the attacker, rendering him immobile while she called the police.*

TAU Taurus. (The astrological abbreviation for the zodiacal constellation of Taurus.) ▸ *TAU (April 21 to May 20)*

taxi taxi cab, itself a shortening of *taximeter cabriolet*. (Clipping. A metered vehicle that transports passengers for a fee.) ▸ *The taxi careened around the corner, almost hitting three pedestrians.*

t.b. trial balance. (A bookkeeping term for a ledger showing the credits and debits to be equal.) ▶ *March 1985 t.b. —final revision*

Tb terbium. (The chemical symbol for Element 65.)

TB tuberculosis. (Initialism. A communicable disease in which nodules form in body tissues, especially the lungs.) ▶ *Kelly died shortly before science brought TB under control.* ▶ *The TB vaccine administered to children is not effective on adults.*

TBA to be announced. (Initialism. Used to describe an undecided aspect of an upcoming event.) ▶ *The next meeting is at 12 noon on April 15th, the location TBA.* ▶ *Date: January 23. Time: TBA* ▶ *In its 25th season, the Regal Theatre Company will present* Hamlet, Private Lives, Equus, Deathtrap, *and a fifth play TBA.*

TBHQ tertiary butylhydroquinone. (Initialism. A preservative in food products. Found in lists of ingredients on food packaging.) ▶ *After eating the chocolate bar, the hypochondriac worried about possible side effects from TBHQ.*

tbsp. See *T.*

Tc technetium. (The chemical symbol for Element 43.)

T-cell thymus-derived cell. (Initialism. A lymph cell of the body that fights against infection and foreign particles.) ▶ *helper T-cell* ▶ *People with immunodeficiency disorders generally have low T-cell counts.*

TD **1.** technical director. (Initialism. In theater, the person who oversees the technical aspects of production.) ▶ *The TD stayed at the theater until 3 A.M., helping the designer hang lights.* **2.** touchdown. (Initialism. A football term for the play made by touching the football to the ground past the opposing team's goal line.) ▶ *Central*

temp.

High's impressive TD in the last ten seconds tied the game.

TDD telecommunication device for the deaf. (Initialism. A device connected to a telephone allowing hearing-impaired people to communicate by telephone lines by using a video monitor; used to indicate the TDD telephone number.) ▶ *The grandchildren bought their grandparents a TDD device so that they would be able to contact the police in case of an emergency.* ▶ *TDD # (312)555-1299*

Te tellurium. (The chemical symbol for Element 52.)

tech. technical. (Sometimes a clipping. Relating to a specialization within a field, especially within industrial arts and sciences.) ▶ *tech. assistant* ▶ *Denise graduated from Cal Tech last year and now has a job in mechanical engineering.*

tech 1. technical [person]. (Clipping. A person with technical knowledge or skills.) ▶ *It won't run. You will have to call in a tech to repair it.* 2. [do] technical [things]. (To perform the duties of a techinal director or manager; to design and manage the technical aspects of a theatrical production.) ▶ *"Did you find someone to tech your show yet?" Jeanne asked the director.*

tel. telephone. (Used in written form, often on letterheads, business cards, advertisements, and signs to indicate a telephone number.) ▶ *Smithco International—tel. (312)555-4040.* ▶ *Free kittens! Tel. (517)555-8431.*

temp. 1. temperature. (Occasionally a clipping. The degree of hotness or coldness.) ▶ *8:00 A.M. temp.—45°* ▶ *"What temp do you want the water at?" Jan asked the head chef.* 2. temporary. (For the time being; not permanent.) ▶ *We regret the temp. inconvenience.*

temp temporary [worker]. (Clipping. A worker hired or contracted from an agency to fill a temporary job need.) ► *While the regular receptionist was on vacation, Dr. Jones was impressed with the temp's congeniality and accuracy.*

Tenn. Tennessee. (See also *TN.*) ► *Memphis, Tenn.* ► *Gov. Joan Davis (Tenn.)*

Ter. AND **Terr.** Terrace. (Used on maps, signs, and in addresses.) ► *1400 N. Sandburg Ter.* ► *Windsor Terr.*

term. terminal. (The last stop of a transit line or any important station along a transit line.) ► *bus term.*

Terr. 1. Territory; Territories. (An area of land ruled by a governing body but not having full status as a state, province, or other principal division.) ► *Northwest Terr.* ► *Dakota Terr.* 2. See *Ter.*

TESL teaching of English as a second language. (Acronym. Pronounced "TEH-sul." Relating to teaching English as a second language. See also *ESL, TESOL.*) ► *Deborah took some TESL courses to help prepare her for teaching in inner city schools.*

TESOL 1. teaching English to speakers of other languages. (Acronym. Pronounced "TEE-sol." A specialist area concerned with teaching English to nonnative speakers.) 2. teachers of English to speakers of other languages. (Acronym. Pronounced "TEE-sol." A national organization dedicated to the advancement of the teaching of English as a second language. See also *TESL.*) ► *A member of TESOL highly recommended a line of textbooks to the college department offering classes in TESL.*

Test. Testament. (A section of the Christian Bible.) ► *Old Test.* ► *New Test.*

Tex. Texas. (See also *TX.*) ▸ *El Paso, Tex.* ▸ *Gov. Sally Smith (Tex.)*

Tex-Mex Texas-Mexican. (Acronym. Mexican-North American food of the type that might be found along the Texas border; Mexican food tailored to North American tastes.) ▸ *Would you like to eat Chinese or Tex-Mex?*

TG transformational grammar. (Initialism. A type of grammar that generates sentences through a series of rules.) ▸ *David dutifully took a TG course, even though he knew linguistic theory had progressed past that stage.*

TGIF Thank God It's Friday. (Initialism. Used on Friday to express relief that the end of the working week is over.) ▸ *TGIF drink specials* ▸ *After the copier exploded and the phone system went dead, the office manager sat in the coffee room muttering, "TGIF."*

Th **1.** thorium. (The chemical symbol for Element 90.) **2.** Thursday. (In the series *Su, M, Tu, W, Th, F, Sa*. See also *T, Thur.,* and *Thurs.*) ▸ *Th Mar 23*

THC tetrahydrocannabinol. (Initialism. The active ingredient in marijuana.) ▸ *THC stays in the bloodstream for thirty days.*

3-D three-dimensional. (Used to describe movies filmed by a special process creating the illusion of depth and to describe related accessories.) ▸ *Jaws 3-D* ▸ *3-D glasses*

3M Minnesota Mining & Manufacturing Company. (The company that manufactures several consumer products such as Scotchguard™ and Post-Its™.) ▸ *3M hired Carolyn to develop products from newly formulated chemical compounds.*

3 R's readin', [w]ritin', and 'rithmetic. (Reading, writing, and arithmetic, the basic fundamentals of a grade school

Thur.

education.) ▸ *The curriculum of the financially strapped school district was limited to the 3 R's.*

Thur. Thursday. (See also *T*, *Th*, and *Thurs.*) ▸ *Watch Chan. 9 next Thur. at 8 p.m.*

Thurs. Thursday. (The same as *T*, *Th*, and *Thur.*) ▸ *Thurs. Mass at 7:15 a.m.*

Ti titanium. (The chemical symbol for Element 22.)

TKO technical knockout. (Initialism. A boxing term for a win awarded to a boxer who has landed sufficient blows to make a knockout inevitable—even though the opponent is not unconscious. By metaphorical extension to other situations relating to any victory that brings down an opponent.) ▸ *The rookie was awarded a TKO in the fifth round after the champion was severely injured.* ▸ *The Coalition Forces TKO'd the Iraqi army less than a week into the war.*

Tl thallium. (The chemical symbol for Element 81.)

TLC tender loving care. (Initialism. Warm attention given to someone or something, such as a baby or a plant.) ▸ *With a little TLC, those droopy geraniums can blossom into the pride of the neighborhood.*

™ trademark. (A legally protected logo, design, or motto used to differentiate a product from other similar products. Compare with ®.) ▸ *Lotus 1 2 3™*

Tm thulium. (The chemical symbol for Element 69.)

TM transcendental meditation. (Initialism. A method of meditation using total physical and mental relaxation to achieve pure consciousness unimpeded by thought.) ▸ *Each evening, Glenn drank a cup of herbal tea and practiced TM in order to forget all of the crises of the day.*

tn. ton. (A unit of weight equal to 2,000 pounds [short ton] or 2,240 pounds [long ton]. A metric ton, or a megagram, is equal to 1,000 kilograms.) ▶ *LOAD WEIGHT ON BRIDGE AHEAD: 12 TN.*

TN Tennessee. (The official two-letter post office abbreviation. See also *Tenn.*) ▶ *Knoxville, TN 37901*

Tnpk. AND **Tpk.** Turnpike. (A limited-access toll road.) ▶ *New Jersey Tnpk.*

TNT trinitrotoluene. (Initialism. A powerful explosive.) ▶ *The railroad crew used tons of TNT to blast a hole through the mountainside.*

TO turnover. (Initialism. A basketball and football term indicating loss of possession of the ball. Found in headlines, statistical tables, and charts.) ▶ *4th Quarter TO Wins Game for State*

TOEFL Testing of English as a Foreign Language. (Acronym. Pronounced "TOE-ful." A standardized test to determine the fluency in English of a nonnative speaker of English. It is required by many universities for admission of foreign students.) ▶ *The university required foreign students to score high on the TOEFL before allowing them to teach undergraduates.*

Tpk. See *Tnpk.*

tr. **1.** transitive. (Pertaining to a verb that takes a direct object. The customary abbreviation is *vt.*) **2.** translated. (Indicates that a writing has been translated from another language.) ▶ The Story of the Stone *(tr. from Chinese by David Hawkes)* ▶ The Boat *(tr.)*

trans(p). transportation. (The way people and products get from one place to another.) ▶ *public trans.* ▶ *The Dept. of Transp. blocked the interstate where the multivehicle crash occurred.*

treas.

treas. 1. treasurer. (The official of a club, company, or organization who is in charge of the finances and accounting of the operation.) ► *Chuck French, treas.* 2. treasury. (The money associated with a club, company, organization, or political entity.) ► *Dept. of Treas.* ► *Sec. of Treas. Ralph Smith*

trib. tributary. (A river that flows into a larger river.) ► *Malakal, Sudan, is a city on the White Nile (a trib. of the Nile).*

trig 1. trigonometry. (Clipping. The mathematical science of the relationships among the sides and angles of right triangles and their practical applications.) ► *Most of the class scored abysmally on the most recent trig test.* ► *The apprentice used trig to calculate the length of the board needed to prop up the flat.* 2. trigonometric. ► *The sine and cosine are two of the most common trig functions.*

tRNA transfer RNA. (Initialism. A form of RNA that combines with messenger RNA to place correctly an amino acid within a chemical chain.) ► *The professor lectured on the exact function of tRNA in the formation of polypeptide chains.*

trop. 1. tropic. (One of the two latitudes about 23.5° north and south of the equator.) ► *Trop. of Cancer* ► *Trop. of Capricorn* 2. tropics. (The land between the Tropic of Cancer and the Tropic of Capricorn.) 3. tropical. (Relating to the tropics; very hot and humid.) ► *Trop. Zone* ► *trop. rain forest* ► *trop. jungle*

TSH thyroid stimulating hormone. (Initialism. A hormone secreted by the anterior pituitary gland that causes the thyroid to make and secrete thyroxin, a hormone that controls body metabolism.)

tsp. See *t.*

TSS Toxic Shock Syndrome. (Initialism. A life-threatening bacterial infection linked to sanitary tampons.) ▶ *The gynecologist told Sarah that her symptoms were indicative of TSS.*

Tu Tuesday. (In the series *Su, M, Tu, W, Th, F, Sa*. See also *T* and *Tue.*) ▶ *Tu January 3*

Tue. AND **Tues.** Tuesday. (See also *T*, and *Tu.*) ▶ *The Frondelles, appearing each Tue. in Feb. at The Front Row!* ▶ *Meet with Carruthers next Tues. at 9.*

Turk. **1.** Turkey ▶ *Ankara, Turk.* **2.** Turkish. ▶ *Turk. cigars* ▶ *Turk. bath*

TV **1.** television. (Initialism. A medium of broadcasting audio and video signals.) ▶ *TV has been a major influence on American culture throughout the last half of the twentieth century.* ▶ *Jerry intended to do his homework, but he stayed glued in front of TV from the moment he came home until he went to bed.* ▶ *Jane went to journalism school to become a TV news broadcaster.* ▶ *The proliferation of cable TV has made the TV antenna a thing of the past.* ▶ *TV dinner* **2.** transvestite. (Initialism. A cross-dresser; someone who dresses as a member of the opposite sex.) ▶ *Thelma realized her husband was a TV when she came home early one night and found him trying on her new lingerie.*

TVA Tennessee Valley Authority. (Initialism. A government corporation established to promote and stimulate economic growth in the Tennessee Valley area.) ▶ *The TVA constructed series of dams to control flooding and generate electric power.*

TWA Trans World Airlines. (Initialism. An international airline.) ▶ *TWA has reduced its routes considerably.*

twp. township. (A political division of a county.) ▸ *The Flint Twp. Business District is centered along Miller and Linden Roads.* ▸ *Evanston Twp. High School* ▸ *Gaines Twp. Fire Station*

TX Texas. (The official two-letter post office abbreviation. See also *Tex.*) ▸ *Galveston, TX 77550*

typo typographical. (Clipping. An error made in typing or transcribing.) ▸ *Reversing two letters is a common typo.*

U

u. **1.** unit. (A division of a larger group, as in the military.) **2.** upper. (Of a higher elevation, for instance, an upstream area of a river.) ▶ *U. Nile*

U **1.** Union. (The faction fighting against the Confederates in the U.S. War Between the States.) ▶ *General Grant (U) eventually became president of the U.S.* **2.** AND **univ.** university. (An institution of higher learning. Usually used in conjunction with the full title of the school.) ▶ *U of M (University of Missouri)* ▶ *SMU (Southern Methodist University)* **3.** uranium. (The chemical symbol for Element 92.)

UA United Artists. (Initialism. A motion-picture company.) ▶ *For a period of time in the 1980s, UA merged with MGM.*

UAE United Arab Emirates. (Initialism. A federation of seven Arab sheikhdoms on the Arabian peninsula along the Persian Gulf.) ▶ *Abu Dhabi, UAE* ▶ *The UAE was aligned with the United States in the Persian Gulf War.*

UAR United Arab Republic. (Initialism. The union of Egypt and Syria from 1958 to 1961. In 1961, the union dissolved, but Egypt kept the name of the United Arab Republic until 1971.) ▶ *The UAR lost the Sinai Peninsula and the Gaza Strip to Israel after the Six-Day War.*

UAW United Automobile Workers. (Initialism. The primary automotive labor union of America.) ▸ *The representatives from the UAW met with officials from GM, Ford, and Chrysler to hammer out a new contract.*

uc upper case. (In typesetting, capital letters.) ▸ *HELLO, THERE! (uc)—hello, there (lc)*

UCLA University of California-Los Angeles. (Initialism.) ▸ *UCLA Bruins*

UCMJ Uniform Code of Military Justice. (The system of military rules used in courts-martial.)

UDAG Urban Development Action Grant. (Acronym. Pronounced "YU-dag." A government program that provides funds to stimulate development in the poorer sections of inner cities.) ▸ *With the help of a UDAG grant, the old theater that had become an eyesore was transformed into a community services center.*

UFO unidentified flying object. (Initialism. Unexplainable objects seen in the sky, often thought to be spaceships from other worlds.) ▸ *The UFO researcher discarded incidents that were easily explained by atmospheric phenomena or hysteria and focused on truly convincing cases.* ▸ *Tom discussed the recurring theme of Cold War-inspired fear that surfaced in 1950s UFO movies.*

UHF ultrahigh frequency. (Initialism. A radio frequency between 300 and 3,000 megahertz. In television broadcasting, the UHF frequencies correspond to channels 14 through 83.) ▸ *In many markets, the new broadcasting network operates on UHF channels.*

UK United Kingdom. (Initialism. The United Kingdom of Great Britain and Northern Ireland.) ▸ *Made in UK*

UL Underwriters Laboratories. (Initialism. The company that approves electrical appliances for use.) ▶ *UL LISTED*

ult. ultimate. (The best. Used frequently in advertising and packaging.) ▶ *Ult. lead-free: $1.56/gal.*

UMW United Mine Workers. (Initialism. The national labor union for miners.) ▶ *The UMW charged the mining company with negligence following the collapse of the mine shaft.*

UN United Nations. (Initialism. An international organization devoted to maintaining global peace, fostering human rights, and solving global crises.) ▶ *Six nations joined the UN in 1991: Estonia, Latvia, Lithuania, the Marshall Islands, Micronesia, and North Korea.* ▶ *George Bush (UN representative, 1971-1973)*

unan. unanimous. (Referring to something agreed upon by all.) ▶ *unan. consent*

UNCTAD United Nations Conference on Trade and Development. (Acronym. A UN program concerned with trade and development issues.) ▶ *UNCTAD helps chart the economic growth of developing nations.*

UNESCO United Nations Educational, Scientific, and Cultural Organization. (Acronym. A UN program that promotes world literacy and the study of cultural development.) ▶ *Through UNESCO, Ellen was trained how to teach illiterate adults how to read.*

UNICEF United Nations International Children's Emergency Fund. (Acronym. A UN program that provides low-cost, community-based health care to children in developing nations.) ▶ *Fillmore Junior High sponsored a raffle and donated the proceeds to UNICEF.*

Unit. Unitarian. (A monotheistic religion tolerant of other religious views. It advocates reason within religion.) ▸ *The Phelps family attended the Third Unit. Church on Main Street.*

univ. 1. universal. (Something that remains constant and true in all environments.) ▸ *univ. grammar* 2. See *U*.

UNIVAC Universal Automated Computer. (Acronym. An early computer of the 1950s.) ▸ *Data on a UNIVAC was stored on magnetic tape.*

UP Upper Peninsula. (Initialism. The more northern of the two peninsulas that make up Michigan.) ▸ *Many of the inhabitants of the UP are of Norwegian or Finnish descent.* ▸ *The Hutchinsons drove up to the UP on the first day of deer season.*

UPC Universal Product Code. (Initialism. The series of lines and bars found on packaging. When a bar code is scanned at a checkout lane at a grocery store, the price of the item is automatically registered and is recorded in a database that controls inventory.) ▸ *Jeanne sent the UPC label from the packs of 25 batteries and received a $10 rebate.* ▸ *The scanner did not properly read the UPC label, so the cashier had to call the deli department for the price of the salami.*

UPI United Press International. (Initialism. An international news agency.) ▸ *The reporter read the news flash as it came over the UPI wire.*

US AND **U.S.** United States [of America]. (Initialism. See also *USA*.) ▸ *The US Senator traveled to Asia on business.* ▸ *After the fall of communism, Ivan could leave Minsk to visit his relatives in the US.* ▸ *Robert would only buy US-built cars.*

USA AND **U.S.A.** **1.** United States of America. (Initialism. See also *US.*) ▸ *Chicago, Illinois, USA* ▸ *Made in USA* ▸ *The USA hockey team faced Czechoslovakia in the Olympic quarterfinals.* **2.** United States Army. (Initialism.) ▸ *Gen. Colin L. Powell, USA*

USAF United States Air Force. (Initialism.) ▸ *Gen. David C. Jones, USAF*

USC University of Southern California. (Initialism.) ▸ *USC Trojans*

USCG United States Coast Guard. (Initialism. A branch of the armed forces that enforces federal maritime law. The USCG is part of the Department of Transportation except during war or as directed by the president, in which case it is a part of the navy.) ▸ *The survivors from the cruise ship accident were rescued by the USCG.*

USDA United States Department of Agriculture. (Initialism. An executive department formed in 1862 to improve farms, conserve natural resources, and inspect and grade the quality of food products.) ▸ *1 dozen USDA grade A large eggs* ▸ *The USDA inspector carefully scrutinized the butcher shop.*

USIA United States Information Agency. (Initialism. A government agency that controls overseas information, including Voice of America Radio broadcasts, and advises the National Security Council of global opinions on U.S. policies.) ▸ *Agents from the USIA disseminated propaganda to bolster support for the candidate backed by the US.*

USMC United States Marine Corps. (Initialism. A branch of the U.S. armed forces trained for land, sea, and air combat.) ▸ *Gen. John R. Dailey, USMC*

USN United States Navy. (Initialism.) ▸ *Adm. Arthur W. Radford, USN*

USNA United States Naval Academy. (Initialism. The educational institution of the United States Navy at Annapolis, Maryland.) ▸ *The proud family hung their children's USNA diplomas in the trophy case.*

USO United Service Organization. (Initialism. A not-for-profit organization that aids people in the armed forces and their families by providing community and family services and recreational activities.) ▸ *The troops were entertained by a USO show starring Bob Hope.*

U.S.S. United States Ship. (Initialism.) ▸ *U.S.S. Constitution* ▸ *The U.S.S. Harrington docked for two weeks in Boston.*

USSR Union of Soviet Socialist Republics. (Initialism. A global superpower nation that was comprised of several Slavic, Caucasian, and Asiatic peoples in fifteen republics. In 1991, the Union ceased to exist. See also *CIS*.) ▸ *Consisting of over 8.6 million square miles, the USSR was the world's largest country.* ▸ *After the dissolution of the Soviet Union, Leningrad, USSR, became known as St. Petersburg, Russia.*

usu. usually. (Often but not always.) ▸ *Nancy plays clarinet, knows French, usu. drives to rehearsal.*

Ut. Utah. (See also *UT*.) ▸ *Provo, Ut.* ▸ *Gov. Ed Norman (Ut.)*

UT 1. Utah. (The official two-letter post office abbreviation. See also *Ut*.) ▸ *Ogden, UT 84401* **2.** Universal Time. (Initialism. Also known as Greenwich Mean Time, *GMT*, which is the basis for global time. *UT* is the standard time of the meridian that passes through Greenwich, England. Local time is determined by adding one hour for each 15° east of 0° longitude and subtracting one hour for each 15° west of 0° longitude. UT is expressed on a 24-hour clock; that is, 1:00 PM is expressed as 1300, 2:00 PM is expressed as 1400, and so on.) ▶ *The eclipse enters totality at 1545 UT.*

UV ultraviolet. (Initialism. Electromagnetic radiation whose wavelength is shorter than violet light and is not a part of the visible spectrum.) ▶ *Anne put on sunblock to protect her skin from UV radiation.*

V

v. **1.** verb. (A word conveying action or a state of being. Found in language textbooks and dictionaries. See also *V.*) ▸ *complex v.* ▸ *to suffocate (v.)* **2.** verse. (A division of a chapter in the Bible.) ▸ *Psalm 105, v. 1: Give glory to the Lord, for He is good: for His mercy endureth forever.* **3.** version. (A variation or modification of an original.) ▸ Das Boot *(English subtitle v.)* ▸ War and Peace *(abridged v.)* **4.** AND **vs.** versus. (In opposition to someone or something; in a contest against someone or something, often a court case.) ▸ *Roe v. Wade.* ▸ *Brown vs. Board of Education of Topeka.* ▸ *Tyson v. Spinks* ▸ *good v. evil.* ▸ *polyester vs. cotton blends.*

V **1.** 5. (A Roman numeral.) ▸ *Article V of the U.S. Constitution outlines the manner in which the Constitution can be amended.* **2.** vanadium. (The chemical symbol for Element 23.) **3.** AND **vel.** velocity. ▸ *V = 55 mph* **4.** verb. (Initialism. A linguistic symbol for *verb*, used in formulas that describe the structure of the syntax of a sentence. See also *v.*) ▸ *aux. + V = VP* **5.** victory. ▸ *The president flashed a V for Victory gesture to the photographers.* **6.** volt. (A unit of electromotive force.) ▸ *The electrical current in the house operated on 220V.* **7.** volume. (The amount of space an object occupies.) ▸ *The formula for the volume of a cube is V = s3, where s is the length of any* *side.* **8.** vowel. (Initialism. A linguistic symbol for particular speech sounds. During the production of vowel sounds, the airflow is not blocked and the vocal cords generally vibrate. See also *C.*) ▶ *V represents any vowel sound, such as* a, e, *and* u. ▶ *Examples of words exhibiting a CV pattern are* bay, me, row, *and* saw.

V-8 1. an internal combustion engine with eight cylinders arranged in two rows of four shaped as a V. (Pronounced "VEE ATE.") ▶ *Randy's new car had a V-8 engine.* **2.** vegetable-eight. (Pronounced "VEE ATE." A protected brand of juice drink made from the juice of eight vegetables.) ▶ *Karen's breakfast consisted of a banana and a glass of sodium-free V-8.*

Va. Virginia. (See also *VA.*) ▶ *Richmond, Va.* ▶ *Gov. Sam Jones (Va.)*

VA 1. Veterans Administration. (Initialism. A government agency in charge of programs for veterans. In 1988, it was granted executive office status and became the Department of Veteran Affairs. See *DVA.*) ▶ *Jimmy's leg was amputated in a VA hospital.* **2.** Virginia. (The official two-letter post office abbreviation. See also *Va.*) ▶ *Alexandria, VA 22301*

Val. valley. (Low land that lies between hills or mountains; the land carved out by a river.) ▶ *San Joaquin Val.* ▶ *Ohio Riv. Val.*

val. value. (The amount of an object's worth.) ▶ *retail val.*

var. 1. variable. (Something that is not constant.) ▶ *var. rate* **2.** various. (Any number of different kinds; an assortment.) ▶ *Fresh Juice $1.50 (var. flavors)*

VAR value-added retailer. (Initialism. A retailer who adds an item of value onto a retail product and resells it.)

VAT value-added tax. (Initialism and acronym. An indirect sales tax levied against products and services at each phase of production based on the value added at that phase, the cost of which is passed on to the consumer. Sometimes referred to as a VAT tax.) ▸ *Congress deliberated a VAT on many kinds of goods as a means of balancing the budget.* ▸ *Did you get a refund of your VAT?*

VC Viet Cong. (Initialism. The Vietnamese military force who overthrew the South Vietnamese government and fought anticommunist troops during the Vietnam Conflict. Also called Victor Charlie, the military representation of the letters *V* and *C*.) ▸ *The eighteen-year-old soldier was ambushed and killed by the VC.*

VCR videocassette recorder. (Initialism. A machine that plays videotapes and records onto videotape.) ▸ *After Carl's VCR was stolen, he began going to the theater to watch movies.*

VD venereal disease. (Initialism. A disease such as gonorrhea, syphilis, genital herpes, chlamydia, and AIDS, spread through sexual contact. *STD* is more current.) ▸ *Sam went to a VD clinic.*

VDT visual/video display terminal. (Initialism. A computer terminal that has a monitor and a keyboard.) ▸ *During the night, a prowler made off with five VDTs from the Design Department.*

V-E Day victory [in] Europe day. (Initialism. May 8, 1945, the day Germany surrendered, ending war in the European theater.)

vel. See *V.*

Ven. Venerable. (A title of reverence in the Anglican and Roman Catholic Churches.) ▶ *The Ven. Reverend William Upton delivered a sermon.*

vert. vertical. (Straight up and down. A control on a television set that helps tune in the picture.) ▶ *vert. hold*

vet 1. veteran. (Clipping. A person who has served in the armed forces.) ▶ *Uncle Bob is a Vietnam vet.* ▶ *The vet suffered from war flashbacks.* 2. veterinarian. (Clipping. A medical doctor in the field of veterinary medicine.) ▶ *Gina and her mom took the dog to the vet to get some shots.*

VFD volunteer fire department. (Initialism. A unit of fire fighters who work without pay in areas that cannot afford a publicly funded fire department.) ▶ *Springfield's VFD held a raffle to assist in the purchase of new equipment.*

VFW Veterans of Foreign Wars. (Initialism. Founded in 1898 after the Spanish-American War. It is an organization of U.S. veterans who have served in foreign wars.) ▶ *Every Friday, the local VFW sponsored a fish and chips buffet followed by a dance.* ▶ *The VFW float at the Independence Day parade was greeted with cheers and applause.*

VGA video graphics array [monitor]. (A type of computer graphics circuitry that drives a computer monitor with very high resolution, or the monitor itself. See *EGA*.) ▶ *VGA monitor* ▶ *The art department designed highly detailed and multicolored graphics on their new VGA terminal.*

VHF very high frequency. (Initialism. A radio frequency between 30 and 300 kilohertz. In television broadcasting, the UHF frequencies correspond to channels 2

VHS

through 13.) ▸ *Brad's old TV received broadcasts only from UHF stations.*

VHS video home system. (Initialism. Trademark. An electronic audio-video recording system and the videocassettes used.) ▸ *The neighborhood video store only offered VHS tapes, so the Johnsons sold their Betamax.*

V.I. Virgin Islands. (A group of 100 Caribbean islands owned by Gt. Britain and the U.S. See also *VI*.) ▸ *St. Croix, V.I.*

vi intransitive verb. (A verb that does not take a direct object. Found in language textbooks and dictionaries.) ▸ *to die (vi)* ▸ *to laugh (vi)*

VI Virgin Islands. (The official two-letter post office abbreviation. See also *V.I.*) ▸ *Charlotte Amalie, St. Thomas, VI 00801*

Viet. 1. Vietnam. (A country in southeast Asia on the South China Sea.) ▸ *Da Nang, Viet.* 2. Vietnamese. (The adjective form of *Vietnam*.) ▸ *Viet. alphabet*

vil. village. (A municipal district, usually smaller than a town.) ▸ *Vil. of Skokie*

VIP very important person. (Initialism. An important official or guest often provided with preferential treatment.) ▸ *The president's family listened to the symphony from the VIP room.*

VIR Virgo. (The astrological abbreviation for the zodiacal constellation of Virgo.) ▸ *VIR (August 23 to September 22)*

VISTA Volunteers in Service to America. (Acronym. A government agency of volunteers assisting low-income Americans by providing food distribution, employment searches, housing, and other public service programs.) ▸

Sarah moved to the Appalachian Mountains shortly after joining VISTA.

viz. *videlicet.* (Latin: namely.) ▶ *Add the dry ingredients; viz., flour, sugar, brown sugar, and salt.*

VJ video jockey. (Initialism. Similar to a radio disc jockey, a broadcaster on a video channel who introduces songs and provides music news.) ▶ *Martha Quinn, one of the first MTV VJs, went on to play Bobby Brady's wife in a reunion series.*

V-J Day. victory [over] Japan day. (Initialism. August 15, 1945, the day the fighting between the Allied forces and Japan ceased and September 2, 1945, when the Japanese formally surrendered.) ▶ *V-J Day heralded the end of World War II and the beginning of the Cold War.*

V.M.D. *Veterinariae Medicinae Doctor.* (Initialism. Latin: Doctor of Veterinary Medicine. See also *D.V.M.*) ▶ *Roger Maxwell, V.M.D.*

VO voiceover. (Initialism. A narrative audio track dubbed on top of a video track.) ▶ *Carol's income came from VO work on national commercials.*

VOA Voice of America. (Initialism. The broadcasting arm of the United States Information Agency, an American-oriented news source transmitted globally in over forty languages.) ▶ *Before the fall of the Iron Curtain, Laszlo listened to Western news broadcast by VOA.*

voc. vocative. (A grammar case found in highly inflected languages such as Latin, referring to nouns, pronouns, and adjectives used in direct address. Found in language textbooks and dictionaries.)

vocab. vocabulary. (A word list, often used as a clipping in language classes.) ▶ *Vocab. quiz on Friday—study now.*

vol. 1. volume. (A sound level, used to label the loudness and softness controls of something that produces noise.) ▶ *vol. control* 2. volume. (The capacity of a container. Often found on packaging.) ▶ *vol. 64 oz.*

VP 1. verb phrase. (Initialism. A linguistic symbol for a group of words functioning as a verb. Found in language textbooks. Sometimes written so that the right leg of the V is the vertical line of the P.) ▶ *Mary underlined the VP of the sentence in red.* 2. vice president. (A position of authority just below the president. The United States vice president is also the president of the senate.) ▶ *Who will the candidate's VP be?*

VRM variable rate mortgage. (Initialism. A mortgage whose interest rate fluctuates with the market. Compare with *ARM*.) ▶ *The developer took a gamble with a five-year VRM, following the advice of a broker who claimed that rates would be stable throughout the decade.*

vs. See *v.*

V.S.O. very superior (or special) old. (Initialism. Used to describe brandy.) ▶ *Royal Extra Fine, V.S.O.*

V.S.O.P. very superior (or special) old pale. (Initialism. Used to describe brandy.) ▶ *Walton's Best, V.S.O.P.*

Vt. Vermont. (See also *VT*.) ▶ *Montpelier, Vt.* ▶ *Gov. Peter Rogers (Vt.)*

vt transitive verb. (A verb that has a direct object. Found in language textbooks and dictionaries. See also *t.*) ▶ *to hit (vt)* ▶ *to touch (vt)*

VT Vermont. (The official two-letter post office abbreviation. See also *Vt.*) ▶ *Burlington, VT 05401*

VTOL vertical takeoff and landing. (Partial acronym. Pronounced "VEE-tall." Aircraft [other than helicopters] that can take off and land vertically.) ▶ *The military has invested substantial money in researching viable VTOL.*

vulg. vulgar. (A linguistic term, characteristic of the general, common speech of a language, as opposed to the standard or literary form of the language.) ▶ Cabellero, *the Spanish word for horseman, is from vulg. Latin* caballus, *meaning "horse."*

v.v. *vice versa.* (Initialism. Latin: reversal of order. The converse. In the example, the *v.v.* indicates that the New Yorkers also went to Boston.) ▶ *The Bostonians went to New York, v.v.*

W

w/ with. (Used primarily in brief notes and classified advertisements.) ▸ *coffee w/ cream* ▸ *eggs w/ bacon* ▸ *3:00—Jones left w/ briefcase. Made phone call.* ▸ *For sale, vacuum cleaner w/ attachments*

W **1.** tungsten. (The chemical symbol for Element 74. The symbol is derived from German *Wolfram*.) **2.** watt. (Unit of electrical power. Wattage is the power of an electrical circuit determined by multiplying the voltage by the amperage.) ▸ *W = V x A* ▸ *75W light bulb.* **3.** Wednesday. (A day of the week. In the series *S, M, T, W, T, F, S* or *Su, M, Tu, W, Th, F, Sa*. See also Wed.) ▸ *M - Toledo, Tu - Akron, W - Pittsburgh, Th - Return home* **4.** AND **W.** west. (A compass direction. Found on maps and signs and in addresses. See also *N, S, E*.) ▸ *Drive past the purple building on the W side of the street and turn left at the next intersection.* ▸ *W. 59th Street.* ▸ *W. Chicago, Illinois* **5.** win(s). (Used in sports statistics. Usually appears along with losses. See L.) ▸ *Cy Young—Inducted into the Baseball Hall of Fame, 1937—511 W/313 L.* **6.** woman. (Indicates sex, used to differentiate between man and woman. See also M.) ▸ *Jane, needing to use the bathroom, walked through the door with the W on it.*

w width. (The dimension from side to side; the opposite of height.) ▸ *w = 36 inches*

WA (The official two-letter post office abbreviation. See also *Wash.*) ▶ *Seattle, WA 98101*

WAC Women's Army Corps. (Acronym. A military organization of women serving in noncombat roles from 1943 to 1978, at which time the WAC was integrated into the U.S. Army.) ▶ *Alice was a WAC during WWII.*

Wash. 1. the state of Washington. (See also *WA.*) ▶ *Walla Walla, Wash.* ▶ *Gov. Anne Thomas (Wash.)* 2. the city of Washington. ▶ *Wash. D.C.*

WASP White Anglo-Saxon Protestant. (Acronym. A Protestant of English or northern European descent. Usually derogatory. See also *AS.*) ▶ *The realtor was hit with charges of steering minorities away from WASP neighborhoods.* ▶ *"His WASPy attitudes on class structure are rather offensive," Jane said of her civics professor.*

WATS Wide-Area Telecommunications Service. (Acronym. A service offered by AT&T providing special networks so that calls can be transmitted between particular areas at a discounted rate.) ▶ *Our company has inbound WATS.*

WAVES Women Accepted for Volunteer Emergency Service. (Acronym. A military organization begun during World War II and established permanently in 1948. An organization of women who serve alongside men in the medical corps and other noncombat roles.)

WBC 1. white blood cell. (Initialism. Also called a leucocyte. It is found in the bloodstream and acts against disease and infection.) 2. white blood count. (Initialism. A blood test that counts the number of white blood cells in a sample.) ▶ *A high WBC is indicative of infection.*

WC water closet. (Initialism. A room equipped with a toilet.) ▶ *Bill called a plumber to fix the leaky pipes in the WC.*

WCTU Women's Christian Temperance Union. (Initialism. Founded in 1874 to improve public morality by advocating abstinence from alcohol and narcotics.) ▶ *The WCTU is headquartered in Evanston, Illinois.*

Wed. Wednesday. (See also *W.*) ▶ *Wed. 7:00 Leave it to Beaver.* ▶ *Wed. 7:30 I Dream of Jeannie.*

WHO World Health Organization. (Initialism. A United Nations agency that tries to solve health problems by coordinating with governments and other UN agencies, in the areas of health education, nutrition, sanitation, pregnancy and postnatal care, sanitation, immunization, and disease prevention.) ▶ *WHO commissioned Cynthia to write a report on the global impact of malaria.*

whse. warehouse. (A large building where inventory is stored.) ▶ *Whse. #5—carpet remnants and fabric swatches.*

W.I. West Indies. (Initialism. The islands between the Caribbean Sea and the Atlantic Ocean from Cuba and the Bahamas south to Trinidad and Tobago.) ▶ *Win a 7-Day W.I. Luxury Cruise Liner Vacation*

WI Wisconsin. (The official two-letter post office abbreviation. See also *Wis.* and *Wisc.*) ▶ *Madison, WI 53701*

WIA Wounded in Action. (Initialism. A term applied to armed forces personnel injured in combat.) ▶ *After the battle, Colonel Spencer listed 214 WIA's.* ▶ *Uncle Hank, a WIA at Midway Island, received a Purple Heart when he returned safely to the States.*

WIC women, infants, and children. (Acronym. A special supplemental food program administered by the Department of Agriculture that helps provide adequate meals to all children.) ▶ *WIC coupon*

WIN 1. Whip Inflation Now. (Acronym. A slogan used by President Gerald Ford in the early 1970s to encourage people to fight inflation.) ▶ *The nostalgia shop was selling WIN buttons for $5 apiece.* 2. work incentive [program]. (Acronym. A program under which recipients of Aid to Families with Dependent Children must register, if employable, to receive aid. See also *AFDC*.)

Wis. AND **Wisc.** Wisconsin. (See also *WI*.) ▶ *Monroe, Wis.* ▶ *Gov. Paul Thompson (Wis.)*

Wisc. See the previous entry.

wk. week. (A period of seven days.) ▶ *wk. 1—Learn the Basics! wk. 2—Become a Master! wk. 3—Earn a Lot of Money!*

WNW west-northwest. (A compass direction, halfway between due west and northwest.) ▶ *Santa Barbara is about 80 miles WNW of Los Angeles.*

w/o without. (Used primarily in brief notes and classified advertisements.) ▶ *salad w/o dressing* ▶ *Lose weight w/o exercise!*

WORM write once, write many [times]. (A type of optical disc computer storage that can be written or recorded only one time, but read back any number of times.) ▶ *I am saving my money for a WORM-drive.* ▶ *Memory is getting cheaper all the time. Someday it will be cheaper to use chip-based memory than WORM or hard-disk technology.*

WP word processing. (Initialism. The use of computers and other office technology to prepare the written output of a company.) ▶ *Patricia took her dictation tape to* *the WP department and asked if she could have the material as soon as possible.*

WPA Works Projects Administration. (Initialism. Originally Works Progress Administration, 1935-1939. A New Deal relief agency that provided work during times of massive unemployment until 1943.) ▸ *The park district fieldhouse was built by WPA workers.*

WPM words per minute. (Initialism. A measure of typing, printing, or reading speed.) ▸ *Secretarial help wanted, 65 WPM minimum.*

WSW west-southwest. (A compass direction, halfway between due west and southwest.) ▸ *Chicago is roughly 250 miles WSW of Detroit.* ▸ *The tornado touched down two miles WSW of the meteorological station.*

wt. weight. (Found on packaging and labeling to indicate the weight of something.) ▸ *Net wt. 32 oz.*

WV West Virginia. (The official two-letter post office abbreviation. See also *W. Va.*) ▸ *Charleston, WV 25301*

W. Va. West Virginia. (See also *WV.*) ▸ *Morgantown, W. Va.* ▸ *Gov. Jenny Davis (W. Va.)*

WWI World War I. (Initialism. A global war from 1914 to 1918 that began with the assassination of Archduke Francis Ferdinand of Austria-Hungary.) ▸ *The U.S. entered WWI after the sinking of the Lusitania.*

WWII World War II. (Initialism. A global war from 1939 to 1945 that began with Hitler's invasion of Poland.) ▸ *The U.S. entered WWI after the bombing of Pearl Harbor on December 7, 1941.*

WWIII World War III. (Initialism. Referring to the next global war.) ▸ *The Persian Gulf War did not become the WWIII some pundits predicted it would become.* ▸ *The* *scientist warned that unless nuclear proliferation were halted and reversed, a WWIII was inevitable.*

WY   Wyoming. (The official two-letter post office abbreviation. See also *Wyo.*) ▶ *Centennial, WY 82055*

Wyo.   Wyoming. (See also *WY.*) ▶ *Casper, Wyo.* ▶ *Gov. Pete Jones (Wyo.)*

X

x **1.** by. (Indicates dimensions.) ▸ *The 4-inch × 6-inch box held Gail's 3-inch × 5-inch notecards.* **2.** times. (Indicates multiplication or strength.) ▸ *12 × 12 equals 144.* ▸ *This lens magnifies the object 10x.* **3.** AND **X** (An algebraic variable.) ▸ *Let X equal the number of people alive today.* ▸ *If 5x − 5 = 0, then x = 1.*

X **1.** Christ. (The first Greek letter of the Greek word for Christ, *Christus*.) **2.** a location (as on a map), in the phrase "X marks the spot." (Initialism.) ▸ *X marks the spot where the treasure was buried.* **3.** ecstasy. (Initialism. A "designer" drug. Drug slang. From the *ecs-* of ecstasy. See *MDMA*. See also *E*.) ▸ *Albert took Leon to an X party at an abandoned warehouse.* **4.** 10. (A Roman numeral.) ▸ *Chapter X—In which the girl drops her matchsticks into the snow.* ▸ *Pope John X.*

Xe xenon. (The chemical symbol for Element 54.)

XL extra large. (Initialism. Size, usually related to clothing. In the series *XS, S, M, L, XL*.) ▸ *The celebrity started a diet when even XL clothing stopped fitting.*

Xmas Christmas. (The *X* stands for *Christ* as in X (sense 1) above.) ▸ *Xmas Sale—25% off all specially marked items.*

X ray. (An electromagnetic radioactive wave. The x refers to an unknown quantity so named because not much was known about X rays when they were first discovered.) ▸ *The doctor took an X ray of the patient's forearm to determine the extent of the bone fracture.* ▸ *The dental X rays indicated that Jane's secondary teeth were coming in straight.*

XS extra small. (Size, usually related to clothing. In the series *XS, S, M, L, XL.*) ▸ *The sales clerk placed sales tags on a rack of XS blouses that were not selling well.*

XT extended; extended [architecture]; extended technology. (Partial initialism. A model or computing power designation designation of a DOS-based computer, somewhere between the *PC* and the *AT* in speed and capacity. See also *AT.*) ▸ *I traded in my old XT on a 486.*

XYZ examine your zipper. (Initialism. Used in informal situations to point out that someone's zipper is not zipped.) ▸ *Horace turned red when Emily whispered "XYZ" in his ear.*

Y

Y 1. YMCA. (See *YMCA*.) 2. YWCA. (See *YWCA*.) 3. yttrium. (The chemical symbol for Element 39.)

Yb ytterbium. (The chemical symbol for Element 70.)

yd. yard. (A unit of linear measurement equal to three feet.) ▸ *A 10 yd. × 4 yd. swimming pool.* ▸ *First down, 10 yds. to go.*

YMCA Young Men's Christian Association. (Initialism. Established in England in 1844, a network of nonprofit corporations that provide athletic, recreational, and educational services, as well as rooms to rent for transients, all at a minimal cost. Further abbreviated as *The Y*.) ▸ *Barry stayed at the YMCA until he got a job.*

YMHA Young Men's Hebrew Association. (Initialism. Established in 1854, an organization providing athletic, recreational, educational services to Jewish men, now largely a constituent of local Jewish Community Centers. See *JCC*.) ▸ *Barry took Hebrew and swimming lessons at the local YMHA.*

yr. year. (A unit of time equal to 12 months or 365 or 366 calendar days, determined by the time it takes for the earth to make one complete revolution around the sun, slightly less than 365.25 earth days.) ▶ *5-yr. loan* ▶ *10-yr. amortization schedule.*

YTD year to date. (Initialism. Found in fiscal statements and other statistical statements referring to items measured from the beginning of the calendar or business year to the current date.) ▶ *YTD figures indicate sales are lagging compared to last year's.* ▶ *Gross Income: $46,200 (YTD)*

YTM yield to maturity. (Initialism. The yield promised when bonds are purchased, assuming that all interest payments will be made in full and on time and that the rate of interest will not change before the bond is sold.) ▶ *The broker quoted a phenomenal 8.5% YTM rate.*

Yugo. Yugoslavia. (A country of eastern Europe comprised of several republics, some of which have declared independence.) ▶ *Zagreb, Yugo.*

yuppie young urban professional. (Acronym. A demographic category for urban, white-collar people in their twenties and thirties, who often have significant amounts of disposable money. Often used derogatorily.) ▶ *The yuppie was a phenomenon of the late 1980s.* ▶ *Some yuppies renovated a dilapidated section of a working class neighborhood, driving up rental prices and displacing the poor.*

YWCA Young Women's Christian Association. (Initialism. Founded in 1855, an organization providing athletic, recreational, and educational services to women at a minimal cost. Further abbreviated as *The Y*.)

YWHA Young Women's Hebrew Association. (Initialism. Founded in 1888 as an auxiliary of the *YMHA*. *YWHA*s are now a part of local Jewish Community Centers.)

Z

z. **1.** zone. (A region or area. Found on maps, tables, and text.) ▸ *flood z.* **2.** zero. (The number 0.) ▸ *absolute z.*

ZBB zero-based budgeting. (Initialism. An accounting term for a budgeting method that requires justification for every dollar to be spent, as opposed to detailing the changes from the previous year's budget. So called because each year the budget is planned from a base of $0.) ▸ *Under President Carter, the government departments began using a ZBB system.*

ZIP Code zone improvement plan. (Acronym. Instituted by the U.S. Post Office on July 1, 1963, a five-digit postal coding system that provides speedier and more efficient handling of mail. In 1981, ZIP Codes were expanded to nine digits.) ▸ *Chicago, IL 60622* ▸ *Chicago, IL 60622-3280* ▸ *The ZIP Code for the Wicker Park Post Office in Chicago is 60622-9998.* ▸ *Anna forgot Tim's ZIP Code, so her letter took three weeks to get to his house.* ▸ *Companies that use a nine-digit ZIP Code receive more efficient service.*

Zn zinc. (The chemical symbol for Element 30.)

zool. zoology (The study of the animal kingdom.) ▸ *Zool. Dept. Chairman—Room 241*

ZPG zero population growth. (Initialism. The goal of organizations trying to prevent overpopulation of earth.) ▶ *China has been attempting to attain ZPG for the past generation.*

Zr zirconium. (The chemical symbol for Element 40.)